Courage of Conviction

Women's Words, Women's Wisdom

LINDA A. M. PERRY
University of San Diego

PATRICIA GEIST
San Diego State University

MAYFIELD PUBLISHING COMPANY
Mountain View, California
London • Toronto

*"I am grateful to the many women and men who
dare to create theory from the location of pain and
struggle, who courageously expose wounds to give
us their experience to teach and guide, as a means to
chart new theoretical journeys."*

bell hooks

Copyright © 1997 by Mayfield Publishing Company

Library of Congress Cataloging-in-Publication Data
Courage of conviction : women's words, women's wisdom / [edited by]
 Linda A. M. Perry, Patricia Geist.
     p. cm.
 Includes bibliographical references.
 ISBN 1-55934-716-3
    1. Women—United States—Biography.   2. Women—United States—
Social conditions.   3. Women—United States—Literary collections.
 I. Perry, Linda A. M.   II. Geist, Patricia.
 HQ1412.C68   1997
 305.4'0973—dc21   96-40937
                                                                        CIP

Manufactured in the United States of America
10 9 8 7 6 5 4 3 2 1

Mayfield Publishing Company
1280 Villa Street
Mountain View, California 94041

Sponsoring editor, Franklin C. Graham; production editor, Carla L. White; manuscript editor, Beverley DeWitt; text and cover designer, Donna Davis; cover art,
Louisa Chase; design manager, Jean Mailander; photo researcher, Brian Pecko;
manufacturing manager, Amy Folden. The text was set in 10.5/13 Sabon by
TBH Typecast, Inc., and printed on 50# Butte des Morts by Banta Book Group.
Text and photo credits appear on page 344, which constitutes an extension of the
copyright page.

Contents

Preface v

Indian Time *María Cristina González* viii

Introduction *Linda A. M. Perry and Patricia Geist* 1

Part One: Women's Words 17

1 Connecticut's Canterbury Tale: Prudence Crandall's Brave Stand *Benjamin Sevitch* 19

2 Frances Ellen Watkins Harper: Recovering What Is Right *Richard W. Leeman* 35

  Ruby *Phyllis Kahaney* 36

3 "I Can and I Will": "Mother" Jones Crusades for Labor Rights *Diane Cypkin* 55

4 Stone Mother: Katie Frazier's Native Tales *Gwendolyn Clancy and Deborah Ballard-Reisch* 69

  Incognito *María Cristina González* 70

5 Margaret Chase Smith: The Spirit of Conviction *Marlene Boyd Vallin* 87

6 Tillie Olsen: Catching a Lifetime in a Phrase *Maureen E. Hoffman* 101

  The Controversial Vision *María Cristina González* 102

7 Confinement in the Sexual Wasteland: The Writings of Aphra Behn and Fay Weldon *Cynthia L. Caywood and Bonnie A. Hain* 113

  One Fantasy *Phyllis Kahaney* 114

8 In My Shoes for Life: A Disabled Woman's Journey *Thuy-Phuong Do* 129

9 Singing Along: The Self-Reflective Power of Carly Simon's Musical Diaries *Thomas Endres* 145

Part Two: Women's Wisdom 165

10 Elation and Devastation: Women's Journeys Through Pregnancy and Miscarriage   *Julie L. Ross and Patricia Geist* 167

Untitled   *María Cristina González* 168

11 The Mystery and Mystique of Natural Childbirth *Lisa Rose Gates* 185

12 Mobilizing Motherhood: Mothers' Experiences of "Visiting" Their Children   *Deborah L. Eicher-Catt* 201

Homecoming   *María Cristina González* 202

13 "Return to Life": Communicating in Families of the Holocaust *Lynn H. Turner* 221

Visit   *Phyllis Kahaney* 222

14 African American Women: Voices of Literacy and Literate Voices   *Cheryl Forbes* 235

That White Thing   *María Cristina González* 236

15 False Eyelashes and the Word of God: Speaking as an Evangelical Woman   *Lynne Lundberg* 253

16 Courageous Talk: Empowering the Voices of Recovering Female Alcoholics   *Kelley R. Chrouser and Jack Kay* 265

Sympathetic Ailments   *María Cristina González* 266

17 "I'm Alive, Thank You": Women's Accounts of HIV/AIDS *Judith Liu, Kathleen Grove, and Donald P. Kelly* 283

Inscribing Your Name in the Book of Life *Phyllis Kahaney* 284

18 Thelma and Louise: Breaking the Silence *Linda A. M. Perry* 301

Interior   *Phyllis Kahaney* 302

19 The Rhetoric of "New Feminism": Searching for a Cultural Backlash   *Delia B. Conti* 321

20 La Malinche Revisited   *María Cristina González* 339

Bird of Paradise   *Phyllis Kahaney* 343

Preface

When we think about courage and conviction, we forget that sometimes the simple act of speaking up takes just that. It takes courage and conviction to be a leader, a writer, a keeper of oral histories, a politician, a poet, or a singer. If you happen to be a woman, it takes extra strength to do these things because women have been historically ostracized for attempting these public roles.

It takes courage and conviction for women to face the emotional devastation of miscarriage, the ecstasy of natural childbirth; to create acceptable new roles for motherhood, defy family taboos and religious sanctions; to find their own voice as they recover from addictions, accept the agony of illness, overcome daily violence; or even to question the direction in which women are headed. But, women of courage and conviction throughout time have forged paths for us and future generations of women to walk—and they continue to do so today. A variety of life choices and circumstances are represented in this book. Also represented are a variety of women: African American, Chicana, Mexican American, Native American, Vietnamese American, disabled, Jewish, evangelical, and White middle-class American women, for example. The group representations, however, were not the issue for us in editing this book; the experiences of women regardless of their class, race, religion, or ethnic background were. In fact, it sometimes seems that in an attempt to claim our independent heritages, what we share is lost. This book is about what women share to one degree or another: personal and public silencing. And, more important, it is about breaking that silence.

We had several goals in mind while editing this book. First, we wanted to provide opportunities for women's stories to be told, and better yet, for women to tell their own stories. There may be more books doing that these days but still not enough. Women's voices are only beginning to be heard, and like most of you, we believe that changes in the social paradigms about gender and sex equality will not occur until women's voices are heard. Women's life stories and experiences are unique from men's; the more of these stories we have an opportunity to hear, the more role models we will have, the wider our perceptual field, and the stronger our convictions to live our feminist scholarship. In this book, we have provided both stories about specific women from the past to contemporary times and opportunities for women to tell their own stories.

A second goal we had in mind was to demonstrate what research could look like if it embraced rather than marginalized the personal, emotional, and feminine. That is, we wanted to provide a forum in which the researcher and the researched might intermingle in ways that turn back our research experiences upon ourselves, enlightening, questioning, and confirming who we are. We wanted to show students that what they choose to study should come from their hearts, their heads, and their souls—that truly exciting discoveries come when the starting place is somewhere near to the researcher's personal interests. As you read the text, note the essays where the authors disclose their own experience with the topic; what they find is also personal and profound. The social sciences, too, are going through a paradigm shift when it comes to research methods. Although they are not abandoning quantitative methods with their often detached "expert" stance, they are recognizing the utility (and validity) of the more up-close and personal, qualitative stance. For those of us who have repeatedly had to defend our methods and, therefore, our research, this book offers an opportunity for legitimizing the newer paradigm and the discoveries made in its use.

Finally, we wanted to offer a book about women's lives that could be used in many contexts. Because this book embraces a variety of narrative forms (storytelling, historical accounts, poems, theory-building, and so forth) it easily can be used as a supplemental text in feminist theory courses. It also could facilitate the teaching of naturalistic/qualitative methods in research method courses. In fact, this text can be used in a variety of disciplines: gender studies, women's studies, history (especially considering the absence of women's histories in most mainstream texts), English, communication, and others. We also wanted to edit a book that our nonacademic friends and family would enjoy reading and by doing so become enriched.

To reach the goals we set for ourselves in the editing of this text, we have tried to weave the past and the present, the personal and the political, the excitement and the devastation, the struggles and the victories. We believe we have reached or even surpassed our goals and have demonstrated what the title of our book, *Courage of Conviction: Women's Words, Women's Wisdom,* suggests about women's lives in everyday and extraordinary circumstances.

Acknowledgments

First and foremost, we thank the women whose stories are told in this volume. It is our hope that the voicing of their experiences will inspire others to speak, to listen, and to be heard. Next, we acknowledge Frank Graham, our Sponsoring Editor at Mayfield Publishing Company, for providing us with continued support. He clearly understood what we wanted to accomplish and stood strongly behind us to do so. His participation has added immensely to the quality of the final project. Another person whose work we greatly appreciate is that of our manuscript editor, Beverley DeWitt. In our opinion, she took our manuscript from great to excellent. Sara Early, Editorial Assistant and Carla White, Production Editor, along with many others, worked long and hard to bring this project together, to provide excellent suggestions, additional photographs, and to obtain necessary permissions—from the mundane tasks to the exceptional feats, the folks at Mayfield have been superb!

Many readers provided advice and suggestions for which we are grateful. We want to acknowledge the supportive feedback we received from Julia Wood, University of North Carolina–Chapel Hill, whose opinion we greatly value. We gratefully acknowledge the support and input of those who reviewed the book: Teri Ann Bengiveno, San Jose State University; Jane Smith Boyd, San Jose State University; Angela E. Hubler, Kansas State University; Jeanne Kohl, University of Washington; Wendy Kozol, Oberlin College; Sandra Krajewski, University of Wisconsin–LaCrosse; and Sydney Langdon, Arizona State University.

We acknowledge those people in our mutual lives who have provided us with the strength, energy, and/or opportunities to have our voices heard. We thank our colleagues and friends who have provided us with many kinds of support throughout this project. Most notably, we appreciate the support of the University of San Diego and San Diego State University. As trite as it may seem, we raise our glasses to each other for being there as mutual friends, colleagues, and participants in this project. It is the balance between our work and our friendship that ultimately provided us both with a strong and clear voice in the outcome of this book.

Finally, we want to each acknowledge those who have supported us individually. Linda wants first to acknowledge those who have had the greatest impact on shaping her voice: most significantly, her grandmother, the late Alice B. Leach whose love, wit, and wisdom carry on; her parents Sid and Jean Perry; her siblings David, Bonnie, Ronnie, and Sandra; her children Holly and Heather; and her granddaughter Ashley. She also thanks her good friends Eric, Judy, Linda, Mabel, Phyllis, Scott, Solluna, and especially her steadfast companion Sweetie Pie, who have nurtured her in a variety of ways, through the good times and the bad since the inception of this book. She gratefully thanks her family and friends for listening closely when her voice was small and feeble and for not quieting it when it was annoyingly loud.

Patricia first and foremost wants to acknowledge her best friend, companion, and confidant—her husband J. C. Martin—who deserves special acknowledgment for his willing, loving, and steadfast support through this and every other project she has initiated, including *equal* parenting of their daughter Makenna. Keeping her centered are Makenna, whose truthful words support every ounce of this book's labor, and Makenna's "little brother" Maile, whose ever faithful, purring, lap presence is welcomed. Her family deserves thanks for visits, talks, and distractions; thank you Denny, Bill, Nicole, Daniel, Pat, Reese, Patsy, Josh, Sullivan, and Lina. Finally, she would like to give special thanks to her early collaborators, Monica Hardesty, Sandra Metts, Linda Putnam, Teresa Chandler Sabourin, and Mary Caccavo who shared with her a collaborative spirit and soulful friendship. And thanks must be given to the continuing spirit and friendship that extends from past into present and future collaborations with colleagues and graduate students, including her work ahead with Lisa Gates, Eileen Berlin Ray, and Barbara Sharf.

Indian Time

This thing called time
Of which you joke as you
Take off your watches
Put away your clocks
So you can be white man on Indian time
Has nothing to do with clocks
Is more to do with the passing of time
Is more to do with the ability to
    Wait.
Not wait as in waiting
For what you want
But *wait*

wait . . .

As in sitting in the presence of,
Sitting in the presence of
What should be
    When it should be
Sitting in the presence of,
The Sacred

waiting.

      —*María Cristina González*

An Introduction

Linda's Story

The beginning of my story is all too familiar. As a graduate student, I was told that if I decided to research the lives of "only" women *and* persisted in using qualitative methods, I would have a lot of trouble getting a job and, certainly, would never get tenure. I got a job, I got tenure, I got full professorship. Perhaps it was a matter of courage, but I tend to believe it was more about naïveté. Although I was a feminist, although I had experienced a lifetime of discrimination (the kind that is the color of everyday life so you don't really notice it), and although I had been keen on seeing the ways in which women were left out of a lot of things, on some level it all seemed too incredulous to be real: "You mean they *really* dropped women out of the subject pool 'cause women messed up the stats?" "So, let's see, women were educated so they would be better wives and better mothers to their sons?" "*How* many women are raped each year?" "NO WAY!"

Well, you see my point. A few years ago I noticed there were few, if any, books that told women's stories (thankfully, since then several have appeared). I decided that once I finished the project on which I was working at the time, I would create a forum for women's stories to be told, for recapturing some of *their* history, to examine *their* lives . . . to make *them* the center of the research. I did not want the focus to be on *how* the research was done ("What do you mean, an N of 1 doesn't matter? Don't *I* matter?"), but on the women themselves.

During the editing of this book, I became the chair of my department and continued as the co-director of the Gender Studies Program at the University of San Diego (which has been very supportive of me throughout the process). A lot happened personally, too. My youngest daughter, Heather, moved to Australia, and my oldest daughter, Holly (mother to my only grandchild, Ashley), went back to school, and I bought a house (well, a little California bungalow if the truth be known). Between these professional and personal events, along with other responsibilities I had taken on, trying

1

to stay active in the field, and trying to have a personal life, I knew I needed help. I called my good friend Patricia immediately. . . . If I was going to bring someone into this project, it needed to be a friend, a woman, a top-notch scholar, and someone who understood my disdain for the way scholarship usually happened. Patricia said yes. And, neater still, she had asked me to help her and her husband, J.C., give birth to their beautiful daughter, Makenna. I guess she wanted a lot of similar things in a birthing partner: a friend, a woman, a top-notch visualization guide, and someone who understood her disdain for the medical model of birth.

In some ways, the development of this book was a lot like giving birth. The idea was conceived; the process was nurtured along the way by me, Patricia, the authors, and many of our friends, family, and colleagues; and the day it was "born" Patricia and I cried. Now that it is done and in your hands, we suspect that the beauty of some of the stories, the poetry and prose, might make you cry too. As my daughter Holly says of purchasing greeting cards, "If it doesn't make you cry, don't buy it."

Patricia's Story

Courage. Is that what it took for me to say yes to Linda when she asked me over three years ago if I would co-edit a book with her? Well, yes, in that I had never edited a book before. And yes, because as usual I already was balancing what seemed like a million other projects. And surely yes, because I had just convinced myself that I had learned how to say no. But in reality—and ironically, considering the title of our book—it was not a courageous act at all to say yes to Linda.

Conviction is what drew me into this project. Conviction is what this book feels like, sounds like, cries like—what it is. And this conviction began for me in the strong *faith* I have in what my friendship and collaboration with Linda could produce. This faith, this assurance, and this intensity are what allowed us to enjoy, even relish, our time together as "sacred waiting," described in the opening poem "Indian Time."

This book re-presents my convictions, a long time in the making: becoming a motherless daughter at the age of 17, searching for a woman's voice, my voice, in the midst of desperately missing my mother's voice; painfully but steadfastly endeavoring to educate myself while life traumas whir around me, confuse me—like my divorce and the death of my grad school confidant, Sylvia—and all the while, gathering words of wisdom from innumerable women who had the courage of their convictions to survive and help me survive graduate school, divorce, death of loved ones, miscarriages, and living so very far away from family members.

And without a doubt conviction helps me remember and listen to:

- my mother's voice
- my daughter's stories
- my friends' wisdom
- my own words

Our Story

And so, we joined our efforts, our commitments, and our voices to offer you *Courage of Conviction: Women's Words, Women's Wisdom.* There have been many changes in the book since our collaboration began. We added essays and lost others; we included poetry and pictures; we even changed the name of the book. But, what we didn't change was our feelings about what we were doing. Although we have always been interested in the final product, it never got more important than the process. Our commitment to it enriched our commitments to each other. And, our commitment to each other has enriched it. The result is a collection of essays, "voices" if you will, that is unique in conception and powerful in essence.

The title of our book comes directly from its content. When we asked ourselves what seemed to be at the core of each essay, several words came to mind. Courage and conviction were among them. *Courage:* The quality of mind or spirit that enables a person to face difficulty, danger, pain— with firmness and without fear. Bravery. *The courage of one's convictions:* To act in accordance with one's beliefs in spite of criticism. The women whose stories are told here all demonstrate true courage *and* the courage of their convictions.

Each reading provides a new "voice," independent of and separate from all the rest. And, although each stands on its own, we prefer to see them as interwoven by these voices, voices that may have gone unheard before. To start you on your way, we want to talk a little more about the idea of "voice" and why it is an important metaphor to think about while reading this collection, describe a few of our ideas about "scholarly" research and writing that brought focus to the women's stories and away from methods, and finally, offer you a brief overview of the essays. But, more than that, we want you to have a seat, listen to the orchestra tune up, and get ready for a symphony.

Listening to Voices in the Wind

When Carol Gilligan wrote *In a Different Voice* in 1982, she introduced the metaphor of "voice" to millions of readers. We can think of voice in many ways: "She has a nice voice," "I gave voice to my opinion," and so forth. But, what the idea of voice did for women was to begin to provide them with a way of reversing what had previously been their lot, silencing. Women's voices have been silenced in a variety of ways. Historically, that silencing is part of patriarchal cultures. One belief is that it began as an attempt to control women's sexuality to keep blood lines pure (men wanted to make sure their property went to their rightful heirs). Another view is that women are the handmaidens of men because that is the way life was dictated by God. A third theory is that women are physically weaker and so need to be protected by men, which explains male superiority. We could go on; there are many theories about why women became subordinated to men and, therefore, silenced.

Regardless of the historical, religious, biological, and social explanations, the result is the same; the silencing and confinement of women have robbed them of a history by undervaluing their life stories and denying them posterity by not acknowledging their work. Silencing has caused women to be economically devalued, professionally limited, and personally abused in a variety of ways. To reverse that silence is to give voice. Hinman (1994) offers us a variety of ways to think about voice as a metaphor. First, he says that it works better than using terms such as *theories* or *perspectives* because they limit diversity or, at the very least, do not allow for individuality. "To speak of voices, however, is immediately to conjure up something concrete, something with tone, texture, and cadence" (p. 329). Hinman further notes:

> Three other characteristics of voices are particularly noteworthy. First, voices combine both emotion and content. *How* something is said is tied

closely to *what* is being said. Voices are *embodied* in a way that theories are not. Second, voices are described and assessed in a wide range of terms, most of which have little to do with "true" and "false" or "right" and "wrong." Voices may be strong or weak, full-bodied or hollow, lilting or deep, strident or sweet, excited or dull, trembling and hesitant, or clear and confident. Third, voices may be different without excluding one another. Think of the way people sing together. Their voices may blend in a choir. They may sing harmony, one voice in distinctive counterpoint to another. They may toss a melody back and forth from one person to another, taking turns singing. One may be the lead singer, others may sing background. There are, in other words, numerous different ways in which voices may interact with one another. (p. 329)

And so it is with the voices singing in these essays. They are distinct from each other but they create a chorus. For us, the metaphor of voice goes one step deeper, however. Providing a platform for voices to sing out is another kind of voice in itself. When we provide opportunities for others to be heard, when we empower others through our works, words, or actions, our own voices ring loud and clear.

Being in the position to provide opportunities for others to empower themselves, to have their own voices heard, does not necessarily mean that our own voices always have been heard by others—or ourselves, for that matter. Gloria Steinem came to this understanding about herself: "I had lost my 'voice,' as writers say. It was as if I had been walking on a plate of glass just above the real world, able to see but not to touch it" (Steinem, 1992, pp. 5–6). Each of us has been told to be quiet, to not talk, to speak in a certain way, and to use particular words (or, as often, to not use certain words). Females, however, have been at the receiving end of silencing more so than males—so much so, many of us have internalized it. We find it difficult to speak out. We don't know why we are afraid, but there is something down deep in our psyche that tells us to hold back our words, especially words of anger, disgust, or recrimination. And, when we are not heard, we become, like Steinem, invisible. Perhaps we are living our daily lives, perhaps we are getting a word in here or there, but we know, sometimes by the ache in our throats, that we are socially mute, publicly silenced, and personally powerless. Yes, we too have been silenced. As Steinem also noted, "I began to understand with a terrible sureness that we teach what we need to learn and write what we need to know" (p. 6). And that, in part, is what helped us to understand the importance of providing a platform for the voices you will read in the following essays and, in the process, provided a voice for ourselves.

Celebrating the Learning
of the Unlearned Language

Are we learning the unlearned language or are we unlearning the learned language when we write as the authors in this volume have—personally, evocatively, emotionally, reflexively? As we continue challenging and deconstructing philosophies of social science and the standards for conducting and writing our research, we are both unlearning a language of traditional science *and* learning an unlearned language that is "innate," untapped, suppressed, confined, and silenced. This unlearned language in our social science, in our methods, in our writing is coming together as the "marriage of the public discourse and the private experience, making a power, a beautiful thing, the true discourse of reason. This is a wedding and welding back together of the alienated consciousness . . . the language you can spend your life trying to learn" (Le Guin, 1989, p. 152). But what exactly are we learning and unlearning? Le Guin (1989) tells us we are learning and unlearning a language "always on the verge of silence and often on the verge of song" (p. 150); we learn this "mother tongue" from our mothers, and we offer it as the truth of our experience:

> The mother tongue, spoken or written, expects an answer. It is conversation, a word the root of which means "turning together." The mother tongue is language not as mere communication but as relation, relationship. It connects. It goes two ways, many ways, an exchange, a network. Its power is not in dividing but in binding, not in distancing but uniting. . . . [I]t flies from the mouth on the breath that is our life and is gone, like the outbreath, utterly gone and yet returning, repeated, the breath the same again always, everywhere, and we know it by heart. (pp. 149–150)

You will find the mother tongue in our book. The diversity of methods the authors in this text utilize to voice women's courage, conviction, and wisdom reflect this turning together—the binding, the uniting—and their heartfelt connection to the women represented in their stories.

The scholarship evidenced in this book attempts to rectify the omissions of women's words, women's wisdom in our journals—omissions that too often occur because of the learned language of what constitutes scholarly writing. Carole Blair, Julie Brown, and Leslie Baxter in their article, "Disciplining the Feminine," point to and critique a constellation of practices that confine our research and writing and silence our passions:

> Notably missing, or at least reduced to virtual silence, is the passion that obviously drives our choices to write about particular topics in particular

ways. Our writings suppress our convictions, our enthusiasm, our anger, in the interest of achieving an impersonal "expert" distance and tone. (p. 383)

In these authors' view, we have all helped to perpetuate the silencing by reinforcing and accommodating ourselves to the rules promoted by academic disciplines. Unlearning this language is vital if we are to move away from writing as "scholarly turns" and toward writing as "extended, interactive, 'scholarly conversations'" (p. 403). The readings in this book move in this direction by voicing the convictions of the authors and the women they write about.

Celebrating the learning of the unlearned language, our authors begin their writings with their own personal narratives describing the sense of connection they have to a particular woman—either historical or contemporary—or to a group of women who have suffered and shared what the authors know all too well. Through their research and their writing, the authors allow us to hear the voices of the women with whom they have conversed, either by revisiting their words in songs, poetry, stories, actions, and speeches or by visiting them in person, one with one. And in hearing these women's words we are breaking silences and opening spaces for opposition, translation, support, and change. Old lessons and new lessons abound for all of us.

Le Guin (1989) too admits that she is continuously unlearning lessons and learning new lessons about the minds, work, words, and being of women and of the mother tongue. Like the readings in this book, her unteachers are historic and contemporary:

I celebrate here and now the women who for two centuries have worked for our freedom, the unteachers, the unmaters, the unconquerors, the unwarriors, women who have at risk and at high cost offered their experience as truth. . . . I have to praise these women and thank them for setting me free in my old age to learn my own language. (p. 151)

We praise and thank our authors for their contributions—theoretical, methodological, and most of all personal. May their words of wisdom endow us with the courage of conviction to learn our own language.

Singing in Harmony: An Overview

Some of the voices in *Courage of Conviction: Women's Words, Women's Wisdom* are strong and sure; others quietly speak to both the optimism and the dissolution that mark women's worlds. These voices may be sung out in a baby's lullaby, vocalized in a public address, spoken in a support group, politicized in a poem, or written in a piece of literature.

There are two parts to this book, each of which addresses women's varied voices. They read a bit differently from each other because they are unique in form. Women's Words, the first part, focuses on historical and/or biographical accounts of achievements of women from the 17th century to contemporary times. An individual woman's life, works, and words are at the center of each reading. The second section of this book, Women's Wisdom, focuses on women's contemporary life experiences, which evolve from direct dialogue with groups of women. Highlighted are the ways in which cultural mores continue to confine women and restrict their voices, the extent to which women's roles are changing, and how their life experiences are beginning to be recognized as important and distinct from male experience. Following are brief overviews of the 20 readings in the two parts and their special contributions to women's empowerment through gaining a voice.

Part One: Women's Words

"Connecticut's Canterbury Tale: Prudence Crandall's Brave Stand" is a story about one woman's attempt to provide an education to African American girls in the early 19th century. During that time, there were virtually no opportunities for women in American public life. Denied the vote, the opportunity to speak in public, the benefits of coeducational education (if they received any college education at all), as well as virtually excluded from every professional and public office, women were patently less than second-class citizens. This book begins with Benjamin Sevitch's look at the saga of Prudence Crandall, a woman who lived in those times. Sevitch notes that there are such strong inequities in the scholarship about women that it makes investigating the lives of women throughout history almost impossible.

Richard Leeman also notes that women's voices are silenced by time. Frances Ellen Watkins Harper is one of those women who, although well known and influential during her lifetime, has been largely forgotten by history. Harper was an extremely influential woman in the African American community (e.g., in the Underground Railroad, National Association of Colored Women) and in predominantly White organizations as well (e.g., Women's Christian Temperance Union, American Equal Rights Association). Her poetry, since devalued for its artistry, was solidly written in the tradition of fireside poets and was immensely popular and widely read in 19th century America. In the writing of "Frances Ellen Watkins Harper: Recovering What Is Right," Leeman offers 20th century readers an opportunity to hear a 19th century voice that has been silenced over time.

"'I Can and I Will': 'Mother' Jones Crusades for Labor Rights" by Diane Cypkin offers us a new look at a woman who defied socially prescribed roles at a time when women's voices were almost completely silent, when just about the only acceptable societal roles women could play were "wife" and "mother." Mary Harris Jones courageously and determinedly forged her own role, disregarding and disdaining all stereotypes. Thus, she became the feisty and fiery speaker who led women, men, and children in their valiant fight for labor rights. "Mother" Jones became a woman to admire then and now.

"Stone Mother: Katie Frazier's Native Tales" by Gwendolyn Clancy and Deborah Ballard-Reisch is about a Paiute woman and her desire to preserve her Native American culture. Although native peoples lived on this continent for thousands of years before the arrival of Euro-American settlers, they, as well as women and other minorities, have been left out of American history. During her life, Katie Frazier became a storyteller and historian to her people, among many other things. One of her greatest concerns was that the traditions, language, memories, and stories of her people were dying out. In this reading, Katie Frazier tells her story and thus provides a voice for herself and a recorded history for her people.

In "Margaret Chase Smith: The Spirit of Conviction," Marlene Boyd Vallin provides us with evidence that women can achieve that to which they put their minds. In addition to being a woman in the ultimate male club, the United States Senate, Margaret Chase Smith did not have the family wealth or the political credentials common to many of her Senate colleagues. With only a high school education and from a remote working class town in Maine, she came to be the first woman duly elected to both houses of the Congress. Her slight physical stature and soft voice disguised a will of granite. Talk of political suicide and recrimination did not deter her from speaking out on the Senate floor against Joseph McCarthy, who had cowed other more seasoned colleagues from making a stand against him and his political beliefs.

Maureen Hoffman's essay, "Tillie Olsen: Catching a Lifetime in a Phrase," demonstrates that Olsen's arduous effort to come to print gives voice (and credence) to the lives of many women. In this essay, women will read their own lives: their marital responsibilities, family demands, financial needs, and desires to succeed in their independent endeavors. Olsen's fiction recounts *their* struggles; her nonfiction argues *their* reality; her very life validates *their* truth. Olsen's success at turning her life (and their lives) into the stuff of literature, award-winning literature no less, is at once astonishing and affirming.

"Confinement in the Sexual Wasteland: The Writings of Aphra Behn and Fay Weldon" is a comparison between the works of the 17th century Behn and the 20th century Weldon. It calls into question the notion that women have made unilateral progress in self-definition over the 300 years that separate the two authors. Cynthia Caywood and Bonnie Hain critique the extent to which Western culture has objectified (and still does) women's bodies, thus denying women an integrated sense of self. Ultimately, this comparison shows that regardless of the dismantling of many patriarchal structures, women are still not liberated from being defined externally.

Thuy-Phuong Do's personal account of being a disabled woman helps us all better understand the lifelong struggles of disabled people in the fight against stereotypes. "In My Shoes for Life: A Disabled Woman's Journey" shows that it is a mistake to think of disabled people only in terms of tragedy. There is much more than sorrow; there is joy, there is the mundane, and there are accomplishments. The disabled are a culture with their own set of norms. Do demonstrates that it is difficult, if not impossible, to see her or other disabled persons as full human beings if we continue to view others through our own able-bodied ethnocentrism.

With Thomas Endres's essay, "Singing Along: The Self-Reflective Powers of Carly Simon's Musical Diaries," our book moves into the realm of popular culture where it demonstrates again that women's voices come in a variety of packages. Popular music has an ability to evoke emotional responses and memory associations more than most any other discursive form. This is particularly true when the artist's words, like Simon's, reflect those of the listener. The experiences of being muted that Simon exposes in her music are typical. Her frustrations over being defined by her parents, siblings, lovers, husband, and children are not unique. She is not alone in her three-decade search for her voice—a voice that she found. While Simon sang her frustrations, she gave voice to countless artists and audience members, female and male alike, who learned to both sing her praises and sing along.

Part Two: Women's Wisdom

Women who have experienced miscarriage often are denied the opportunity to talk about and grieve their loss openly. Julie Gray and Patricia Geist's essay, "Elation and Devastation: Women's Journeys Through Pregnancy and Miscarriage," tells the story of one woman and her search to make sense of and seek healing for her tragic losses. In her search, she interacts with other women who have experienced miscarriages, allowing us to share their stories and giving them a forum to express their pain. As such, this reading allows us to hear the voices of a group of women frequently silenced by even their closest friends and family.

Lisa Gates in "The Mystery and Mystique of Natural Childbirth" considers why women choose natural childbirth methods when less painful, drug-assisted methods are available. Interestingly and ironically, natural childbirth is often viewed as a mysterious, "radical" approach to bringing children into the world. Gates takes us into a conversation with mothers who have attempted to give birth naturally within the hospital context. She answers such questions as, What exactly is "natural" childbirth? and Why would *anyone* in her right mind choose the often long, arduous, painful process of natural childbirth? The challenge of childbirth is a pivotal and profound life experience. In this essay we hear the stories of several women and how they chose to meet that challenge.

Contrary to many prior feminist accounts of motherhood that unwittingly universalize women's experience, "Mobilizing Motherhood: Women's Experiences of Visiting Their Children" explores a unique mothering situation that reflects contemporary circumstances. Deborah Eicher-Catt explains that for most noncustodial mothers, the status of noncustodian necessarily silences them. Many become reticent about discussing openly their perceived "deviance" from socially prescribed norms of behavior. Although their worlds as mothers are similarly shattered, they typically lack sufficient channels of communication through which they can voice their concerns to one another. This essay offers readers the opportunity to hear about the personal, social, and cultural implications of attempting to "mobilize" a new vision of motherhood and of beginning a dialogue concerning the issues involved in this adaptation of a rigidly defined role for women.

In "'Return to Life': Communicating in Families of the Holocaust," Lynn Turner says that two characteristics of survivor families are their resilience and their desire to establish family life. However, communication in survivor families may be impaired by one of two responses to the topic of the Holocaust: Either the topic is taboo or it is invoked incessantly. Even in families where silencing is the norm, daughters learn lessons about the Holocaust and about "being female" from their parents. By sharing the conversations of four daughters raised in Holocaust survivor families, Turner helps us begin to understand the focus these families place on life and rebirth, even in the face of death.

Profound and moving statements about voice and voicelessness come from female students in the classroom. Although they may gain voice in that small public forum, many seldom get heard outside of it. Cheryl Forbes notes that students in general are voiceless, female students are particularly voiceless, and women of color are the most silenced. The stories of four such women are presented in "African American Women: Voices of Literacy and Literate Voices." Forbes's uncovering of these hidden voices has deep implications for the way we teach, write, and think about what it means to be a teacher working with women. These representative voices also have deep implications for what it means to have a public voice and a private voice and for the appropriate relationship between the two.

The most distinctive difference between feminist analysis of women's speech and other methods of inquiry, Lynne Lundberg explains, is that feminist theory allows us to recognize that female speakers need to break down the barriers imposed by a male-dominated world before they can be heard. For women raised in religious traditions that devalue and even forbid women to speak in public, these barriers are even more powerful because they are ordained by God. "False Eyelashes and the Word of God: Speaking as an Evangelical Woman" exposes the limitations that most religions place on women. The evangelical tradition in America, however, is a unique case study because 19th century evangelical churches were among the first to allow women to speak in public, whereas the present-day church silences women. Lundberg was raised in the evangelical church and attests to the difficulty of setting aside the church's prohibition in order to speak.

Women recovering from alcoholism are somehow "displaced" in the rather voluminous quantity of scholarly work on the topic. Kelley Chrouser and Jack Kay note that although much is known about emotional responses to alcoholism, psychological changes, and environmental conditions, little is known about how women "talk" in recovery. "Courageous Talk: Empowering the Voices of Recovering Female Alcoholics" shows that women in recovery have a story to tell, that they are courageous, and that their "talk" is what shapes who they become.

HIV/AIDS hits women particularly hard. Women who have been socialized to be the nurturers find themselves in need of being nurtured. People who contract this disease are often thought of as "bad" people, so these women constantly work to construct their self-images as "good" and to present themselves to others as such. The process of coping with this medical tragedy is complicated because of the stigma attached to HIV/AIDS. Women with AIDS become invisible because the media limit their coverage of AIDS victims in general (unless the individual is famous) and seldom discuss female victims. Consequently, the social perception of women with HIV/AIDS is normally that they are sex-industry workers. "'I'm Alive, Thank You': Women's Accounts of HIV/AIDS" by Judith Liu,

Kathleen Grove, and Donald Kelly shows that there are no clear distinctions between "us" and "them." If seemingly ordinary White, middle-class women can become infected, then given the wrong set of circumstances, anyone can.

The potential for being a victim of violence is a daily reality for most women. Whether a woman is walking down the street, going out for the evening, driving down the highway, or walking into her home, the threat is ever present. The movie *Thelma and Louise* demonstrates daily encounters with violence that range from the psychological abuse of an arrogant and domineering husband to the come-ons of a flirtatious and dangerous would-be rapist. As viewers of this movie, women have a brief opportunity to ride along as Thelma and Louise counter men's attacks on their self-images, identities, and safety. Linda Perry argues in "*Thelma and Louise: Breaking the Silence*" that as they watch this film women experience vicarious vindication for having to live their lives "on guard."

Delia Conti demonstrates in "The Rhetoric of the 'New Feminism': Searching for a Cultural Backlash" that the greatest threat to the advancement of women's issues is women themselves. The decisions women must make about work, family, and societal roles are, at their core, moral issues that create and reflect life dilemmas. Women must reexamine their dominant mode of arguing about these issues and reassess the most effective rhetorical strategy for overcoming division among themselves. Women's strategies must take themselves, men, and government policies into consideration on issues such as balancing work and family.

Our book concludes with "*La Malinche* Revisited." In many ways, this piece by María Cristina González captures the issues addressed throughout this volume. Her work demonstrates the profound ways her personal history as a sexually abused, multicultural Catholic bilingual Texan Chicana with a Ph.D. has blended to create lenses that enable others to see poignantly the realities of voices that are not always heard. No matter how many identities we might have or which ones we choose to emphasize, it is always traumatic to have the right to voice them silenced. González tells us that "*La Malinche* Revisited" took 37 years to write; we think it speaks for itself.

Getting Ready to Listen

Each essay in *Courage of Conviction: Women's Words, Women's Wisdom* makes a special contribution to the literature by, for, and about women. In addition, the artful poetry of Phyllis Kahaney and María Cristina González offered throughout the book deepens our understanding of women's lives. Combined, they create a chorus of women's voices, interwoven through their stories and stories about them. We ask you to sit back and enjoy the process of "hearing" all of these women's voices, perhaps for the first time. Our hope is that, like gaining an ear for music, the reading of these stories will train your ears to hear and listen to women's voices regardless of their origin.

Discussion Questions

1. Why do you believe that Perry and Geist began this book with their own personal narratives? How does it affect your perception of them? Of what they want to accomplish? Of what to expect in the remainder of the book?

2. In what ways do you see speaking out as courageous? By looking at the Contents, can you see the same two themes of courage and conviction? What other themes might have evolved?

3. Have you ever felt silenced? Under what circumstances do you continue to feel as if you do not have a voice? What about the situation might change if you voiced your opinion?

4. Do you agree that women are more silenced than men in American culture? Is this true in most cultures? In what ways are women silenced? How has silencing affected women's lives?

5. What are some examples of situations in which someone provided opportunities for others to have a voice? Do you agree with Perry and Geist that that action was a voice in and of itself?

6. In your experience, what forms of writing do you find most rewarding or most capable of expressing your passion?

References

Blair, C., Brown, J. R., & Baxter, L. A. (1994). Disciplining the feminine. *Quarterly Journal of Speech, 80,* 383–409.

Gilligan, C. (1982). *In a different voice.* Cambridge: Harvard University Press.

Hinman, L. (1994). *Ethics*. Fort Worth, TX: Harcourt Brace.

Le Guin, U. K. (1989). *Dancing at the edge of the world: Thoughts on words, women, places*. New York: Harper & Row.

Steinem, G. (1992). *Revolution from within: A book of self-esteem*. Boston: Little, Brown.

Part One

Women's Words

Part One of this volume, Women's Words, focuses on biographical accounts of women and their achievements from the 17th century to contemporary times. The stories depict women who have been forgotten or devalued in history, who have accomplished a lot with virtually no opportunities, who have redefined their socially prescribed roles, who have devoted their lives to preserving and affirming women's realities, and who have striven to be recognized for who they were and what they contributed to American culture.

An individual woman's life, words, and work are at the center of each reading. Through her life's example, each of these individuals provides opportunities for women of the past, the present, and the future to be heard, to gain a voice. The women discussed in this section of the book overcame silencing based on stereotypes, threats, indignities, public humiliation, recrimination, objectification, arrest, and even arson. The authors of each of these essays begin with their own personal narratives describing the sense of connection they have to the women—either historical or contemporary—about whom they have written.

Connecticut's Canterbury Tale

Prudence Crandall's Brave Stand

Benjamin Sevitch, Ph.D.[1]

Department of Communication
Central Connecticut State University

Prudence Crandall, 1838

*P*rudence Crandall was not a typical person. She not only knew the difference between right and wrong, she was willing to endure all manner of threats, indignities, public humiliation, arrest, incarceration, and even arson to pursue what was just and decent. Because of limitations placed on women in her lifetime, what we know about Prudence Crandall has been told mostly by men. However, I believe that the depiction we have of her is relatively free of gender bias. To me, the most remarkable thing about Connecticut's Canterbury Tale is the extraordinary courage and perseverance of Prudence Crandall. The everyday, mundane events, such as obtaining food and water, were for her an ordeal. I cannot help but wonder how any person, of either sex and any century, would have been strong enough to endure what she did to live a principled life.

This is a story about Prudence Crandall, a brave woman who tried to establish a school for Black girls in a small town in Connecticut. For her troubles she was confronted with bigotry, slander, incarceration, violence, and finally, arson. After months of living in daily fear, she was driven from her home with a sense of personal failure. In short, it is a story typical of the tribulations encountered by many who were sympathetic to the abolitionist movement in early 19th century America, when bigotry and violence were hardly behavioral aberrations. What is perhaps not typical is the courage that this woman demonstrated in the face of the forces mounted against her.

Prudence Crandall was born on September 3, 1803, in Hopkinton, Rhode Island, to Quaker parents (Adams, 1930). Ten years later the family sold their property and settled on a farm in Canterbury, Connecticut, about 10 miles west of the Rhode Island border. After attending the Friends' School at Providence for 4 years, Prudence taught school in Plainfield, the next town 4 miles east of Canterbury, where she immediately became popular with students and parents alike (May, 1869).

Canterbury was a thriving community in the 1830s. With a population of almost 1,500, the town stood on a rise of land near the Quinebaug River and served as a major transportation center through which the Hartford and Providence road intersected the Norwich and Worcester turnpike (Kimbell, n.d.). Farmers and businessmen prospered, and Canterbury boasted the largest Temperance Society in Windham County (Larned,

1880). All that was lacking was a school for the young ladies of the community. To meet that need, a group of the more substantial citizens asked Prudence Crandall to establish such a school. Advancing her money to purchase a large house on the Canterbury Green that had been left vacant by the death of a prominent lawyer, these people became the school's "Board of Visitors," what today we would call trustees.

And so in November of 1831, Prudence Crandall, a 28-year-old spinster Quaker schoolmistress, opened her school, which soon was populated by girls from the best families in Canterbury as well as from neighboring towns (Kimbell, n.d). For the next year the school flourished and its teacher was held in unimpeachable repute. What happened to change this idyllic scenario is best described in a letter written by Prudence many years later to the historian of Windham County:

> I had a nice colored girl, now Mrs. Charles Harris, as help in my family; and her intended husband regularly received *The Liberator* [William Lloyd Garrison's radical abolitionist newspaper, published in Boston]. The girl took the paper from the office and loaned it to me. In that the condition of the colored people both slaves and free was truthfully portrayed, the double-dealing and manifest deception of the Colonization Society were faithfully exposed, and the question of Immediate Emancipation of the millions of slaves in the United States boldly advocated. Having been taught from early childhood the sin of Slavery, my sympathies were greatly aroused. Sarah Harris, a respectable young woman and a member of the church (now Mrs. Fairweather, and sister to the before-named intended husband), called often to see her friend Marcia, my family assistant. In some of her calls I ascertained that she wished to attend my school and board at her own father's house at some little distance from the village. I allowed her to enter as one of my pupils. By this act I gave great offence. The wife of an Episcopal clergyman who lived in the village told me that if I continued that colored girl in my school it could not be sustained. I replied to her, *That it might sink, then, for I shall not turn her out!* I very soon found that some of my school would leave not to return if the colored girl was returned. Under these circumstances I made up my mind that if it were possible I would teach colored girls exclusively. (Larned, 1880, p. 491)

It was not surprising that Prudence Crandall, with her Quaker upbringing, should embrace the abolitionist cause. The Friends had always been vigorous opponents of slavery.

But equality was not the principal concern of the parents of Canterbury. They came to Prudence and demanded that Sarah Harris be expelled

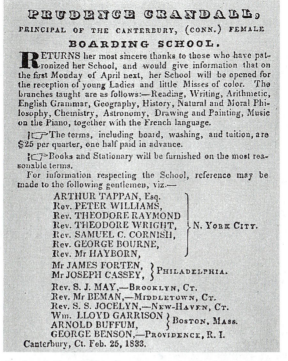

PRUDENCE CRANDALL,
PRINCIPAL OF THE CANTERBURY, (CONN.) FEMALE
BOARDING SCHOOL.

RETURNS her most sincere thanks to those who have patronized her School, and would give information that on the first Monday of April next, her School will be opened for the reception of young Ladies and little Misses of color. The branches taught are as follows:—Reading, Writing, Arithmetic, English Grammar, Geography, History, Natural and Moral Philosophy, Chemistry, Astronomy, Drawing and Painting, Music on the Piano, together with the French language.

☞The terms, including board, washing, and tuition, are $25 per quarter, one half paid in advance.

☞Books and Stationary will be furnished on the most reasonable terms.

For information respecting the School, reference may be made to the following gentlemen, viz.—

ARTHUR TAPPAN, Esq.
Rev. PETER WILLIAMS,
Rev. THEODORE RAYMOND
Rev. THEODORE WRIGHT, } N. YORK CITY.
Rev. SAMUEL C. CORNISH,
Rev. GEORGE BOURNE,
Rev. Mr HAYBORN,

Mr JAMES FORTEN, } PHILADELPHIA.
Mr JOSEPH CASSEY,

Rev. S. J. MAY,—BROOKLYN, CT.
Rev. Mr BEMAN,—MIDDLETOWN, CT.
Rev. S. S. JOCELYN,—NEW-HAVEN, CT.
Wm. LLOYD GARRISON } BOSTON, MASS.
ARNOLD BUFFUM,
GEORGE BENSON,—PROVIDENCE, R. I.
Canterbury, Ct. Feb. 25, 1833.

Prudence Crandall's advertisement in The Liberator, *1833, announcing the opening of her school in Canterbury, Connecticut, to "young ladies and little misses of color" and offering the names of leading abolitionists as references.*

immediately because they "would not have it said that their daughters went to school with a nigger girl" (Kimbell, n.d., p. 3). Rather than yield to the local pressure, Prudence wrote to Garrison in January 1933 and visited him in Boston later in the month. In February, parents and pupils were informed that the Canterbury Female Boarding School would be closed until the first Monday in April, when it would reopen for "young ladies and little misses of color" (May, 1869, p. 42). To guarantee that there would be enough Black students to warrant the continuance of the school, Miss Crandall placed an advertisement in *The Liberator* on March 2 (Garrison, 1885).

By this time Canterbury was thoroughly aroused with Prudence Crandall's intentions. A committee from the Board of Visitors called on her to dissuade her from her venture. Esquire Frost tried to convince her of the impropriety of her idea and delicately hinted at the danger that might ensue from "these leveling principles and intermarriage between the whites and blacks." Prudence answered that "Moses had a black wife," which effectively ended the conversation (Larned, 1880, p. 492).

When private persuasion failed, public action was tried. In characteristically New England fashion a town meeting was called for March 9 to devise some scheme for escaping the crushing calamity of a "school for nigger girls" (Larned, 1880, p. 493). News of the Canterbury school had now reached the Reverend Samuel J. May, a Unitarian clergyman and abolitionist who lived in Brooklyn, Connecticut, just 6 miles north of Canterbury. May had written Crandall offering his support, and on March 4, Prudence replied, asking May to act as her attorney. He accepted and came to the meeting with his abolitionist friend, George W. Benson. The day before the meeting Prudence learned that Arnold Buffum, a fellow Quaker and the principal lecturing agent of the New England Anti-Slavery Society, was in Norwich, Connecticut. She visited Buffum and persuaded him to come to Canterbury the next night.

Attorney Asael Bacon moderated the town meeting, which packed a thousand people into the Congregational Church. Speaker after speaker slandered Prudence Crandall and her supporters in abusive language, describing her undertaking as "a plot against the peace and prosperity of the village" (Kimbell, n.d., p. 5). State Attorney Judson, whose house on Canterbury Green stood next to Miss Crandall's, then continued the attack. The idea of having "a school of nigger girls so near him was insupportable" (May, 1869, p. 45). By this time Buffum and May thought it was appropriate for someone to speak on Prudence's behalf. They passed her powers of attorney over to Judson, who, according to May:

> instantly broke forth with greater violence than before, accused us of insulting the town by coming there to interfere with its local concerns. Other gentlemen sprang to their feet in hot displeasure; poured out their tirades upon Miss Crandall and her accomplices, and, with fists doubled in our faces, roughly admonished us that if we opened our lips there, they would inflict upon us the utmost penalty of the law, if not a more immediate vengeance. (May, 1869, p. 45)

The moderator ruled that they could not address the meeting and warned them that they would be prosecuted if they tried to do so. The resolutions were passed; the meeting was adjourned. May stood up in his pew and cried out, "Men of Canterbury, I have a word for you. Hear me!" After briefly rebutting the vicious attacks against Prudence, he yielded the floor to Buffum, but very quickly the trustees of the church appeared and ordered everyone out of the sanctuary (May, 1869, p. 46).

By now Prudence Crandall had become a cause célèbre in abolitionist circles. Garrison wrote: "Miss Crandall must be sustained at all hazards. . . . In Boston, we are all excited at the Canterbury affair" (1885, p. 782). The Reverend Simeon Jocelyn of New Haven reported to Garrison:

> We are all determined to sustain Miss Crandall if there is law enough in the land to protect her. . . . She is a noble soul and has no doubt more praying friends in the United States drawn to her by her persecution than the whole number of the population in Canterbury. (Garrison & Garrison 1885, p. 340)

When Prudence reopened her school, the battle lines were clearly established, but the townsfolk now shifted their strategy.

Early in its history, Canterbury had passed a law against vagrants. All persons warned to leave town by the selectmen must either post a bond guaranteeing that they would not become a burden upon the town or else be subject to a fine of $1.67 for each week they remained. If, at the end of 10 days, the vagrants had neither paid the fine nor left town, the whipping post was to be invoked: they were to be stripped to the waist and whipped on the naked back not to exceed 10 strokes (May, 1869). This harsh old law was suddenly revived. On the day after her arrival, Eliza Hammond, a 16-year-old pupil from Providence, was warned to leave town. Eliza refused to pay the fine and declared that she would rather take the whipping than give in. Fortunately, May posted a $10,000 bond, which easily protected all the students, and the first victory in the struggle went to Prudence Crandall, but not for long (May, 1869).

After a second town meeting on April 1, Canterbury petitioned the Connecticut General Assembly to adopt a law forbidding schools to admit "Negroes" from outside the state. Prudence Crandall's school had now become a matter of concern for the entire state. Connecticut's infamous Black Law was passed by the state Senate and House of Representatives and signed by the governor on May 24, 1833. It declared that "no person shall set up or establish in this State any school, academy, or literary institution for the instruction of colored persons who are not inhabitants of this State" (Larned, 1880, p. 496), and the law established a schedule of stiff fines for violations. Church bells rang in Canterbury, and a canon was fired to signal the town's victory.

Prudence Crandall's father was sent a letter threatening him and the other members of his family with a fine of $100 if they should attempt to visit her. Miss Crandall, the epistle said, would "be taken up the same way as for stealing a horse or burglaring. Her property will be taken but she will be put in jail, not having the liberty of the yard. There is no mercy to be shown about it" (Larned, 1880, p. 497). On June 27 the sheriff appeared at the school with a warrant for the principal's arrest. Prudence was taken to the local court, where Justice Adams presided. The arraignment did not take long. She was committed to stand trial at the August session of the Superior Court. Bond was established at $300, but to the surprise of everyone, no one posted it. The Justice demanded that a messenger be dispatched to the Reverend May informing him that unless he provided the requisite surety, Prudence would be jailed. May denied the request but traveled immediately to the site of the local jail in Brooklyn. When the jailer arrived with Prudence in tow, May told her: "If now you hesitate, if you dread the gloomy place so much as to wish to be saved from it, I will give bonds for you even now." "Oh no," she promptly replied, "I am only afraid they will not put me in jail" (May, 1869, p. 55).

May's refusal to post bond and Prudence's willingness to go to jail were designed to attract popular sympathy to their cause. The jail was small and not much used. Everyone knew that two years earlier it had been occupied by a condemned murderer, one Oliver Watkins, who had strangled his wife with a whipcord and was taken from the Brooklyn jail to his hanging (McCain, 1986). Recognizing the trap before them, two of Prudence's adversaries beseeched May one final time: "It would be a damn shame, an eternal disgrace to the State, to have her put into jail, into the very room that Watkins had last occupied." "Certainly, gentlemen, and you may prevent this, if you please," May replied. But they protested, "We are not her friends; we are not in favor of her school: we don't want any more damn niggers coming among us. It is your place to stand by Miss Crandall and help her now." "She knows we have not deserted her," May responded; and the very next day bond was posted and Prudence released (May, 1869, pp. 55–57).

But now the campaign of public persecution escalated. Whenever she and her pupils went for a walk, a crowd of noisy hoodlums trailed along behind, hooting, jeering, and blowing tin horns. Her house was splattered with rotten eggs. Her students were never certain when stones would be thrown at them, day or night. The local merchants signed an agreement not to fill her orders. Doctor Harris refused to call at her house. The trustees of the Congregational Church declined to seat her pupils. Someone threw a shovelful of manure into her well, and no one would supply her with fresh water (Garrison & Garrison, 1885). Everything seemed to be going against Prudence Crandall.

But the citizens of Canterbury had underestimated the recalcitrance of their schoolmistress. Prudence met each situation as it arose with ingenuity. She found a sympathetic storekeeper in the nearby village of Packerville and a friendly "Negro" in Norwich. The Black man volunteered to bring her supplies from the grocer and to transport her pupils back and forth from the school. When the doors of the Congregational Church were closed to her students, she found that they were welcome to attend Baptist services in Packerville (Larned, 1880). The water problem was more difficult to solve. She had only one well, and when it became polluted, it looked like the school might be forced to close. But her father came to the rescue, ignoring the threats made against him. Each day he carried a few pails of water from his house to the school.

The Reverend Samuel May, in the meantime, was busily preparing for the upcoming trial of Prudence Crandall. He contacted Arthur Tappan, a wealthy New York City merchant who frequently contributed to abolitionist and temperance causes. Tappan, who had been following the Crandall case in the pages of *The Liberator,* instructed May by letter:

> This contest, in which you have been providentially called to engage, will be a serious, perhaps a violent one. It may be prolonged and very expensive. Nevertheless, it ought to be persisted in to the last. . . . Consider me your banker. Spare no necessary expense. Command the services of the ablest lawyers. See to it that this great case will be thoroughly tried, cost what it may. I will cheerfully honor your drafts to enable you to defray that cost. (May, 1869, p. 58)

A few weeks later the philanthropist appeared unannounced at May's doorstep to prepare for Prudence's defense. They traveled to Plainfield, where Miss Crandall had begun her teaching career, and purchased a printing shop that had recently gone out of business. Then they engaged a promising 23-year-old law student, Charles C. Burleigh, to edit a weekly paper devoted to supporting Prudence Crandall, abolitionism, and temperance. *The Unionist* started publication on July 25, 1833, and ran for almost 2 years (May, 1869).

The trial of Prudence Crandall, for the crime of operating a boarding school for colored girls, began on August 23, 1833, at the Windham County Courthouse in Brooklyn. Acting on the advice of Arthur Tappan, May had hired three distinguished members of the state bar, William Wolcott Ellsworth, Calvin Goddard, and Henry Strong. Ellsworth headed the team. He was then serving as a United States Congressman from Connecticut, and his father, Oliver Ellsworth, had been the second Chief Justice of the United States Supreme Court. Three prosecutors, led by Andrew T. Judson, provided the opposition.

The prosecution began by introducing evidence to establish the fact that the school did exist and that Prudence Crandall did indeed instruct certain colored girls who were not inhabitants of Connecticut. Over the objection of the defense, some of the students were called to the stand. After presenting 14 witnesses, including pupils, friends, and relatives of Prudence, Judson rested his case.

The defense began by conceding that Prudence had broken the Black Law. Their case rested on the argument that the law was unconstitutional. Ellsworth claimed that free Negroes were citizens and therefore enjoyed the same essential rights, such as those to free movement and education, that they enjoyed in the states from which they came. Judson countered by denying that colored persons were citizens of those states where they were not enfranchised. In fact, he argued, if it were not for the protection provided by the current law, the southern states might free all their slaves and send them to Connecticut, which probably made a sobering impression upon some of the jurors. In his charge to the jury, Judge Joseph Eaton observed that "the law was constitutional and obligatory on the people of the State" (May, 1869, pp. 68–69). After being out for several hours, the jury returned without a verdict. Eaton gave further instructions, but the jury returned again and announced that it was hopelessly deadlocked. Seven jurors were for conviction, and five for acquittal (May, 1869).

Under normal procedures, a hung jury would have meant an automatic continuance of Prudence's case until the next term of County Court, scheduled for December 1833. But in October, Chief Justice David Daggett of the Supreme Court of Errors was sitting as the trial judge of the Superior Court at Brooklyn. Daggett was a former mayor of New Haven who, according to Reverend May, "was known to be hostile to the colored people, and a strenuous advocate of the Black Law" (May, 1869, p. 69). Confident of obtaining a conviction with Daggett on the bench, the prosecutors successfully moved the Crandall case to the Superior Court docket. The second trial opened on October 3, 1833, with the opposing legal teams intact. The evidence and arguments were essentially the same as before.

Judge Daggett's charge to the jury left no doubt about the verdict they would return:

> The persons contemplated in this act are *not citizens* within the obvious meaning of the constitution of the *United States,* which I have just read. Let me begin, by putting this plain question. Are *slaves citizens*? At the adoption of the constitution of the *United States,* every state was a slave state. . . . We all know that slavery is recognized in that constitution as it

is; and it is the duty of this court to take that constitution as it is, for we have sworn to support it. The *African* race are essentially a degraded caste, of inferior rank and condition in society. Marriages are forbidden between them and whites in some of the states, and when not absolutely contrary to law, they are revolting, and regarded as an offence against public decorum.

To my mind, it would be a perversion of terms, and the well known rule of construction, to say that slaves, free blacks, or *Indians*, were citizens, within the meaning of that term, as used in the constitution. God forbid that I should add to the degradation of this race of men; but I am bound by my duty, to say they are not citizens. (*Crandall v. The State*, 1834, pp. 344–345)

The jury returned a verdict of guilty, and Prudence Crandall's lawyers filed an immediate appeal to the Supreme Court of Errors.

Despite the ordeals of two trials and the disapprobation of her neighbors, Prudence continued to operate her school. Garrison used *The Liberator* to urge all colored parents who could afford it to send their daughters to Canterbury. He assured them that their children would be well cared for and properly instructed. Attendance had increased from 14 to 17 students, and two new teachers had been added to the faculty: Miss Crandall's younger sister, Almira, and William H. Burleigh, brother of the editor of *The Unionist* (Larned, 1880).

On July 22, 1834, the case of *Crandall v. The State* was heard before the Supreme Court at Hartford, Connecticut. Ellsworth and Goddard represented Prudence for the third time, but now Windham County attorney Chauncey F. Cleveland joined Judson on the state's behalf. Ellsworth again argued that the Black Law was unconstitutional because Prudence's students were citizens of their respective states. If they were White, he contended, it would be conceded that they would be deemed citizens; therefore, Connecticut's law was based solely upon a distinction of color. Judson and Cleveland countered the argument directly. They asserted that it was not novel that citizenship rested upon skin color and cited Indians as an example. Moreover, they cited various laws that had defined citizens as free White persons. Their final point concerned the right of the state to regulate education and to control the influx of outsiders.

Both sides obviously sought a determination of the constitutionality of Connecticut's Black Law. Instead, the case was adjudicated on a technicality. Justice Thomas Scott Williams, writing for the Court, held that Prudence was not charged with establishing a school contrary to law. He noted, "It is, however, no where alleged that the school was set up without license, or that the scholars were instructed by those who had no license" (*Crandall v. The State,* 1834, p. 367). On that minor point all of the justices agreed except one lone dissenter, Chief Justice Daggett, who had presided over the second trial and, amazingly, did not recuse himself when the case came up on appeal. The conviction of Prudence Crandall was reversed.

Elated by her triumph in Hartford, Prudence married the Reverend Calvin Philleo, a Baptist minister from Ithaca, New York, a month later (Kimbell, n.d.). But news of the Supreme Court's decision did not please the townsfolk of Canterbury. On September 9, 1834, a fire mysteriously erupted at her house. Although quickly extinguished, the fire had the desired effect of panicking Prudence and her pupils. The same night a band of men with heavy iron bars broke all the windows in the house (Larned, 1880). The next morning Reverend May was summoned to Canterbury, and he vividly described the scene:

> Never before had Miss Crandall seemed to quail, and her pupils had become afraid to remain another night under her roof. The front rooms of the house were hardly tenantable; and it seemed foolish to repair them only to be destroyed again. After due consideration, therefore, it was determined that the school should be abandoned. . . . I felt ashamed of Canterbury, ashamed of Connecticut, ashamed of my country, ashamed of my color. (May, 1869, p. 71)

Prudence sold her house as quickly as possible and left Connecticut forever (Larned, 1880). She and her husband moved to Illinois, where he died in 1874. She then traveled with her brother, Hezekiah, and took up residence in the small town of Elk Falls, Kansas (Adams, 1930).

Fortunately, there is a happy epilogue to this story. In 1838, at the request of William Lloyd Garrison, the managers of the New England Anti-Slavery Society voted to ask Prudence to sit for a portrait. That oil painting, by artist Francis Alexander, eventually came into the possession of Reverend May, who, on the very day of his death, donated it to his old friend Andrew Dixon White, president of Cornell University (Garrison, 1885). The painting hangs today in the library of Cornell.

After Prudence left Connecticut, the citizens of Canterbury changed their minds about Black people and, through their politicians, vigorously opposed the extension of slavery in the United States. According to the historian of Eastern Connecticut, "Miss Crandall did not succeed in teaching many colored girls, but she *educated* the people of Windham County" (Larned, 1880, p. 502). After the Civil War, Connecticut supported and quickly ratified the 14th Amendment to the Constitution in 1868, which affirmed full rights of citizenship upon Black people.

In 1886, more than 50 years after Prudence left Canterbury, the citizens of that town took steps to expiate the sins of their parents. They petitioned the General Assembly of Connecticut as follows:

> We, the Undersigned, Citizens of the State, and of the Town of Canterbury, mindful of the dark blot that rests upon our fair fame and name, for the cruel outrages inflicted upon a former citizen of our Commonwealth, a noble Christian Woman (Miss Prudence Crandall, now Mrs. Philleo) at present in straightened circumstances, and far advanced in years, respectfully pray your Honorable Body to make such late reparation for the wrong done her, as your united wisdom, your love of justice, and an honorable pride in the good name of our noble State, shall dictate.
>
> It will be remembered that she stands in the Records of the Court as a convicted criminal, and suffered unnumbered outrages in person and property, for benevolent work, that now to its great honor, the General Government itself is engaged in.
>
> We respectfully suggest that you make a fair appropriation in her behalf, which shall at once relieve her from any anxiety for the future, and from the official stigma that rests upon her name, and purge our own record from its last remaining stain, in connection with the colored race. (Petition of the Citizens of the Town of Canterbury, 1886)

The petition contained 112 signatures. The State Legislature awarded Prudence an annuity of $400. Three years later, on January 28, 1889, Prudence Crandall Philleo died in Elk Falls in her 86th year (Adams, 1930). Her epitaph, however, will not be found in Kansas. If you travel to Canterbury, Connecticut, you will see a lovely restored big white house on the village green. It is owned by the Connecticut Historical Commission and was dedicated as a museum in May 1984 (Stenza, B7). A plaque on the outside reads:

In This House
PRUDENCE CRANDALL
Held a School
For Negro Girls
1833

Discussion Questions

1. If Prudence Crandall had been allowed to speak on her own behalf at the Canterbury town meetings, what do you think she would have said?

2. What 20th century woman reminds you most of Prudence Crandall? Why?

3. If you had lived in Canterbury when Prudence did, how would you have responded to her school? Would you have been willing to help her? If so, how?

4. Do you fault Prudence Crandall for placing her pupils in jeopardy when actions were taken against the school? At what point is the protection of the students more important than the existence of the school?

5. If the school in Canterbury had had male students and a male teacher, do you think that the anti-abolitionist forces would have been as brazen? Was it easier in the 19th century to intimidate a woman than a man? Has that condition changed in the 20th century?

6. How is Prudence Crandall's school similar to or different from contemporary single-sex schools, African American schools, or other groupings of students in educational settings?

References

Adams, J. T. (1930). Crandall, Prudence. In *Dictionary of American biography*. New York: Scribner's.

Crandall v. The State. 10 CONN 339–372 (1834).

Garrison, W. P. (1885, September). Connecticut in the Middle Ages. *Century Illustrated Monthly Magazine*, pp. 780–786.

Garrison, W. P., & Garrison, F. J. (1885). *William Lloyd Garrison, 1805–1879: The story of his life, told by his children* (vol. 1). New York: Century.

Kimbell, J. C. (n.d.). *Connecticut's Canterbury tale*. Hartford: Plimpton Press.

Larned, E. D. (1880). *History of Windham County, Connecticut.* Worcester, MA: C. Hamilton.

May, S. J. (1869). *Some recollections of our antislavery conflict.* Boston: Fields, Osgood, & Co.

McCain, D. R. (1986, September). The last hanging. *Connecticut Magazine,* pp. 124, 126–128.

Petition of the Citizens of the Town of Canterbury, Conn., and others to the Connecticut General Assembly for aid for Miss Prudence Crandall. (1886, January). *House Petition No. 48.* Hartford, CT: State Printing Office.

Stenza, L. (1984, May 5). Black women's school dedicated as museum. *Hartford Courant,* p. B7.

Endnote

The author acknowledges the Board of Trustees of the Connecticut State University for granting permission to print this essay based on the article, "Connecticut's Canterbury tale: Prudence Crandall and her school," published in the *Connecticut Review,* Vol. X, No. 1, Summer 1987.

2

Frances Ellen Watkins Harper

Recovering What Is Right

Richard W. Leeman, Ph.D.[1]

Department of Communication Studies
University of North Carolina, Charlotte

Frances E. W. Harper

Ruby

What's her name I ask
my best friend Bertha Rose
and Bertha Rose says
"Ruby, she's our maid"
and Ruby's like a dream
to me, at night her
skinny arms and shiny hair
become a glory, God Himself
could come right up through
her wide mouth on Sunday
when I hear her singing
to the Lord, or see her wash
her car with such a love
I name it Baby, that's
how she caresses it,
rubs it down with
grease she tells me she calls
wax. Oh, yeah, I'm telling
Bertha Rose, I want to be like
her, I want to grow up just
like that—pretty, strong,
a woman men breathe for, a woman
with a voice like glitter
but Bertha Rose tells my Mamma
and pretty soon Ruby's gone,
not even a goodbye, and Tuesdays
now I go to Miss Lucy's to dance
with boys in fresh pressed pants,
and in the South, my Mamma
tells me, girls are ladies,
Missy, and I know what she
means, no music on your
tongue like honey, no grease
on the car, no man black as night
surrounding you until your morning
dawns, cold, white, bleached in sunlight.

    —*Phyllis Kahaney*

Frances Ellen Watkins Harper was a well-known poet and orator in the 19th century. Part of her excellence lay in how skillfully her discourse was executed; part, in how uniformly she gave voice to those who were otherwise voiceless in American society. Yet, defining Harper's unique voice was a major obstacle in writing this essay (aside from the scarcity of materials, especially oratorical). I sensed a strong, independent voice, yet many of Harper's arguments, themes, and language are found in other 19th century discourse. Therefore, it was difficult to capture in words Harper's ability to combine these "common" elements to produce her powerful poetry and speeches. Indeed, she was the "ideal orator" described by Quintilian: a good [wo]man speaking well.

In *Early Black American Poets*, William Robinson calls Frances Ellen Watkins Harper an "orator poet" (1969, p. 3). However, because she applied her skill as a poet to her public speaking, Harper could also be called a "poetic orator." Equally comfortable with either mode of discourse, hers was an eloquent and generally lyrical voice for change in 19th century America. Although famous in her own time, Frances Ellen Watkins Harper has been generally overlooked in ours.

Part of the problem of studying Frances Harper's work is that we know little about her life. Born a free Black in Baltimore in 1825, she came from humble, though comfortable, origins. She was orphaned at the age of 3 and raised by her aunt and uncle. In her uncle's school, the William Watkins Academy for Negro Youth, she studied the Bible, the classics, and elocution until the age of 13. She then went to work as a live-in domestic, where her employer's wife, taken with her intellect, allowed Frances full use of the family-owned book shop. Thus educated, in 1846, at the age of 21, she published her first book of poetry, *Forest Leaves*, of which no copies have been found. When the Fugitive Slave Law was passed in 1850, Watkins left the slave state of Maryland and moved to Columbus, Ohio, where she taught at Union Seminary and continued to write and publish her poetry. About two years later, when the Union Seminary was faced with financial difficulties, she took another teaching position in Little York, Pennsylvania.

In 1854 Frances Ellen Watkins left teaching to work for the cause of abolition. Although the full reasons are unclear, her decision was probably predicated upon a combination of factors. Most schools that served African Americans were in economic trouble, and the two where Watkins taught were no exceptions. The year before, Maryland had passed a law prohibiting free Blacks from entering the state. The law thus prevented Watkins from visiting relatives and friends who had remained in Baltimore. Watkins herself pointed to a singular instance as her motivation for joining the abolition movement. A free Black, visiting in Maryland, had unwittingly violated that state's new law. He was arrested, convicted, and sold into slavery to a Georgia owner. He escaped once and was recaptured, but subsequently died from the hardships involved. William Still reports that Watkins wrote to a friend that "upon that grave I pledged myself to the Anti-Slavery cause" (Still, 1872, p. 758).

In Philadelphia, Watkins found no suitable employment on behalf of the cause, and so moved to New England where greater opportunities presented themselves. In August of 1854, she was invited to deliver her first lecture, "The Education and the Elevation of the Colored Race." By her own accounts, she was soon speaking "every night," and within a month the Maine Anti-Slavery Society hired her to lecture throughout New England. In 1857 she was retained by the Pennsylvania Anti-Slavery Society to speak to audiences in the Great Lakes states. She continued to tour until November of 1860, when she married Fenton Harper and settled on a farm near Columbus, Ohio, purchased partially with the money she had earned as a lecturer and poet. Widowed in 1864, Frances sold the farm to pay off outstanding debts and moved to New England with her daughter, Mary. She had never stopped writing poetry, but now she resumed her professional lecturing.

Through her poetry, Harper had addressed issues other than abolition, such as temperance ("The Drunkard's Child," 1854a) and poverty ("Died of Starvation," 1854b). Although abolition had dominated her antebellum discourse, she now turned her energies to these and other societal problems. Civil rights and women's issues—such as suffrage, legal equality between the sexes, and temperance—especially aroused her concern and attention. Harper spoke at many organizations' conventions as a member and an officer—among them the Congress of Colored Women in the United States, the National Council of Negro Women, the National Council of Women, the American Equal Rights Association, and the Woman's Christian Temperance Union. She continued to travel the lecture circuit, including a southern tour in 1866. Throughout the last three decades of the 19th century, as a poet, a speaker, and a novelist (*Iola Leroy,* 1892a), Harper worked to better America. In 1901 she retired from public life, quietly living out her remaining years until her death in 1911 at the age of 85.

Throughout the last six decades of the 19th century, Frances Ellen Watkins Harper was a virtual whirlwind of activity. Across ten volumes, published between 1846 and 1900, Harper's poetry addressed the problems of the day: slavery and lynching, drinking and sexual double standards, illiteracy and war. From 1854 until 1900 Frances Harper was also a well-known, widely traveled platform lecturer. At that time she could be observed at numerous conventions, from antislavery society meetings to equal rights conventions, and when she didn't attend as a delegate, she was there as an officer of the organization.

All that my yearning spirit craves
Is—Bury me not in a land of slaves.

("Bury Me in a Free Land" Harper, 1864, p. 178)

Of 36 prewar poems still extant, Frances Harper wrote about slavery in 16 of them.[2] During this period, antislavery themes were even more dominant in her lectures. Although other issues—poverty, women's issues, temperance—captured her attention as well, it was abolition that dominated her antebellum discourse.

As were most other abolitionists, Harper was first concerned with confronting White prejudice and establishing the humanity of the slave. However, it was typical of Harper's poetic style that she did not, in either her poetry or her oratory, dwell upon arguments that would "prove" the race's claim to equality. Rather, her discourse *assumed* African Americans' place in the human race, and throughout her work there ran a thread that implicitly reinforced equality. First, familial relationships implicitly affirmed the slave's humanity. Harper's poems "The Slave Mother" (1854c) and "The Fugitive's Wife" (1854d) were typical. In the former, Harper describes a mother's anguish at an auction as she is separated in slavery from her son. The latter poem describes a wife's loyal support of her husband as he decides to flee slavery, leaving his wife and children behind.

Next, Harper argued that African Americans' accomplishments were a source of evidence of their humanity. In "The Colored People in America" (1857a), Harper described some of their successes:

> We have papers edited by colored editors, which we may consider it an honor to possess, and a credit to sustain. We have a church that is extending itself from east to west, from north to south, through poverty and reproach, persecution and pain. (p. 100)

Heroic deeds provided additional proof of the African American's humanity. In "The Tennessee Hero," Harper depicted a fugitive slave who chose death over betraying fellow plotters.

> Though fetters galled his weary limbs, / His spirit spurned their thrall //
> And towered, in its manly might, / Above the murderous crew. . . . And
> what! oh, what is life to me, Beneath your base control? / Nay! do your
> worst. Ye have no chains / To bind my free-born soul. (1857b, p. 80)

Although Harper implicitly argued the logic of slavery's injustice, she
actively sought to communicate the full meaning of its barbarism.

Both her poetry and her oratory utilized "point of view," traditionally
a poetic resource, to frame her audience's perspective of slavery. "The
Slave Mother," for example, employed a second-person perspective to
place the audience at the scene of a slave auction: "Heard you that shriek?
It rose / So wildly on the air. . . . Saw you those hands so sadly clasped— /
The bowed and feeble head?" (1854c, p. 4). As Harper took her audience
through the sale of the slave mother's son, she asked them to "see" the
injustice of slavery through the lens of a representative event.

In instance after instance, Harper sought to intensify her audiences'
response to slavery. In her poetry, families were torn apart, heroes were
murdered, and death was a peaceful escape from the evils of slavery. Perhaps her most horrific poem was "The Slave Mother: A Tale of the Ohio"
(1857c), which, like several others, was based on a true incident. Margaret
Garner, a fugitive slave, had fled with her children across the frozen Ohio
River, but trackers had followed them. Knowing that she had no legal
recourse to sanctuary, Garner began to kill her children rather than surrender them back to slavery.

> Then, said the mournful mother, / If Ohio cannot save, / I will do a deed
> for freedom, / She shall find each child a grave. // I will save my precious
> children / From their darkly threatened doom, / I will hew their path to
> freedom / Through the portals of the tomb. (1857c, p. 85)

Garner was stopped before she could turn her knife on her boys and herself, but not before she had killed her baby girl. By telling such stories—
some true, some archetypal—Harper sought to intensify the audience's
appreciation of slavery's "deadly doom."

Besides emphasizing the emotional content of her stories, Harper used
the traditional abolitionist charge of hypocrisy to intensify her audiences'
reactions to slavery. Slavery violated two beliefs dearly held by most Americans: Christianity and liberty. Worse, slavery blasphemously used Christianity to justify itself. Thus, in "Bible Defence of Slavery" Harper told the
audience to "Let sorrow breathe in every tone, / In every strain ye raise; /
Insult not God's majestic throne / With th' mockery of praise" (1854e, p.
5). Hypocrisy of a sort is laid at the non–slave owner's door as well for

failure to recognize the sins of the slavers: "Oh! when ye pray for heathen lands, / And plead for their dark shores, / Remember Slavery's cruel hands / Make heathens at your doors!" (p. 5). For a country that viewed itself as a beacon of religion to the rest of the world, the claim that Americans were the heathens was a serious charge indeed. It was also a charge that motivated to action many of those who sided with the abolitionist cause.

Finally, Harper's poetic language was not simply ornamentation. By layering different levels of meaning within her discourse, Harper supplied subtextual commentary on her subjects. For example, in the speech "Could We Trace the Record of Every Human Heart" she personified the slave states to engage them in dialogue:

> Ask Virginia, with her hundreds of thousands of slaves, if she is not weary with her merchandise of blood and anxious to shake the gory traffic from her hands, and hear her reply: "Though fertility has covered my soil, though a genial sky bends over my hills and vales, though I hold in my hand a wealth of water-power enough to turn the spindles to clothe the world, yet, with all these advantages, one of my chief staples has been the sons and daughters I send to the human market and human shambles." (1857d, p. 3)

"Fertile soil," "genial sky," and "wealth of water-power" all speak to Virginia's natural resources, which, subtextually, are spurned by a greedy, lazy people who sell their "sons and daughters" instead. By personifying Virginia, Harper simultaneously condemns the community as a whole while maintaining a sense of their personal responsibility. Harper invited the audience, sometimes explicitly, sometimes subtextually, to adopt a perspective that unmistakably condemned slavery. Harper would undertake a similar task of audience education when she spoke to the issue of African Americans' civil rights.

But hark! from our Southland are floating
Sobs of anguish, murmurs of pain.

("An Appeal to My Countrywomen" Harper, 1900, p. 385)

Given Frances Harper's early focus on abolition, her concern with post-slavery conditions in the South is scarcely surprising. Indeed, in many details her later discourses on civil rights mirrored her earlier poetry and oratory on abolition.

Fundamentally, Harper's appeals were grounded in the claim that African Americans were equals with Whites. However, although her poetry continued to implicitly argue such equality, her oratory directly confronted the northern prejudice that permitted southern violations of the 15th Amendment. "Aunt Chloe" is a six-part poem in which the title character describes the pain of losing her sons to slavery, her hidden hope that the North would prevail, the joy of emancipation, the challenge of learning to read and of building a church, and the happiness of her reunion with her children (1872). Aunt Chloe's experiences—personal and emotional— clearly communicate her humanity. The act of becoming literate, however, did more: it signaled her equality, both intellectually and spiritually.

Harper's oratory was more direct in its insistence that the ex-slaves, and all African Americans, were the political, intellectual, and spiritual equals of Whites. Asked to speak on the topic of "Duty to Dependent Races" at the 1891 National Council of Women of the United States meeting, Harper first challenged the organization's presumption that Blacks were "dependent":

> I deem it a privilege to present the negro, not as a mere dependent asking for Northern sympathy or Southern compassion, but as a member of the body politic who has a claim upon the nation for justice, simple justice, which is the right of every race. (1891, p. 86)

As with abolition, Harper told stories of achievement, but unlike "Aunt Chloe," these stories were nonfiction. A surviving portion of "Coloured Women of America," a speech delivered to the 1878 Women's Congress, gave report after report of the material and intellectual accomplishments of ex-slaves, all of them women. Like the story of Aunt Chloe, these women's lives spoke of hard work, persistence, thrift, and most of all, hope for a better life.

Harper argued that African Americans were also equal because, time and again, they had answered the country's call to arms. In her poetry and her oratory, Harper employed an argument that would be echoed by African American orators through two world wars. "Can it be said," Harper asked the National Council of Women, "that [the African American] lacks patriotism, or a readiness to make common cause with the nation in the hour of peril?" (1891, p. 88). In answer, Harper's speeches and poems recounted Blacks' military service in the Revolution, the War of 1812, and the Civil War. The question was, who was the truer citizen? Southern rebels, simply because they were White? Or African Americans, who had pledged themselves to America and had fulfilled that pledge on the battlefield? In a candidly rhetorical poem, "An Appeal to the American People," Harper framed the question sharply:

> But today the traitor stands / With the crimson on his hands / . . . Asking you to weakly yield / All we won upon the field, / To ignore, on land and flood, / All the offerings of our blood, / And to write above our slain / "They have fought and died in vain." (1871a, p. 6)

Harper was equally at ease posing the question poetically in her rhetoric, as she did in "We Are All Bound Up Together":

> But let me tell you there is a depth of infamy lower than that. It is when the nation, standing upon the threshold of a great peril, reached out its hand to a feebler race, and asked that race to help it, and when the peril was over, said, You are good enough for soldiers, but not good enough for citizens. (1866, p. 218)

Scenic elements lend themselves to poetic language, and Harper took advantage of that rhetorical potential when describing the history of her race, a history that justified full civil rights.

Finally, Harper made a case for African Americans' right to equality under the law by linking her claims to similar claims advanced by women at this time. She advanced this claim only in her speeches, but given her frequent opportunities to speak before suffrage and women's rights conventions, her argument was strategic. Most interesting about Harper's rhetoric here was its directness. "You white women speak here of rights," she told the Eleventh Women's Rights Convention in 1866, "I speak of wrongs" (p. 218). She went on to detail some of those wrongs, misdeeds committed out of prejudice against herself and other African Americans. Her list included Whites-only streetcars, segregated railways that consigned all Blacks—male and female—to ride in the smoking cars, and the denial of voting rights to the ex-slaves of the South. She concluded with a unique argument in favor of women's rights, challenging her audience while also suggesting that women could bring an important perspective to American politics:

> Talk of giving women the ballot-box? Go on. It is a normal school,[3] and the white women of this country need it. While there exists this brutal element in society that tramples upon the feeble and treads down the weak, I tell you that if there is any class of people who need to be lifted out of their airy nothings and selfishness, it is the white women of America. (1866, errata page)

African Americans, Harper was saying, lived in a situation far less tolerant and tolerable than the White women she addressed. If her audience felt oppressed—and Harper acknowledged in other passages that women had a right to feel so—then how much more did African Americans warrant equal treatment within the law?

Harper employed the rhetorical strategies she had used in the pursuit of abolition on behalf of civil rights. Once again, in her oratory as in her poetry, Harper had cause to charge southerners with crimes of inhumanity and northerners with sins of indifference. Harper chose to tell true stories in poetic form to make a distant problem vivid. The title poem of her ninth volume of poetry was tragically representative. "The Martyr of Alabama" told the story of Tim Thompson, a Black youth ordered to dance by a group of Whites. When he refused to do so because it was against his religious beliefs, he was knocked down, danced upon, shot, and killed:

> Heard they aright? Did that brave child / Their mandates dare resist? / Did he against their stern commands / Have courage to resist? // Then recklessly a man (?) arose, / And dealt a fearful blow. / He crushed the portals of that life, / And laid the brave child low. // And trampled on his prostrate form, / As on a broken toy; / Then danced with careless, brutal feet, / Upon the murdered boy. (1894, p. 149)

Harper captured the incredulity of the men on being contradicted by the young Black child and suggested the anger they probably experienced when the lines of caste were violated. The question mark after "man (?)" was obvious commentary, as was her choice of the terms "trampled," "careless," "brutal," and "murdered." The metaphor of the broken toy—that the White men were like children whose toy had gotten broken on them—was subtler, even ironic, poetic commentary. Through the story itself and the words she used to tell that story, Harper screamed "injustice" as clearly and forcefully as she could.

As slavery had been un-Christian, so, too, was the South's systematic violation of African Americans' rights. In "Duty to Dependent Races" Harper contrasted Christian words with Christian actions. Noting a historic tendency toward persecution—the Inquisition, anti-Semitism, and, of course, American slavery—Harper claimed that it was "a degenerate Christianity" that denied Blacks their civil rights: "It is the pride of Caste which opposes the spirit of Christ," she told the women in her audience (1891, pp. 90, 91). With further antitheses, Harper continued to juxtapose words against deeds. "What I ask of American Christianity is not to show us more creeds, but more of Christ; not more rites and ceremonies, but more religion glowing with love and replete with life" (p. 91).

Although most of Harper's poetry was New Testament in theme—Christ will save the world through love—when addressing civil rights, her verse put forward an Old Testament tone: God will punish the sinners. Her picture was metaphorical, however, for she focused on the retribution God had already visited upon the South in punishment for slavery. As in Scripture, God had warned the people of their wicked ways: "Judgment slumbered. God in mercy / Stayed his strong avenging hand; / Sent them priests and sent them prophets, / But they would not understand" (1871b, p. 40). Having refused to listen, the people were then punished: "Then God arose in dreadful wrath, / And judgment streamed around his path; / His hand the captive's fetters broke, / His lightnings shattered every yoke" (1895a, p. 163). The Civil War had brought God's wrath upon the southern sinners. By analogy, slavery in the form of civil rights violations would ultimately come to the same end.

Civil rights, then, was indeed a matter of "simple justice" for Harper. In her poetry and her oratory, she argued that her race was entitled to such rights because of their humanity, their citizenship, and their Christianity. She challenged northern audiences to remove the prejudice that caused them to turn a blind eye toward southern transgressions. She was not entirely successful, but then no African American orator, poet, or essayist was. It should be enough to say that she raised her voice as loudly and as powerfully as she knew how. In addition to arguing for justice between the races, Harper lifted her voice in support of justice between the sexes.

And what is wrong in woman's life
In man's cannot be right.

("A Double Standard" 1895b, p. 178)

Frances Harper's interest in women's issues fell into three categories: women's equality, social feminism, and temperance. Generally, Harper addressed women's equality more through her oratory than her poetry. Perhaps the hallmark of Harper's women's rights speeches was her directness. As noted earlier, for example, at the Eleventh Women's Rights Convention she endorsed the ballot for White women in order that they be "lifted out of their airy nothings and selfishness." In fact, Harper began this speech by confessing that, more concerned with problems of her race, to date she had not identified much with the women's rights movement. However, she then went on to recount her own unequal treatment under the law as a widow: "Had I died instead of my husband, how different would have been the result! . . . No administrator would have gone into his house, broken up his home, and sold his bed, and taken away his means of support" (1866, p. 217). As with the African American, justice denied to "the weakest and feeblest of [society's] members" would bring "the curse upon its own soul" (p. 217).

Harper's directness, however, also led her to note that suffrage would not be a panacea for all of America's problems. Although some would undoubtedly criticize Harper's beliefs, her realistic pragmatism served to strengthen her larger claims for women's rights. "Justice is not fulfilled," Harper said, "so long as woman is unequal before the law" (1866, p. 217).

Women's equality was a subject that also occasionally captured the attention of Harper's poetry. In 1892, Harper delivered a lecture entitled "Enlightened Motherhood" to the Brooklyn Literary Society, in which one passage condemned society's sexual double standard:

> I hold that no woman loves social purity as it deserves to be loved and valued, if she cares for the purity of her daughters and not her sons; who would gather her dainty robes from contact with the fallen woman and yet greet with smiling lips and clasp with warm and welcoming hands the author of her wrong and ruin. (1892b, p. 288)

"A Double Standard" (1895b), a poem attacking sexual double standards, illustrates the interrelationship between Harper's poetry and her oratory. In it, Harper uses imagery, writing poetically from the "fallen woman's" point of view:

> Can you blame me that my heart grew cold / That the tempted, tempter turned; / When he was feted and caressed / And I was coldly spurned? / Would you blame him, when you draw from me / Your dainty robes aside, / If he with gilded baits should claim / Your fairest as his bride? (1895b, p. 177)

Harper concluded the poem with a direct claim of equality: "And what is wrong in woman's life / In man's cannot be right" (p. 178).

Although Harper's lectures leaned toward the romantic and poetic in tone and argument, they were not without their practical side, promoting women's confidence in being their own persons. "Marriage should not be a blind rushing together of tastes and fancies," Harper told her Brooklyn audience (1892b, p. 286). Women should choose their husbands carefully, holding men to higher standards than was the current custom: "Is it not madness for a woman to trust her future happiness . . . in the unsteady hands of a characterless man . . . ? (p. 287). This argument echoed one

Harper made 38 years earlier in her poem "Advice to the Girls": "Wed not a man whose merit lies / In things of outward show, / . . . But marry one who's good and kind, / And free from all pretence" (1854f, p. 14).

In all of Harper's practical advice for self-improvement, temperance was a dominant theme. "Characterless" men were usually those who drank alcohol. The most important thing mothers could teach their sons was abstinence from moral degradation, of which drinking was a prime factor. Indeed, temperance was a remarkably consistent theme of Harper's poetry. In her 1854 volume *Poems on Miscellaneous Subjects,* Harper included two temperance poems: "The Drunkard's Child" (1854a) and "The Revel" (1854g). She wrote again about temperance in three 1887 poems: "Nothing and Something" (1887a), "Signing the Pledge" (1887b), and "Save the Boys" (1887c). Finally, in her last volume of poetry, *Idylls of the Bible* (1901a), Harper included two more temperance poems: "The Fatal Pledge" (1901b) and "The Ragged Stocking" (1901c).

Harper's temperance poetry was almost invariably tragic, describing the woes that result from the use of alcohol. In "The Drunkard's Child" the alcoholic father was called from the "haunts of vice" in order to see his son die (1854a, p. 8). Implicitly, the child's death had resulted from the father's dissipation. Finally now, in death's wake, "burning tears like rain / poured down his bloated face; / Where guilt, remorse and shame / Had scathed, and left their trace" (p. 9). In "The Fatal Pledge" a woman tempted her fiance, a recovering alcoholic, with a toast of wine to celebrate their engagement. He succumbed to the temptation and ended up in a "drunkard's grave" (1901b, p. 52). Consistently, Harper's temperance imagery demonstrated the wreck and ruin that comes from drink (see, for example, 1887a; 1901b). Only "The Ragged Stocking" (1901c) avoided a terrible sense of tragedy, as a reformed drunkard told of becoming sober and buying small gifts for his child's Christmas stocking. The stocking then became a talisman of the alcoholic's reform.

Harper's temperance appeals were typical of the era. Her poems were primarily written from the point of view of those who had "fallen." One drink led to the path of ruin, and so saloons were snares, seducers, and dens of vice. Mothers had a special responsibility to raise their sons as teetotalers, in order that they never take a drink or enter a saloon. Christianity stood in direct opposition to alcohol. The closing statement in "Duty to Dependent Races" revealed the relationship Harper saw between some of her reform efforts: "When [Christ's] religion fully permeates our civilization, and moulds our national life, the drink traffic will be abolished, the Indian question answered, and the negro problem solved" (1891, p. 91).

Conclusion

Frances Ellen Watkins Harper's poetry and oratory reveal a simultaneous unity and diversity. The similarities lie in their rhetorical nature, the issues addressed, the impressive command of language, and the imagery that each utilized. Harper did adapt, however, to her audience, her message, and her medium of communication. She did not address the National Council of Women in the same way she did the Brooklyn Literary Society. Her civil rights message was similar to, but not identical with, her arguments for abolition. Her oratory incorporated more third-person points of view, whereas her poetry used more first-person perspectives. Like most successful rhetors, Harper understood the importance of adapting to the particular rhetorical situation. And Harper was successful.

In his 1872 book *The Underground Rail Road,* William Still called Harper "one of the ablest advocates of the Underground Rail Road and of the slave" (p. 755). William Nell, writing in *The Liberator,* referred to Harper as "eloquent" (1858, p. 3). The *Portland (Maine) Daily Express* published this report of a speech she delivered immediately following the Civil War:

> She spoke for nearly an hour and a half, her subject being "The Mission of the War, and the Demands of the Colored Race in the Work of Reconstruction;" and we have seldom seen an audience more attentive, better pleased, or more enthusiastic. . . . We shall attempt no abstract of her address; none that we could make would do her justice. . . . We have seen no praises of her that were overdrawn. We have heard Miss Dickinson,[4] and do not hesitate to award the palm to her darker colored sister. (Still, 1872, p. 760)

Historians and literary critics have argued that Harper was not only eloquent and well received but that hers was a voice that pushed gently but firmly for a radical change in American values. Maxwell Whiteman, in an introduction to a reprinted volume of *Poems on Miscellaneous Subjects,* contended that Harper's oratory contained the seeds of the concept "Black power" (1969, n.p.). Maryemma Graham, another literary critic, argues that Harper's "social protest poetry" provided a "profound challenge to American democracy" (Graham, 1988, pp. 1ii, xxxv). Melba Joyce Boyd calls Harper's activism radical politics and Black feminism and accurately identifies the common thread woven throughout her discourse: "[Harper] is ever suspicious of government and persistent in her critique of individual or social domination over the human spirit for the purpose of material, political, or personal gain" (1994, p. 29). Frances Smith Foster summarizes Harper's unity of message and diversity in style this way:

As a writer and lecturer, [Harper] was a complex and confounding figure. Her language was "chaste," her literature was "moral," and contemporary reporters rarely failed to note her "slender and graceful" form and her "soft musical voice." [Harper] was by all accounts very ladylike in her public appearances. However, on the podium, as William Wells Brown says, "Her arguments are forcible, her appeals pathetic,[5] her logic fervent, her imagination fervid, and her delivery original and easy." (1990, p. 15)

Frances Harper wanted a world in which Black and White and male and female were equal. She wanted an America that treated all humans—others as well as herself—with dignity and compassion. She wanted, as she called it, "simple justice." It was this message that provided the central unity behind her diverse styles and arguments. It was this message that she consistently sounded in her poetic oratory and her oratorical poetry.

Discussion Questions

1. In what ways did Harper's civil rights discourse resemble her earliest abolitionist discourse?

2. Frances Harper at heart was a storyteller. Which story did you find most surprising? Why? Which one did you find most disturbing? Why?

3. Did you like the pieces of Harper's poetry that you read? Why or why not? Do you think reading her poems in their entirety might change your reaction in any way?

4. In what ways does Harper's "voice" seem typical of 19th century America? In what ways does her "voice" seem more typical of our own time?

5. Do you think Harper's rhetoric of challenge was effective with her audiences of White women? Why or why not?

6. Why was temperance considered a "women's issue"?

7. Why do you think Harper's temperance stories were usually tragic?

References

Boyd, M. J. (1994). *Discarded legacy: Politics and poetics in the life of Frances E. W. Harper 1825–1911*. Detroit: Wayne State University Press.

Foster, F. S. (Ed.). (1990). *A brighter coming day: A Frances Ellen Watkins Harper reader.* New York: The Feminist Press at the City University of New York.

Graham, M. (Ed.). (1988). *The complete poems of Frances E. W. Harper.* New York: Oxford University Press.

Harper, F. E. W. (1854a). The drunkard's child. In M. Graham (Ed.). (1988). *The complete poems of Frances E. W. Harper* (pp. 8–10). New York: Oxford University Press.

Harper, F. E. W. (1854b). Died of starvation. In M. Graham (Ed.). (1988). *The complete poems of Frances E. W. Harper* (pp. 16–17). New York: Oxford University Press.

Harper, F. E. W. (1854c). The slave mother. In M. Graham (Ed.). (1988). *The complete poems of Frances E. W. Harper* (pp. 4–5). New York: Oxford University Press.

Harper, F. E. W. (1854d). The fugitive's wife. In M. Graham (Ed.). (1988). *The complete poems of Frances E. W. Harper* (p. 19). New York: Oxford University Press.

Harper, F. E. W. (1854e). Bible defence of slavery. In M. Graham (Ed.). (1988). *The complete poems of Frances E. W. Harper* (pp. 5–6). New York: Oxford University Press.

Harper, F. E. W. (1854f). Advice to the girls. In M. Graham (Ed.). (1988). *The complete poems of Frances E. W. Harper* (p. 14). New York: Oxford University Press.

Harper, F. E. W. (1854g). The revel. In M. Graham (Ed.). (1988). *The complete poems of Frances E. W. Harper* (p. 11). New York: Oxford University Press.

Harper, F. E. W. (1857a). The colored people in America. In F. S. Foster (Ed.). (1990). *A brighter coming day: A Frances Ellen Watkins Harper reader* (pp. 99–100). New York: The Feminist Press at the City University of New York.

Harper, F. E. W. (1857b). The Tennessee hero. In F. S. Foster (Ed.). (1990). *A brighter coming day: A Frances Ellen Watkins Harper reader* (pp. 79–81). New York: The Feminist Press at the City University of New York.

Harper, F. E. W. (1857c). The slave mother: A tale of the Ohio. In F. S. Foster (Ed.). (1990). *A brighter coming day: A Frances Ellen Watkins Harper reader* (pp. 84–86). New York: The Feminist Press at the City University of New York.

Harper, F. E. W. (1857d, May 23). Could we trace the record of every human heart [Speech of Miss Watkins to the New York City Anti-Slavery Society, May 13, 1857]. (Available from *National anti-slavery standard*, p. 3).

Harper, F. E. W. (1864). Bury me in a free land. In F. S. Foster (Ed.). (1990). *A brighter coming day: A Frances Ellen Watkins Harper reader* (pp. 177–178). New York: The Feminist Press at the City University of New York.

Harper, F. E. W. (1866). We are all bound up together. In F. S. Foster (Ed.). (1990). *A brighter coming day: A Frances Ellen Watkins Harper reader* (pp. 217–219, plus an errata page). New York: The Feminist Press at the City University of New York.

Harper, F. E. W. (1871a). An appeal to the American people. In F. E. W. Harper. *Poems* (pp. 5–6). Philadelphia: Merrihew and Sons. Reprinted 1975. New York: AMS Press.

Harper, F. E. W. (1871b). Retribution. In F. E. W. Harper. *Poems* (pp. 40–41). Philadelphia: Merrihew and Sons. Reprinted 1975. New York: AMS Press.

Harper, F. E. W. (1872). Aunt Chloe. In M. Graham (Ed.). (1988). *The complete poems of Frances E. W. Harper* (pp. 117–131). New York: Oxford University Press.

Harper, F. E. W. (1878). Coloured women of America. *Englishwoman's Review, 15*, 10–15.

Harper, F. E. W. (1887a). Nothing and something. In M. Graham (Ed.). (1988). *The complete poems of Frances E. W. Harper* (pp. 141–142). New York: Oxford University Press.

Harper, F. E. W. (1887b). Signing the pledge. In M. Graham (Ed.). (1988). *The complete poems of Frances E. W. Harper* (pp. 145–147). New York: Oxford University Press.

Harper, F. E. W. (1887c). Save the boys. In M. Graham (Ed.). (1988). *The complete poems of Frances E. W. Harper* (p. 140). New York: Oxford University Press.

Harper, F. E. W. (1891). Duty to dependent races. In R. Foster-Avery (Ed.). (1990). *Transactions of the National Council of Women of the United States* (pp. 86–91). Philadelphia: Lippincott.

Harper, F. E. W. (1892a). *Iola Leroy; Or, shadows uplifted*. Philadelphia: Garrigues Brothers.

Harper, F. E. W. (1892b). Enlightened motherhood: An address by Mrs. Frances E. W. Harper before the Brooklyn Literary Society. In R. Foster-Avery (Ed.). (1990). *Transactions of the National Council of Women of the United States* (pp. 285–292). Philadelphia: Lippincott.

Harper, F. E. W. (1894). The martyr of Alabama. In M. Graham (Ed.). (1988). *The complete poems of Frances E. W. Harper* (pp. 147–150). New York: Oxford University Press.

Harper, F. E. W. (1895a). Then and now. In M. Graham (Ed.). (1988). *The complete poems of Frances E. W. Harper* (pp. 163–166). New York: Oxford University Press.

Harper, F. E. W. (1895b). A double standard. In M. Graham (Ed.). (1988). *The complete poems of Frances E. W. Harper* (pp. 176–178). New York: Oxford University Press.

Harper, F. E. W. (1900). An appeal to my countrywomen. In F. S. Foster (Ed.). (1990). *A brighter coming day: A Frances Ellen Watkins Harper reader* (pp. 385–386). New York: The Feminist Press at the City University of New York.

Harper, F. E. W. (1901a). *Idylls of the Bible*. Philadelphia: Author. Reprinted 1975. New York: AMS Press.

Harper, F. E. W. (1901b). The fatal pledge. In F. E. W. Harper, *Idylls of the Bible* (pp. 51–52). Philadelphia: Author. Reprinted 1975. New York: AMS Press.

Harper, F. E. W. (1901c). The ragged stocking. In F. E. W. Harper, *Idylls of the Bible* (pp. 48–50). Philadelphia: Author. Reprinted 1975. New York: AMS Press.

Nell, W. C. (1858, September 17). Letter to the editor. *The Liberator*, p. 3.

Robinson, W. (1969). *Early Black American poets*. Dubuque, IA: Wm. C. Brown.

Still, W. (1872). *The underground rail road*. Philadelphia: Porters and Coates.

Whiteman, M. (1969). Introduction. In F. E. W. Harper, *Poems on Miscellaneous Subjects*, M. Whiteman (Ed.). Philadelphia: Rhistoric.

Endnotes

1. The author wishes to express his appreciation to the University of North Carolina, Charlotte, for financial support for his research on Harper.

2. Eleven others covered Christian themes, three addressed women's issues, three spoke about poverty, two about temperance, and one was a eulogy.

3. "Normal schools" were postsecondary schools that trained teachers.

4. An allusion, probably, to Emily Dickinson (1830–1886), a well-known American poet.

5. "Pathetic" is meant here in its original sense: full of emotion.

"J Can and J Will"

"Mother" Jones Crusades for Labor Rights

Diane Cypkin, Ph.D.

Department of Literature/Communication
Pace University

"Mother" Jones with the children marching against child labor, 1903

*J*t is hard to decide what the "hook" was that convinced me I had to research "Mother" Jones. But I am certain that her chutzpah was a good part of the reason. I have always respected people, especially women, who get out there, speak out, and do. And she did and kept right on doing until her golden years. No "I can't," "They won't let me," or "I'm too old" statements from her. Her rhetoric ran more toward "I can and I will!" Yes, I do like that. I think we all do. Surely, too, her instinctive theatricality captivated me. My own background in theater acting and directing on and off Broadway is probably the cause. "Mother" Jones shrewdly used drama and its innate emotive abilities to make people feel and then act on those feelings. Hence, they were moved to improve life for themselves and others. "Mother" Jones was a great woman who challenged people in her time and continues to challenge us to this day and in many ways!

I have said I hate violence; I favor drama. We must wake the sleepers somehow, and where blindness can be healed by shock we must provide the shock. Sometimes it hurts a little, but it helps the patient, for lo! it makes him see. ("Mother" Jones, cited in Foner, 1983, p. 510)

On July 7, 1903, the press, and through the press the nation, witnessed the beginning of a 22-day real-life drama. "Mother" Jones's "army" was on the march. Some 300 individuals, "one third . . . little girls, and the remainder . . . young men and boys" (Camp, 1970, p.1), embarked on a 125-mile overland crusade. They were marching from Kensington, Pennsylvania, to Oyster Bay, New York, to see the President. The primary goal of this "army" of Pennsylvania mill workers was to focus national attention on the evils of child labor. In addition, they hoped to pressure the President into enacting federal child labor legislation that "worked." And, indeed, the crusade, determinedly and deliberately directed by the 73-year-old fiery orator Jones, would leave an indelible impression. In fact, it would rouse the nation to "the wail of the children" ("'Mother' Jones Speaks," 1903, p. 10).

Ironically, Jones's own early history did not particularly foreshadow the lusty labor agitator and self-proclaimed "hell-raiser" she would become (Featherling, 1974, p. 10). She was born simply Mary Harris in Cork, Ireland, in May 1830. True, Mary's "paternal grandfather was hanged in the fight for Irish freedom." True, too, her father "was forced to flee the country [Ireland] for agitating." Yet, aside from emigrating from Ireland to America at the age of 8, Mary's life was like any other child's. Reunited in America (Mary's father had fled Ireland alone), the family moved to Canada, where her father had been hired as a railroad construction worker. There, too, Mary went to parochial and public school, majored in education and dressmaking, and discovered a "talent for debating" (Featherling, 1974, p. 3). After graduation, she was employed, first, as a schoolteacher in Canada. Later, in America, she worked as both a teacher and a dressmaker. In 1861, while teaching school in Memphis, Tennessee, Mary met George Jones. He was a proud member of Local 66, Iron Molders International Union. She married him, and was soon a regular hausfrau raising four children.

In 1867, however, tragedy completely transformed her life. In that year a murderous yellow fever epidemic ravaged Memphis. Before the angry wrath of the epidemic was sated, Mrs. George Jones was left widowed, childless, and bereft. Need brought her to Chicago, where she started a dressmaking business. Need, too, made her ever more aware of the great disparity between the wealthy and the poor around her. Resentment grew and with it the urge to act.

Thus, when the Chicago fire burned her out, she became involved in the Noble Order of the Knights of Labor. This was an early labor organization "not so much a union as a mass fraternal lodge" (Featherling, 1974, p. 6). They were dedicated to improving the lot of the worker—whether pay, hours, or working conditions. And they did so through cooperation, organization, and education (Austin, 1949, pp. 86–88). Jones was mightily stirred by all these ideas and became a faithful believer in the Knights' cause. Moreover, she came to consider the leadership "martyrs and . . . saints" (Parton, 1969, p. 14). It wasn't long before Terence V. Powderly, leader of the organization and dubbed "Grand Master Workman," in fraternal terminology, noticed her. He especially appreciated her "quick brain and an even quicker tongue" when her outspokenness was brought home to him at a meeting (Featherling, 1974, p. 10). Impressed, he put her to work.

For the next 50 years, Jones could be found wherever labor strife was at its hottest—always organizing. Indeed, Jones, never a true rank-and-filer (Featherling, 1974, p. 154) but rather a down-to-earth "individualist" (Darrow, 1969, p. 5), quickly became a familiar figure. In 1877, under the aegis of the Knights, she was called to Pittsburgh to help striking railroad employees. Before this battle was over, it involved the nation. In 1885 she led a "Poor People's March" in Chicago. From the 1890s on, she most frequently worked for the United Mine Workers. They called her to the coal fields of West Virginia and Pennsylvania, smoldering cauldrons of anger and violence. By 1902 she was nationally renowned.

Why was this 5-foot, white-haired, spectacled, grandmotherly looking woman such an effective organizer? Why was her very appearance—forever costumed in a reserved black bonnet and dress—always anxiously awaited? Why did the laborer love this woman who threw all her "possessions in an old black shawl" (Sickels, 1968, p. 55) and came whenever her boys called? The answer appears to lie in the personal admiration the workers—her audience—had for her. After all, it was they who would lovingly nickname her "Mother." The answer also lies in her masterful oratory and her skillful direction of the speech-performance event.

Yes, "Mother" Jones led a fearless life, idolized by the worker. Death threats while organizing in the Dietz coal fields of Norton, Virginia, in 1891 didn't stop her (Parton, 1969, p. 24). Warrants served in the striking coal fields of Arnot, Pennsylvania, in the early 1900s left her defiant. In fact, she publicly taunted the warrant server, saying, "Keep it [the warrant] in your pill bag until I come for it. I am going to hold a meeting now" (Parton, 1969, p. 36). During the same period, she was no less courageous in Kelly Creek, West Virginia. There, again, she publicly dared "the [coal] company's lap dogs" to come and "hang her" (Parton, 1969, pp. 47–48). Arrest didn't lead to surrender, nor did "the wrath of governors, presidents, and coal operators" (Foner, 1979, p. 281). The workers, impressed by her fortitude, respected "Mother."

Moreover, her oratorical abilities were quickly legendary. Biting words were frequently profane. Caustic retorts were to the point and earthy. "[P]athetic and beautiful word pictures" (Foner, 1983, p. 95) were carefully interspersed. And all this she delivered in true revivalist fashion, with an Irish lilt. Accused of swearing, she would answer: "You've got to talk a language people can understand. The public is the sleepiest damn bunch you ever saw. You've got to wake them up! Then you get action!" (Foner, 1983, p. 536). Fired by a brash fury, her retorts became no less famous than she. Challenged to name the college she graduated from, she resentfully answered, "I graduated from the college of hard knocks" (Featherling, 1974, p. 139). Questioned as to whether she had secured a legal permit to speak publicly, she defiantly responded that it was "Patrick Henry, Thomas Jefferson, and John Adams" (Wertheimer, 1977, p. 346) who had given her permission. Moved, she moved others to see their own lives of endless, cruel, and sunless toil. She painted for her listeners never-to-be-forgotten visual pictures—haranguing them to act while sympathizing with their plight.

Invigorated by conviction, Jones's narrative method of oratory was premeditated and highly directed, as was the entire speech-performance event. Whenever possible, she began by warming up her audience with music played on a treasured phonograph. Sometimes a brass band would escort her into the rally (Foner, 1983, p. 39). Stepping up to the podium—or whatever was serving as one—she began to address the crowd. Working it much like a fundamentalist preacher (Featherling, 1974, p. 170), she modulated the intensity of her voice to a low murmur. The pacing began. The eyes behind the spectacles began to dart and flash. Gesticulating (Long, n.d., p. 6) and shaking her fist, she "rais[ed] her clenched and trembling hands" heavenward (Chaplin, 1972, p. 120). Then sympathy with the workers' plight turned to outrage at the employers and more so at the workers before her. If things were bad, they (the workers) had let them get that way. With wit snapping, anger fuming, and righteousness blazing, she whipped her audience into a frenzy. Shaming them, she boasted of her own fearlessness. Finally, she placed the responsibility for change and improvement in their lives squarely on their own shoulders (Foner, 1983, p. 39). Fight! Unionize! and life would be worth living.

The response to this "Celtic blend of sentiment and fire" (Featherling, 1974, p. 8) was as exciting as the presentation. Audiences, many sharing her Irish background, cried at her sad renditions of their lot and laughed at her punctuating anecdotes. They freely interjected agreement with her varied emphatic statements and roared with rage at injustices brought home to them. In sum, all agreed, here was a speaker who knew their lives well.

Yet, this was only just part of the entire speech event as orchestrated by Jones. An audience energized by her was led to protest, either immediately or a day or two following her appearance. Jones's trademark and specialty was the march, led by bands, flags, and women carrying "domestic armaments," usually mops, brooms, pots, and pans. Unique and effective, this technique of organizing miners' wives into strike battalions was utilized in coal mining regions. For example, in Arnot, Pennsylvania, in the 1900s, the strategy proved very successful. There, housewives dressed in frightening rags, and so armed, determinedly made for the mines their husbands were striking. The uproar they caused scared away not only the mules, but also the strike-breaking scabs brought in by management. Women in other striking coal mining regions noted their success and did no less (Foner, 1979, pp. 281–282; Parton, 1969, pp. 34–36).

Thus, "Mother" Jones's outstanding words and actions, utilizing men, women, and children, crossed state boundaries. They were meant to. Real-life drama, enacted by the workers, publicized their case. Indeed, the public aroused would, she felt, always support the worker's right to a decent life with decent pay. Yes, Jones had a deep respect for public opinion and what public support could do.

Jones's interest in the issue of child labor was an outgrowth of her work in mining regions and employment in southern textile mills. She found that coal operators were eager to take advantage of a cheap and easily dominated labor pool. Thus they encouraged miners to file false affidavits stating their children were of legal age to work in the mines. In Pennsylvania in 1900, for example, the legal age was 14. Need made miners willingly agree to the lie, because even a small additional income was beneficial. The result—in Pennsylvania alone—was thousands of 9- and 10-year-olds set to work in dark and dangerous mines. Moreover, these children worked from 10 to 14 hours a day, for an average daily wage of 60 cents (Parton, 1969, pp. 127–131; Spargo, 1968, pp. 163–167).

The lure of cheap, docile labor was even more enticing to the textile mills dotting the nation. Working in an Alabama factory in 1894, Jones found 6- and 7-year-olds laboring 14 hours a day. In a Tuscaloosa, Alabama, rope factory she discovered a 9- and a 10-year-old slaving at night alongside their father running 155 spindles. For 12 hours work, each child earned 10 cents. And these cases were not the exception. They were the rule (Foner, 1983, pp. 453–455; Spargo, 1968, pp. 148–153).

In May of 1903, 600 mills in Philadelphia and the surrounding area were struck. Led by the General Executive Committee of the Central Textile Workers Union, 100,000 textile workers walked off their jobs. Of these, 16,000 were children under 16. What were the workers' grievances? Initially, one of the major issues was working hours. Employees wanted a reduction of hours from 60 to 55 a week. Even a proportionate decrease in wages—from the $2 a week for children and $13 for adults—would have been accepted. Soon, however, the issue of child labor in these factories became as important, if not more important ("Big Textile Strike," 1903; Featherling, 1974, p. 48).

In mid-June, "Mother" Jones appeared on the scene. On June 17, 1903, she held a mass rally in front of Philadelphia's City Hall. Her purpose: to draw attention to the injustices visited on the children grinding their lives away at the mills. Surely once this aberration was recognized it would be quickly rectified!

Dressed in her usual grandmotherly fashion, Jones led in her actors: the suffering children of the mills, weak and scarred. Displaying them on a platform, she began her harangue. She cried that "Philadelphia's mansions were built on the broken bones, the quivering hearts, and drooping heads of these children." She accused officials of neglect and wealthy manufacturers of "moral murder," enjoying life at the expense of these little ones.

She threatened that "[s]ome day the worker will take possession of your city hall, and when we do, no child will be sacrificed on the altar of profit" (Parton, 1969, p. 72). Unfortunately, newspaper interest quickly flagged, as did public interest. Jones realized that more dramatic measures were called for (Foner, 1979, p. 284; Parton, 1969, pp. 72–73). As history would have it, this "scene" was just the prologue.

On July 7, the main event—a 22-day, real-life, pageantlike drama—began. "Mother" Jones convinced the union leadership that success would be brought about by organizing a march. Mill children, a multitude of striking mill children bound for the President, vacationing at Oyster Bay, New York—this, she claimed, was what had to be done. It would raise money for the continuation of the strike and publicize the demands of the strikers. Plus, it would rouse the nation to the evils of child labor and pressure legislation on the issue. Agreeing to Jones's plan, an "army" of about 300, composed of children and their adult sympathizers, left Kensington, Pennsylvania, that day (Camp, 1970, p. 1). All along the 125-mile, three-state route, Jones intended to give speeches, with demonstrations and concerts provided by her "cast"-"army" (Camp, 1970, pp. 9–10). No, she undoubtedly felt, the nation could not ignore the strike, nor more important, the plight of the children. A grandmotherly woman leading her brood of wronged little ones . . . it was the stuff of drama (Featherling, 1974, p. 50; Foner, 1979, pp. 284–285; "No Pity Is Here," 1903).

A lesser leader would have been disappointed by the first day's outing. Insufficient accommodations and provisions and a stifling heat decimated the ranks, leaving fewer than 100 to enter Bristol, Pennsylvania. Yet, "Mother" Jones's determination did not waiver. Bristol was a mill town. There was sure to be a sympathetic audience here for her crusade and the crusaders (Camp, 1970, pp. 11–12; Featherling, 1974, p. 50).

Indeed, both Bristol, Pennsylvania, and Trenton, New Jersey, the next stop on the march, were tremendous successes. Thousands came to see the little "army" march in and stayed for the rally. In Bristol, Jones thundered against child slavery in the mills and conquered the borough ("Fate of Strike," 1903; "'Mother' Jones Army Meets," 1903). In Trenton, condemning the wealthy manufacturers and the even wealthier who sponsor them, Jones cried, "What is the use of bringing a lot of children into the world to make money for plutocrats, while their little lives are being ground out in the mill and workshop" ("'Mother' Jones in Trenton," 1903)? This "army" would show the millionaires in New York, including John D. Rockefeller and J. Pierpont Morgan, what injustices they were perpetrating ("We're Going to Dine," 1903). Applause welcomed her words ("Army Crosses Delaware," 1903).

The following day, in Princeton, New Jersey, Jones "customized" her fiery rhetoric to suit her academically oriented audience (Parton, 1969). The result was not one of "overwhelming gratitude." Speaking opposite the campus, she displayed her little "army." Then Jones fumed at the "rich [who] robbed these little children of any education" so that they might send their own on to institutions of higher learning (Parton, p. 76). She showed her audience children who could barely read or write because their lives were being sacrificed to the mills. She pointed to little James Ashworth, a 10-year-old member of her crusade, stooped and slight, and cried, "Here's a textbook on economics" (Parton, p. 77). Ashworth was giving away his life so that they, the children of the wealthy, could go to school (Wertheimer, 1977, p. 348). "[The] young men at Princeton [, she said, were] but a lot of bums who think they know more than the President of the United States. They are wasting money. . . . The money ought to go to organized labor" ("Bums, Says Mother Jones," 1903, p. 7). Since hearty agreement and donations were lacking, Jones was quick to depart Princeton and push on.

With undiminished energy, Jones went on to address crowds in New Brunswick, New Jersey ("Mother Jones Says," 1903), Rahway, New Jersey ("Mother Jones in Triumph," 1903), and Elizabeth, New Jersey ("Mother Jones Asks," 1903). And it was from Elizabeth that Jones sent her first "official notice" to President Theodore Roosevelt. In summary, her letter castigated the federal government for not passing the 8-hour workday bill. Had that bill been law, she claimed, the strike in Kensington, Pennsylvania, might very well have been averted. Most important, however, the note dealt with the issue of child labor. Appealing, Jones wrote:

> We ask you, Mr. President, if our commercial greatness has not cost us too much by being built upon the quivering hearts of helpless children. We who know of these sufferings have taken up their cause and are now marching towards you in the hope that your tender heart will counsel with us to abolish this crime. . . . The manufacturers have threatened to starve these children and we seek to show that no child shall die of hunger at the will of any manufacturer in this fair land. ("Mother Jones Asks," 1903, p. 1)

The answer to this letter was communicated by way of the press. "'President Roosevelt would probably be willing to meet Mother Jones if she made a request in the usual way' but he objected to 'having his castle stormed'" (Camp, 1970, p. 21). Intrepid, "Mother" Jones moved on to Newark, speaking to a supportive crowd numbering 2,500 (Camp, 1970, p. 22; "Mother Jones and Army," 1903), and from there to Paterson.

In Paterson, rumor spread that Secret Service men had been dissuading members of the "army" from continuing ("Mother Jones Fears," 1903). In addition they paid her an unofficial visit and expressed the same sentiment ("Agents Threaten," 1903). This only made Jones more adamant. So Roosevelt didn't want to see her. He was sending his men to stop her. Burning with an indignation and vengeance directed at the President, she asked a Paterson audience of several thousand, "Will you vote next time for an aristocratic president, who will not listen to the wail of suffering childhood?" (Foner, 1979, p. 287). And just about all the audience—good unionists—said no as they eagerly fought to get close to the brave, defiant crusader (Foner, 1979, p. 287).

On July 20, in a speech during a side trip she took on her own, Jones continued her tirade against the President. Addressing the New York City Social Democratic Party at Sultzer's Westchester Park, she steadfastly announced to her audience of 4,000:

> There is one thing I must tell you, and that is, that I am going to complete the journey to Oyster Bay with my army to see the President. . . . I am going there to find out if he is the President of the capitalists only, or whether he is the President of the workingmen too. If he is the President of the capitalists only, he will be wiped out at the next election. ("'Mother' Jones in the City," 1903)

Then, on the afternoon of July 23, 1903, Jones and her "army" entered New York City itself ("'Mother' Jones Arrives," 1903). There she would hold one of her most unusual rallies—at Coney Island. On July 27, the *New York Times* reported that "'Mother' Jones and her army were the central attraction yesterday afternoon at Bostock's trained animal show at Coney Island" ("'Mother' Jones Speaks," 1903, p. 10). An audience, anxious to see the event, quickly filled the building way before the 4:30 starting time. Heralded, "Mother" Jones and her "army" appeared. She gave her speech on "a chair in the midst of the audience" ("'Mother' Jones Army in," 1903). In the meantime, her "army" was placed on stage in a cage, recently freed of Bostock's usual animal performers. The backdrop, heartily approved of by Jones, was a painted set of the Roman Colosseum. Flanking the scene were Emperors, thumbs down to the encaged. This, Jones felt, was a true-to-life metaphor of the relationship between "the aristocracy of employers" and the worker. Her speech to the crowd, frequently interrupted by the roar of lions, was as bold as ever. She and her "army" were going to see the President. They were going to ask him to pressure Congress to pass a bill to protect these children. Fifty years ago a war had been fought to stop "the selling of black children on the block.

Today the white child" was being sold into slavery to the manufacturer. The President, she declared, must "hear the wail of the children" and act ("'Mother' Jones Speaks," 1903).

On July 29, Jones arrived at Oyster Bay, New York. Eager to realize her goal of meeting the President, she was anxious to emphasize the more peaceful nature of her visit. Thus, she was accompanied by only five members of her "army" on this venture. Nonetheless, the President would not see her. She was directed to write a letter to him outlining her mission ("Mother Jones at Oyster," 1903). In fact, Jones would write two letters to Roosevelt. In them she pleaded the case of the little ones working "twelve hours a day in an unsanitary atmosphere, stunted mentally and physically" ("Mother Jones Writes," 1903). The President's answer was reported in the Philadelphia North American on August 4 ("President Replies," 1903). There Mr. Roosevelt noted that he was in "heartiest sympathy" with her cause, but that the issue of child labor was a state concern. Rebuffed, Jones was initially defiant. She threatened to continue her crusade: "The matter is not dropped here" ("Mother Jones Bitter," 1903). Yet, the march was over. Jones held a few more speeches in the New York–New Jersey area, and then she and her "army" headed home ("President Replies," 1903).

At first glance, it would appear that Jones's 125-mile crusade had been a total failure. The marchers disbanded, and on August 17, the defeated Kensington strikers all returned to work. Yet, analysts and historians agree that Jones's 22-day drama was fruitful. It was, undoubtedly, instrumental in the increasing amount of child labor legislation that followed. Soon after the march, a number of states (including those visited by Jones on her march) enacted stricter and more enforceable child labor laws. Within the first 20 years of this century, almost all the states of the nation addressed the issue in legal terms. Although federal legislation lagged behind, it, too, stumblingly appeared (Featherling, 1974, pp. 56–57; Smith, 1967, p. 303). Indeed, "Mother" Jones's dramatic, well-publicized, history-making march had roused a nation to the plight of the children. And once roused, the nation answered the cry!

Discussion Questions

1. Would a "Mother" Jones be successful today? In what ways?

2. How might Jones present herself differently to today's public, or would the "goodly grandmother" role prove effective?

3. How would people respond to Jones's language today? How might she change it? Why?

4. How might Jones's use of the media differ? Would the public forum still be central?

5. In what areas of political, economic, or social life could we really use a "Mother" Jones today? What specifically could such a woman do? What beliefs might she give voice to?

6. Is there anyone today doing this work? Are their tactics similar to or different from "Mother" Jones's? In what ways?

References

Agents threaten "Mother" Jones. (1903, July 19). *North American,* pp. 1, 4.

Army crosses Delaware. (1903, July 11). *New York Tribune,* p. 1.

Austin, A. (1949). *The labor story.* New York: Coward-McCann.

Big textile strike in Philadelphia. (1903, June 1). *New York Times,* p. 1.

Bums, says Mother Jones of students. (1903, July 12). *New York World,* p. 7.

Camp, H. C. (1970). *Mother Jones and the children's crusade.* Unpublished master's thesis, Columbia University, New York.

Chaplin, R. (1972). *Wobbly: The rough-and-tumble story of an American radical.* New York: DaCapo-Plenum.

Darrow, C. (1969). Foreword. In M. F. Parton (Ed.), *The autobiography of "Mother" Jones.* New York: Arno & *The New York Times.*

Fate of strike is in union's hands. (1903, July 9). *Philadelphia Inquirer,* pp. 1, 16.

Featherling, D. G. (1974). *Mother Jones: The miners' angel.* Carbondale: Southern Illinois University Press.

Foner, P. S. (1979). *Women and the American labor movement: From colonial times to the eve of World War I.* New York: Free Press.

Foner, P. S. (Ed.). (1983). *"Mother" Jones speaks.* New York: Monad Press.

Long, P. (n.d.). *Mother Jones: Woman organizer, and her relations with the wives of workers, working women, and the suffrage movement.*

Unpublished manuscript, Cornell University, New York State School of Industrial Labor Relations.

Mother Jones and army here. (1903, July 17). *Newark Evening News,* pp. 1, 36.

"Mother" Jones army in a cage at Coney. (1903, July 27). *North American,* p. 5.

"Mother" Jones army meets armed foes. (1903, July 9). *North American,* p. 2.

"Mother" Jones arrives. (1903, July 24). *New York Times,* p. 5.

Mother Jones asks President's counsel. (1903, July 16). *North American,* pp. 1, 2.

Mother Jones at Oyster Bay. (1903, July 29). *Newark Evening News,* p. 1.

Mother Jones bitter towards Roosevelt. (1903, August 6). *North American,* p. 3.

Mother Jones fears sleuths. (1903, July 18). *Newark Evening News,* p. 1.

"Mother" Jones in the city. (1903, July 20). *New York Times,* p. 10.

"Mother" Jones in Trenton. (1903, July 11). *New York Times,* p. 1.

Mother Jones in triumph enters Rahway's door. (1903, July 15). *North American,* p. 2.

Mother Jones says rich steal a living. (1903, July 13). *New York World,* p. 2.

"Mother" Jones speaks to Coney Island crowd. (1903, July 27). *New York Times,* p. 10.

Mother Jones writes plea to Roosevelt. (1903, July 31). *North American,* p. 3.

No pity is here, so "Mother Jones" will lead textile workers through country to win sympathy. (1903, July 7). *North American,* pp. 1, 15.

Parton, M. F. (Ed.). (1969). *The autobiography of "Mother" Jones.* New York: Arno & *The New York Times.*

President replies to Mother Jones. (1903, August 4). *North American,* pp. 1, 6.

Sickels, E. (1968). *Twelve daughters of democracy.* New York: Books for Libraries Press.

Smith, R. E. (1967). The march of the mill children. *Social Service Review, 41*, 298–303.

Spargo, J. (1968). *The bitter cry of the children.* Chicago: Quadrangle Press.

We're going to dine with Teddy. (1903, July 11). *New York World*, p. 12.

Wertheimer, B. M. (1977). *We were there: The story of working women in America.* New York: Random House, Pantheon Press.

4

Stone Mother

Katie Frazier's Native Tales

Gwendolyn Clancy, M.A.
Deborah Ballard-Reisch, Ph.D.

*Department of Speech Communication
and Theatre
University of Nevada, Reno*

Katie Frazier at Pyramid Lake

Incognito

So distanced from their selves
That when they see
For the very first time
Their own faces
When they sense
For the very first time
Their own spirits
They believe it is something
Indian.

   —*María Cristina González*

F or many years, Mrs. Katie Frazier worked to preserve the folkways of her people, the Pyramid Lake Paiute tribe, by teaching traditional dance, language, and crafts to Indians and non-Indians alike. She later became interested in having her own life story recorded for this same purpose. At the time of her death in 1991, many hours of audiotape, as well as several hours of film and videotape, had been recorded.[1] To date, anthropologists, filmmakers, historians, and scholars and students from several disciplines have drawn from the original recorded material. Our various efforts have resulted in a documentary film, slide presentations, and academic papers. I, with Deborah Ballard-Reisch, my steadfast collaborator, offer here my own experiences documenting Katie's life, in honor of her desire to share her story with all of us.

I first met Katie Frazier, a woman of almost legendary status in our part of the West, late in 1988. She was an elder of the Pyramid Lake Paiute Tribe, whose reservation lay just 40 miles northeast of Reno, where I lived. No one really knew how old she was, but she had been around longer than even the very oldest in our midst. She knew things about the old days and the old ways, such as how her people had found food and survived in a harsh and rugged land and how they had adapted to the coming of the White settlers. Katie Frazier was a window into these forgotten times, and I was looking forward to getting to know her.

Today, I was to go to her house on the reservation. Leaving Reno, a 24-hour town of neon signs and burgeoning population, I drove through miles of open sagebrush country interspersed with small sharp canyons, and up and over a final rise. Pyramid Lake suddenly spread out in front of me, a bright patch of striking blue, sapphire/turquoise in shade, and filling the horizon.

Driving along its sandy shores, I reached the tiny town of Nixon and found the compact, mint-green government-built house belonging to Katie Frazier. She welcomed me in and gestured to a chair. I sat down and studied her as covertly as possible. A small woman, she was barely 5 feet tall, with a medium build. Today she wore a flowered cotton housedress, with a bright-colored scarf over her shoulders. Her straight, salt-and-pepper colored hair was gathered in a long, tidy braid fastened with a beaded barrette. She was clearly very old, with a face deeply furrowed, but her movements were purposeful and strong, and the impression was one of vitality.

She was watching me, with a slight roguish look in her eyes, and I knew instantly that I hadn't fooled her with my nonchalance. Feeling foolish and caught out, I smiled tentatively, and she smiled back. In that moment she became "Katie" to me, not the formal "Mrs. Frazier" I'd expected to call her. Somehow the name Katie fit her—it caught her sparkle, her spontaneity, her responsive nature. As I looked at her, I reflected that each of us has a story to tell, a story affected by our perceptions, our feelings, our thoughts, and our actions. I wanted to know Katie's.

This essay tells part of Katie Frazier's story, and through her, the story of adaptation and change experienced by her people, the Pyramid Lake Paiutes of northern Nevada, since their first contact with Euro-American settlers traveling to the California gold rush of the 1850s. I approach her story chronologically, through her life span, so that her experiences can speak not only of her reality, but of the reality of her people.

Historical Overview

Nestled within the high desert of northern Nevada lies a blue-green expanse of water 25 miles long, 11 miles wide, and 630 feet deep called Pyramid Lake. It is the center of the aboriginal homeland of the Pyramid Lake Paiutes. Researchers and anthropologists estimate that the people of this region lived as seminomadic, peaceful hunters and gatherers for thousands of years, until the Euro-American migration of the mid-1800s. Over the next few decades, their lives were to undergo unprecedented change as they first had to deal with the destruction of the resources on which they depended and then were restricted to a reservation, where agents of the federal government attempted to acculturate them.

Archeological finds indicate the people of this region engaged in a highly stable material culture which has lasted, according to various estimates, 4,000 years (Knack & Stewart, 1984), 8,000 years (Wihr, 1988), and for the current inhabitants, the Northern Paiutes, since A.D. 1400 (Janik & Anglin, 1992).

The Paiutes originally referred to themselves as the "Neh-muh," which means "The People" (Harner, 1974). They made few distinctions between members of various groups until later, when they became primarily affiliated with their predominant food source (Fowler & Liljeblad, 1986). The Pyramid Lake Paiutes were called Kuyuidokata (Wihr, 1988) because they ate the cui-ui fish of the lake. "Kuyuidokado territory incorporated about

2,000 square miles, including both Pyramid and Winnemucca lakes" (Knack & Stewart, 1984, p. 16).

The Kuyuidokata were hunters and gatherers who traveled continually with the seasons to harvest the fruits of the land and to hunt game (Fowler & Liljeblad, 1986). Consequently, their social and political structures were informal, with the primary affiliation being "kin-and-clique" composed of nuclear and extended family members as well as friends and acquaintances (Malouf, 1966). The membership of these groups changed from season to season depending on the availability of food. The organization and process of their lives were centered around the quest for sustenance. In general, kin-and-clique tasks were divided primarily along gender lines, with women responsible for gathering berries, seeds, and roots and men responsible for hunting. Both shared responsibility for communal activities like fishing and collecting pine nuts. They were an egalitarian and cooperative people who adapted to the harsh, uncertain life-style of the desert. As a people, the Paiutes lived a simple, seminomadic life.[2] After contact with Euro-American settlers, the lives of the Paiutes were changed forever. Katie Frazier's story reflects those changes.

Katie Frazier's Story

Katie Frazier was born around 1890 near what is now Doyle, California. At that time, many of the traditional birthing rituals were still practiced. Women gave birth in special huts accompanied by female relatives. New mothers were confined for 21–25 days following the birth of a child. They were forbidden to eat meat and were bathed regularly, as were their newborn babies (Brink, 1969).

One afternoon, we decided to drive across the nearby California border to the area where Katie was born. We took the back way, bouncing over seemingly endless miles of dusty, washboard dirt roads, the kind that meant a wheel alignment would be needed all too soon. Two hours later we reached the tiny ranching town of Doyle and cruised its main street while Katie tried to recall family stories about the spot her mother had chosen to give birth.

I was born somewhere around here. My mother had a little camp back there—born in a little tepee. My mother and my grandmother tended to me, I think. And I guess I looked kind of funny to them. My grandma didn't take care of me much; she just pushed me aside, and she took care of my mother. My grandma thought I wasn't going to live, because I was weak. I was born before time, and I didn't have no eyelashes, and I didn't have no fingernails, and I didn't have hardly any hair. Now they call the babies like that premature babies. She just pushed me aside and took care of my mother.

She wasn't going to take care of me, because she thought I wasn't going to live, I guess. And an old lady came along to her to see what was going on, and she said, "Oh, my, why don't you take care of this baby girl? Someday when she grow up, she might make coffee for us." So she took care of me—the old lady. She cleaned me up and laid me by my mother. That's what my mother told me. That's the way they took care of me.

I wouldn't have lived if this old lady didn't come along and clean me up, put me by my mother. My mother said I couldn't nurse. She had to use a rabbit fur dipped in milk out of her breast, and then she put it in my mouth, and I sucked that milk off the rabbit fur. And then I got along pretty good.

I was struck by the irony of Katie's story. She was bright and vital, nearly a century after she had been left aside to die.

We turned homeward. Katie sat relaxed and at ease in the passenger seat of my minivan. As she looked about, pointing out landmarks and events of a time long past, I sensed that she was equally at home in the present and in the past. Surely here was an individual with an extraordinary ability to adapt to her world. One of the enduring qualities of the Pyramid Lake Paiutes is their adaptability, attributable to their egalitarian life-style, their independence, and life circumstances that demanded continual adaptation to the changing characteristics of the desert in which they made their primary home (Wihr, 1988).

On a crisp December day, along with a few friends and family members, we walked along the beach on the east shore of Pyramid Lake, near the conical rock outcropping that had earned the lake its name. Bundled snugly in a warm jacket, Katie moved boldly along with the aid of her cane. At her side toddled a great-granddaughter, dragging a stick horse.

As a young child, Katie was always scrambling about over the rocks. She'd earned the name Tisiponah, which Katie told us meant "small one always running" in Paiute. The name still seemed to fit. We seated ourselves in the lee of a large tufa formation, which sheltered us against the cold breeze. The formation is a special one. Its shape resembles a woman seated next to a basket, gazing off to the east, and it is called the Stone Mother, in tribute to the Paiute founding story of a woman whose tears filled the lake and turned her to stone.

Warming her hands over a small campfire, Katie lapsed into telling a story in Paiute. She began by uttering the standard opener "*Ish i gah,*" meaning "listen up." Only the older members of our group understood the language, and they laughed when the story was done. One of her listeners, an elderly woman who could have passed as a contemporary but was actually a good 20 years younger, complained, "My mother never did tell me anything like that, stories or anything." Katie said:

Your mother wasn't the talking kind. You didn't make any trouble when you go to bed. That's why your mother didn't have to tell you story. (She laughed.) *Like my mother used to tell us, "Get your pillows all ready, and put your head on your pillow, and I'll tell you a story." Just like you have a baby, where you put rockaby baby, you rock him, then you put him to sleep like that—sing to him. That's the way my mother used to do to us. But she had to lay down with us, and my mother usually go to sleep before we do!*

Katie laughed and looked around the group, enjoying the memory.

We'd get willows, my mother used to go get willows, about like that. (She points to a pole someone had dragged in to feed the fire.) *And then she'd put it so far apart, just like when you make house, and it makes pretty good-size house, just for the family. And then they leave a space for the door . . . then they go get little willows, and weave it like that, together. And they put it on outside, and then—*

The old woman interrupted, "Tepee, they put canvas, or something around it, for tepee." Katie responded impatiently, "Well, that was lately, but before, and they just had willows. And at first, they had sack—" The old woman interrupted again, uttering the Paiute word "*kanni.*"[3]
Katie resumed her narrative:

Well, that's what I'm talking about, the kanni. And then they put the sack around it, to make it tight, and so it won't get no wind or air in it. And the willows are thick anyway, they'd just weave it close, and then sometimes they, if we live like out here, my mother'd go get sagebrush, and she just pile it on top of each other to make it windproof and warm. Then they put sack around it, to keep it all together, so wind won't blow it. Then they cover it with the dirt all around, about that high, all around with willow, just like cement blocks. And you know, the wind can't blow it over? And it's warm, that's our winter house.

They go get tules, and they weave that together, and they put it inside, like a carpet, or rug. And we sit around on that. And then we eat—here, and all around, wherever we sit—like a picnic. Of course in the old times, we never had no dishes. My mother'd cook something in the frying pan, and we'd all get around that frying pan, and we eat just like chickens. No plates, or anything, we'd just use bread for our spoon. And that was all.

The old woman laughed, "No washing dishes." Katie nodded, "Uh huh, save us washing dishes. That's why the Indian children don't know how to wash dishes—to this day!" Both women laughed at their joke. The toddler had fallen asleep in her mother's arms, and the rest of the group sat contentedly around the campfire. By now the sun had lowered over the lake, casting a warm golden light on their faces. The sky and water filled with pinks and purples of sunset.

Katie sighed contentedly, "That was happy life. Nobody bother, nobody come around scare us." She gazed off to the east. The rays of the setting sun glanced off the Stone Mother figure behind Katie, and I was suddenly startled. Katie's profile, silhouetted against the white backdrop of the tufa, looked uncannily similar to the Stone Mother.

Katie's people traditionally relied primarily on plants, willows, tules, and sagebrush for the construction of their homes and sleeping mats. A rabbit blanket was the most commonly used skin product, and other hides were reserved for special uses (Wheat, 1967). They were a basket, not a ceramic, culture, primarily because materials for making baskets were abundant; ceramics were heavy and breakable, not well conditioned to a people who needed to carry their possessions continually from one place to another (Knack & Stewart, 1984). Homes, also, were temporary shelters, constructed quickly and out of available materials (Wheat, 1967).

The availability of the materials necessary for subsistence was greatly reduced once Euro-American settlers began to compete with the Paiutes for resources. This competition continued even after the reservation was established, as more and more White settlers viewed the boundaries of the reservation as limitations on their personal freedom (Knack & Stewart, 1984). Squatters became common soon after the government set aside land for the reservation (Harner, 1974). In 1924, the squatters were permitted, by the Secretary of the Interior, to purchase the land which they had inhabited, from the Paiutes, for $1.25 per acre. One payment was made but the balance was never received (Knack & Stewart, 1984). The government did not force the squatters either to move or to pay the required amount.

Still, in many ways, the Paiutes of Pyramid Lake adapted to contact with Euro-American settlers. Katie's earlier story makes reference to one change, the use of hides to insulate winter homes. Upon contact with Euro-Americans, the Paiutes indicated a willingness to learn agriculture, to have the federal government start schools, and to learn the benefits of a "White" way of life. The first school opened on the Pyramid Lake reservation in 1878. The first year, 18 students attended. The next year, 52 were enrolled (Brink, 1969). In 1890, the Stewart Indian School was opened. Girls were taught to sew, cook, can, and bake; boys to use hammers, nails, and saws and to shoe horses and mend harnesses. Both boys and girls were taught to read and write a little and to count money. The children were spanked, however, if they spoke in their own language (Wheat, 1967).

When Katie was about 8, she was shipped off to the Stewart Indian School, much against her will. Katie notes, "I yelled loud when my mother left me and walked out." Katie was sad and lonely. But she adapted and soon excelled. The school wanted her to stay and teach, but she left to have a family of her own.

The children of Katie's generation learned valuable lessons from both worlds. "The boarding school attempted to provide full-time instruction in 'White civilization' and many of the graduates of the school . . . had a better understanding of the nature of the outside world" (Wihr, 1988, p. 177). They learned "traditional Paiute crafts and lore from their parents and western 'culture' and three 'R's' from their White teachers" (Wihr, p. 177).

Over the years Katie did many things to support her family, such as working as a domestic for White families. After a while, she moved to the reservation, and the years passed. By the time I met her, she'd outlived two husbands and all but three of her children. As Katie aged, she became increasingly interested in practicing the old ways. She volunteered in the elementary school on the reservation, teaching traditional dance, and she taught Paiute to both youngsters and adults. At home, she liked to work on traditional crafts. The importance of crafts, lore, and the traditional ways was evident in Katie's day-to-day life.

One summer afternoon, she and two of her friends worked on projects at the kitchen table by the window. It was summer, and a light breeze stirred the white gauze curtain behind their heads. The table was covered with handcrafts in various stages of completion. All three were busily sewing. I was quite interested in getting them to talk about their work. Katie began:

I'm making baby shoes. These materials are made out of deerskin. (Holding up the tiny moccasins.) *You have to work hard to fix the deerskin so you can make nice things out of it. You can make bags, beaded bags, out of it, and nice shoes, and little baby shoes and gloves. You get a hide and scrape it. Soak it first for about four or five days. And lots of times a dog gets away with it if they know where it's put.*

She glanced at the door, where her half-coyote/half-husky was standing, gazing in with a hopeful look. He caught her meaningful glance and slunk away.

We just make a lot of things like that, and the people come to our house. The White people come from town, and sometimes they catch me without any, because I sell them out. And the Indians around here, they buy little shoes like this all the time, because they like little shoes for their kids, their little babies. And the little girls in school like them for dancing.

The woman working to Katie's left said, "And there isn't too many people here that make cradleboards—a very few." She gestured to the traditional item used to carry newborn babies. It is made of willows and buckskin, and decorated with beads. "Most people go out, you know, out of the reservation to pick willow, cut willow," she continued. "When they can't find it around here, they go elsewhere, because there's a certain kind they use." Katie broke in:

And then when you try to go get willows, the farmers are pulling the willows. They're killing the willows. They sprayed some kind of chemical on there. They were killing mosquitoes, sprayed with some chemical . . . stuff . . . the ladies that work the willows, they say their mouth gets sore. So they quit getting the willows, you know, on the outside. You can get on the reservation, but you can't find very much willows around here. The rivers are drying, too. They say willows won't grow unless it's where they get a lot of water.

A silence fell over the three women. They bent their heads over their work and sewed quietly. The only sound was the buzzing of a cicada outside the open window.

Later that fall, we drove to a spot on the west side of Pyramid Lake where Katie frequently gathered willows. On that trip, my husband and 4-year-old son accompanied us. We turned off the main road onto a dirt lane and began to climb slowly into a canyon. My son began to complain and squirm in his seat. Katie chuckled and told him we'd be there soon and then he could get down:

We used to roam all over here, a lot of little children. Every day we used to go way up there to that rock that's sticking up in the hill. And we'd stay there, and then one of the bigger girls used to scare us. She'd say, "All these bones laying around there are all people that died here. Look at them moving!" And she'd run. She'd say, "You died!" She'd run, and then we would all run behind her crying. The next day we'd go up again. (She chuckled.) We never learn.

The road was now following alongside a streambed.

They called this canyon See-hoo, because the willows grow here. "See" is the willow, and "hoo" is the water coming down the canyon . . . going down the river, like a river. That's a "hoo." There's no stop to it. And all the ladies, they have a day they all come up here and pick willows to make baskets, and they sell them down here. Nowadays they are hard to find. All the streams are dry where they grow.

We rounded a bend and suddenly had to stop before a large green metal gate, the kind you see on farms and ranches throughout the West. Stretching the full width of the road, it was locked with a large padlock. Nailed to a nearby tree was a large "No Trespassing" sign. Katie climbed out of the car and with the aid of her cane, she walked to the gate and peered through the metal bars. Then she walked slowly over to the streambed we'd been following. It was bone dry. On the near bank stood a small clump of willows. They looked tired and dejected.

See, there's no water in the stream going down here. They've got it all dammed up there to try to hold the water for farming, which they shouldn't do. Hardscrabble Creek used to be running water like a river—a little stream.

She turned and looked up the road, past the metal gate. The hillside had fallen into shadow. Against this somber background, bright curtains of water backlit by the afternoon sun sprayed rhythmically from hidden irrigation lines.

I never thought that anybody out here would take our place up here. We thought this was our home forever and ever. I feel real bad about it. I don't know who gave them permission to get up here and lock their gates up. We used to come up here when no gate was here. I think it's awful the way they take our land away, and then they have no use for us at all. The Indians just never tried to fight the White people; they just moved when somebody come in—just like they were scared of them.

Katie turned away from the gate and walked to the clump of willows. She took a pocket knife out and began sawing at the tough, dust-covered shoots.

The Paiutes adapted to contact with Euro-American settlers by building a booming fishing industry. The Lahontan cutthroat trout, described in 1844 by Colonel Fremont (the first White man to see Pyramid Lake) as the best-tasting fish he had ever eaten, were particularly prized. The issue of water rights became a crucial one for the Paiutes in 1913, when the water of the Truckee River (upon which the fishing industry, as well as the growth of willows, depended) was largely diverted for the Newlands Agricultural Project. Although it was estimated that Pyramid Lake needed an annual average flow of 400,000 acre-feet of water to maintain the fisheries, water rights granted were based on agricultural land; the Paiutes were awarded a mere 30,000 acre-feet annually, far below what was needed to prevent the lake from drying up (Rusco, 1992). As a result, the cutthroat trout died out completely, the cui-ui were endangered, and Winnemucca Lake dried up.

The Paiutes, who had developed a thriving economic system, now became wards of the government, their existence subsidized by outside forces. The Paiutes have been struggling to regain economic independence ever since, principally through the development of a fish hatchery program facilitated by the federal government. The Negotiated Settlement signed by President Bush in November 1990, although it did not return water rights to the tribe, will go a long way in preserving the fish hatchery program, which replaced the natural fishing industry that was destroyed when Truckee River water was diverted (Rusco, 1992).

One day Katie was particularly irritated because a Paiute acquaintance had refused to speak Paiute with her:

> I think the Paiute people here are losing their language. That's what I think. Or either they don't want to speak it, or they're ashamed of it! Even the old ladies, pretty near as old as I am talk English, even if they talk broken English. It sounds so silly. But they won't talk Paiute.
>
> And the kids, they don't speak it. They say, "Oh, we don't know what you're saying." They won't try to learn. It's a wonderful language, but I don't know how we're going to revive it again. I'd like to see all that come back before I leave.

And so, discouraged and yet optimistic, Katie Frazier ushered us all into her world. I was only one of many people hungry for a glimpse into that world. Young and old, Indian and non-Indian, urban and country, untutored and academic, we sought her out, asking a myriad of questions, practicing the unfamiliar Paiute words, recording her stories, videotaping her motions as she fashioned traditional garments or danced the old dances. And she welcomed us all, for she was eager to pass along what she knew. The older she became, the more she could see that her culture was slipping away. Maybe we would be the bearers of her story.

It was now early winter. We were walking in the cemetery near Katie's house, among the white stones and plastic flowers carefully placed in tribute. Now and then Katie paused, leaning on her cane to gaze at a name. A full harvest moon rose behind her, huge upon the horizon. Katie began to talk about her mother.

She was always playing games with us. She was a good runner and a good horsewoman. We couldn't beat her at anything. And she'd try us every way. Of course, she knows she can always get the best of us. She liked to live in the open place. When we were traveling, she find a nice place on the road or out on the hills and say, "Let's stop there. There's a nice place." And then she'd make camp with sagebrush, and make fire, and she'd heat rocks. She'd make a little house about the size of that bush, and cover it up with her blankets. She'd bring her hot rocks in there and take a bucket of water in, and she'd set on a cloth, and she'd pray for herself and all of us. And then she gets out, and she looked so nice and clean! Whenever we stopped, she'd always do that.

I know my mother lived a happy life. That's why she lived to be an old lady. She lived to be 110 years old when she died. We played cards, and she says, "I'm feeling sleepy." And so we stopped playing cards. I fixed her bed for her and she went to bed. And the next morning about 5:00 I heard her moving around, and I thought maybe she wanted to go to the potty, or something. And I got up and I asked her. And she looked at me, she smiled at me, and she didn't say anything. And she turned over, still smiling, and she just went to sleep. She wasn't sick at all. Passed away. And she was still smiling when we buried her.

Katie stopped talking. The moon had risen higher in the sky, and it bathed us all in a silvery light.

I think if people live a happy life, then I think they die happy, they don't suffer. But I think if you abuse your life while you're young and living, why, I think you get punished for that somewhere, and you suffer for it. I always think that myself, too.

We were back in Katie's house on the reservation. Katie was talking as she worked on her old, black, treadle sewing machine. Late-afternoon sun streamed in the west-facing window, and a radio played softly. The mood felt peaceful, unhurried.

I don't know what would happen if I die. I'd like to know that. I've tried to live a happy life, and I think that's why I'm living so long. And I'm not afraid of death if I have to die today. I'd be willing to go. I don't know how my children feel about that, but that's the way I feel.

"Where do you think you go after you die?" I asked.

I don't know, but it's a beautiful place, and it smells beautiful like flowers all over. They always say that.

"What will you see when you go to the . . . ?"

I don't know.

"Will you see people you know?"

I have to go there and see. [Said with a gentle chuckle.] *Then I'll come back and tell you!*

She looked up from her work and directly into my eyes. Her eyes twinkled mischievously, but she also looked wise, as if she were letting me in on a big, wonderful secret.

In early August of 1991, I got a phone call from Katie's daughter. A few mornings earlier her mother, smiling, had quietly slipped away. I drove to the gym in Nixon, the only building that could hold the hundreds of relatives and friends and neighbors who had come to pay final tribute to Mrs. Katie Frazier.

It was an open casket ceremony, and during the service I agonized over whether to walk past her, one last time, or to remember her alive, vibrant and wise. I chose to walk past, and was glad I did. Katie lay peacefully, a familiar smile on her lips. Although her eyes were closed, I sensed her impish, wise spirit, promising to let us know what lies ahead.

Discussion Questions

1. What themes do you see in Katie's story? How do they reconcile with your images of women? of Native American women?

2. How do you think the egalitarianism of Katie's culture benefited the Paiutes? Hindered them? How might this have benefited women in their culture?

3. How do you think Katie's culture, heritage, and life experiences affected her as a woman?

4. Respond to the "Stone Mother" as a symbol. In what ways is it powerful? What are the implications?

5. Why do you think that at this time in history so many people were "hungry" for a glimpse into Katie's world? Why do you think she welcomed the many people who sought her out?

6. What are the implications of "giving voice" to a Native American woman?

7. In many ways the Paiute people adapted themselves to White culture. Through Katie's eyes, what benefits were there? What negative impact did she sense? Do you agree with her view? Why or why not?

References

Brink, P. J. (1969). *The Pyramid Lake Paiute of Nevada.* Unpublished doctoral dissertation, Boston University, Boston.

Fowler, C. S. (1986). Subsistence. In W. L. d'Azevedo (Ed.), *Handbook of North American Indians: Great Basin* (vol. 11, pp. 64–97). Washington, DC: Smithsonian Institution.

Fowler, C. S., & Liljeblad, S. (1986). Northern Paiute. In W. L. d'Azevedo (Ed.), *Handbook of North American Indians: Great Basin* (vol. 11, pp. 435–465). Washington, DC: Smithsonian Institution.

Harner, N. S. (1974). *Indians of Coo-yu-ee Pah (Pyramid Lake): The history of the Pyramid Lake Indians of Nevada.* Sparks, NV: Western Printing and Publishing.

Janik, C. A., & Anglin, R. M. (1992). Nevada's unique wildlife oasis. In P. Goin, R. Dawson, & J. M. Winter (Eds.), *Dividing desert waters: Nevada Public Affairs Review* (no. 1, pp. 54–59). Reno, NV: Senator Alan Bible Center for Applied Research.

Knack, M. C., & Stewart, O. C. (1984). *As long as the river shall run.* Berkeley: University of California Press.

Malouf, C. (1966). Ethnohistory in the Great Basin. In W. L. d'Azevedo (Ed.), *The current status of anthropology research in the Great Basin* (pp. 1–38). Social Sciences and Humanities Publication 1. Reno, NV: Desert Research Institute.

Rusco, E. (1992). The Truckee-Carson-Pyramid Lake water rights settlement act and Pyramid Lake. In P. Goin, R. Dawson, & J. M. Winter (Eds.), *Dividing desert waters: Nevada Public Affairs Review* (no. 1, pp. 9–14). Reno, NV: Senator Alan Bible Center for Applied Research.

Wheat, M. M. (1967). *Survival arts of the primitive Paiutes.* Reno: University of Nevada Press.

Wihr, W. S. (1988). *Cultural persistence in western Nevada: The Pyramid Lake Paiute.* Unpublished doctoral dissertation, University of California, Berkeley.

Endnotes

1. The authors wish to thank JoAnn Peden for her commitment to seeing that Katie's memories were recorded, the University of Nevada Oral History Program for transcribing the interview tapes, and the University of Nevada Special Collections Library for research assistance and access to photographic archives.

2. There were primarily four seasons, which lent themselves to four differing organizational patterns. From midwinter to spring, the people organized themselves into small villages typically composed of several kin and clique. This organization was conducive to effective fishing during the winter spawning runs of the Lahontan cutthroat trout (Wihr, 1988).

   The spring spawning runs of the Lahontan cutthroat trout and of the cui-ui were a time of congregation. Members of other bands came from miles around to participate in the abundant fishing. Although Paiutes did have typical hunting territories, they were not territorial and shared openly with one another any abundant resources.

   In summer, groups typically broke down into individual kin and clique to exploit the scattered resources of the land more effectively; gathering seeds and plants, hunting, fishing, and trapping were primarily solitary activities during this season.

   From fall to midwinter, larger groups often formed, at least for short periods, when game concentrated at lower elevations and hunting drives with a larger number of hunters were most effective. A major ceremony of the fall involved the pine-nut harvest. Piñon gathering, like the spawning runs of the trout and cui-ui, was a time of plenty. "The entire winter subsistence of the group depended on the productivity of the trees and the rapid labor of the people" (Knack & Stewart, 1984). The harvest was followed by a communal rabbit hunt and, again, the people scattered to smaller kin and clique for the cold months of winter (Wheat, 1967).

3. The dome-shaped, mat-covered house known as "kani" (*kanni* in Paiute pronunciation) was the most common winter structure for most of the Nevada Northern Paiute groups. Conical in form, it was cov-

ered with tules or grass and built over a framework of willow poles. A smoke hole was left in the top, and a doorway was placed on one side, usually facing east or away from prevailing winds. Inside the kani, in the center, was a fire for cooking and warming. The size of the house varied with the size of the family, but 8–15 feet in diameter seems to have been the standard (Fowler, 1986).

5

Margaret Chase Smith

The Spirit of Conviction

Marlene Boyd Vallin[1]

Department of Speech Communication
Pennsylvania State University, Berks Campus

Margaret Chase Smith, 1946

H istorically, women all too often have accepted the cultural norm rather than challenge it. Hence, women opted for a subordinate role in society because they were told that was their place. Submissively, they donned their aprons, as their mothers had done before them, and retreated to the kitchen, stifling all attempts to dream. That was not the case for the pragmatic Margaret Chase Smith. As an American, she firmly believed that in this land of opportunity she could do whatever she chose. When she was told by powerful men and many of her friends that the Senate was no place for a woman, she became even more determined. Morality was her strength, motivating her to have the courage of her convictions. She proved her detractors wrong with her indomitable spirit.

*O*n June 1, 1950, Margaret Chase Smith, junior senator from the state of Maine and the only woman member of that prestigious body, rose from her seat on the Republican side of the chamber and delivered her famous "Declaration of Conscience" speech.[2] Undeniably feminine with her slight stature, soft voice, and trademark rose pinned neatly to her lapel, the lady from Maine stood stalwart, like the patriots on Concord Bridge. There was "a serious national condition" that needed to be addressed (Smith, 1972, p. 12), and, in characteristic Yankee fashion, Margaret Chase Smith rose to do the job.

The oldest of six children born to Carrie Murray and George Chase, Margaret Chase lived in Skowhegan, a small working-class city in northwestern Maine, where the Kennebeck River dominates the rugged terrain and the long, harsh winters temper one's character. Driven by the need to help her financially strained parents, she left high school in the spring of her senior year, two months before graduation, to take a job offered to her by Clyde Smith, then Skowhegan's First Selectman—$12 a week to record tax payments in the town's books.

Over the years, her work experience followed the traditional pattern for women of her generation—schoolteacher, telephone operator, bookkeeper, office manager. Eventually, however, she broke from tradition. She became active in public life, of sorts, as a charter member of the local chapter, and later president, of the State Federation of Business and Professional Women's Clubs, and as representative of her county on the Republican State Committee.

Such achievements for a woman—particularly one like Margaret Chase, who never went to college—were considered unusual at the time. Most women generally got married right out of high school. Like those of their mothers before them, their hopes to make a difference in this world lay in the realm of family. Their chamber for effecting positive change was the kitchen. Life as it "ought to be" was broadcast by such popular television productions as *The Donna Reed Show, Leave It to Beaver,* and *Father Knows Best.* Simply stated, Americans tended to believe that life was better for everyone when women devoted their lives to raising families. According to the cultural dictates of the time, women had one life-style choice—to marry or be labeled an "old maid."

Margaret did marry. On May 14, 1930, at the age of 32, she became the wife of Clyde Smith, now a seasoned politician, 22 years her senior. By that time, Margaret had enjoyed a good degree of popularity in Skowhegan from her jobs at the telephone company and for the local newspaper, the *Independent Reporter.* Her marriage to Clyde plunged her into the whirlwind of political life.

When Clyde was elected to the United States House of Representatives in 1936, Margaret saw Washington for the first time. She became his secretary, traveling with him, helping him with his speeches, and prepping him with background material on important issues. In 1940, a severe heart attack left her husband unable to run for reelection. The Maine Republican Party chose Margaret to run instead. On April 7, 1940, Clyde Smith died. Maggie was back on her own again, but in a different venue—not the secure world of small-town New England, but the complex arena of national politics.

When Representative Smith expressed an interest in running for the Senate in the election of 1948, she was not encouraged to do so. One woman friend, newspaper correspondent May Craig, reflected the reaction of many others by responding, "Margaret, you have reached your peak—you can go no further—so you must adjust yourself to going downhill from now on" (Smith, 1972, p. 4). Her own party did not support her candidacy. Maine's other senator, Owen Brewster, an ultraconservative, believed that Margaret's place was in the House (Graham, 1964, p. 50). Another politician remarked, "The little lady has simply stepped out of her class. The Senate is big-league stuff. Nobody in Maine can get into the Senate without a political machine, fat campaign funds, the right business connections and the help of the powers-that-be. Margaret hasn't got any of these things" (Graham, 1964, p. 47).

Obviously, those doubting individuals did not know Margaret Chase Smith very well. *She* knew she could be a good senator and was determined to put the decision to the voters. No entrenched attitudes designating women to subordinate roles were going to derail her ambition. She always identified herself as a *person* who happened to be a woman; gender was a secondary trait (Vallin, 1992). With characteristic independence and determination, she soundly defeated her three powerful opponents in the primary race and went on to win the Senate seat by the biggest majority ever given a Maine candidate (Graham, 1964, p. 58). She had become the first woman to win a seat in the United States Senate and the first woman ever to serve in both houses of Congress.

On June 1, 1950, Senator Smith was moved to deliver her first major speech to that bastion of men, the traditional decision-makers of our democracy. She believed that fundamental American principles were being abused and it was her duty to speak out. Smith was always a take-charge person, and when she was given a job to do, it was going to be done. That's all there was to it. She had made a covenant with the people, and that bond would be upheld. That was how she had been raised—with simple yet strong values of trust and honesty; that was the attitude of her constituency—the hardworking, decent folks of Maine who struggled proudly to eke out a living in the smaller towns and villages. Accordingly, Smith was convinced that she must make her speech, "Declaration of Conscience," to the Senate.

In resolute, measured terms she launched a 15-minute attack on her colleagues for allowing themselves to be "held hostage" by one of their own—Joseph McCarthy. Known as the "Quiet Woman," for she believed that one should speak only if there was something worth saying, the 52-year-old senator fixed her clear blue eyes on the gentlemen on both sides of the aisle, those Republicans and Democrats who were rendered mute in the face of McCarthy's witch-hunting tactics, especially his blatant abuse of the privilege of senatorial immunity.

In spite of the fact that she was already regarded as a person of few words, she explained at the outset of this speech that the urgency of the issue dictated a simple rather than eloquent style:

> I speak as briefly as possible because too much harm has already been done with irresponsible words of bitterness and selfish political opportunism. I speak as simply as possible because the issue is too great to be obscured by eloquence. I speak simply and briefly in the hope that my words will be taken to heart. (Smith, 1972, p. 13)

Actually, in the Senate chamber, where rousing oratory reminiscent of the grand style was the historical norm, Senator Smith's simple, direct style and soft, almost solemn delivery were indeed eloquent. She warned her listeners, "It is a national feeling of fear and frustration that could result in national suicide and the end of everything that we Americans hold most dear" (Smith, 1972, pp. 12–13).

Many Americans were convinced that the Communists were bent on the overthrow of all governments. Such talk was hot copy in the popular press. For example, the featured article of the June 2, 1947, issue of *Newsweek*, "The Communist Party in the U.S.," informed its readers of the growing Communist membership in labor unions, of an increase in Communist publications, and of the effectiveness of the American Labor Party, considered a pro-Communist organization, which was represented by Vito Marcantonio in the United States Congress. The following week, June 9, 1947, *Newsweek* published "How to Fight Communism," by J. Edgar Hoover, head of the Federal Bureau of Investigation. Hoover promoted the need for vigilance by underscoring the increase in Communist Party membership and the deceitful methods being employed by the Communists. For example, he alerted Americans to the formation of "front organizations," such as American Youth for Democracy (which had formerly been known as the Young Communist League). He urged all Americans to fight Communism with truth and justice.

Few attempts were made to modify the situation. In a speech delivered in May of 1948, Justice William O. Douglas warned against undue concern about Communism. He advocated the need to counteract fear based on ignorance and a demand for better understanding of the "threat" (Douglas, 1948). However, the fear prevailed and grew to suspicion bordering on national paranoia. Books, television programs, and films—in fact, all forms of the popular media—focused on the rising "Red Scourge" and promoted the national mind-set of "Better dead than Red."

In 1950, while Americans were watching the "happily ever after" exploits of their favorite television families, they were becoming increasingly tense over the fear of the spread of Communism, that Communists were planning to overthrow their government. Ever since the rise and success of Bolshevism in Russia with its talk of world domination, a "Red Scare" had pervaded the American psyche. This fear grew to its greatest intensity during the Cold War years. The overtly aggressive behavior of the Soviet Union under Josef Stalin after World War II, resulting in the "Stalinization" of a number of countries and the creation of the "Iron Curtain," as well as the disruptive actions of the Soviet Union in the United Nations contributed to an almost phobic reaction to any references to Communism and the USSR.

The Communists were suspected of being everywhere. Basing his activities on that allegation, Senator Joseph McCarthy, Republican from Wisconsin, embarked on a personal crusade to drive the traitors out. His plan, detailed at length in his book, *McCarthyism: The Fight for America* (McCarthy, 1952), convinced millions of Americans that his was the strategy needed to safeguard America. The one issue of McCarthyism in particular that seemed to have galvanized public opinion was that loyal Americans did not want any department of the federal government infiltrated by people with pro-Soviet feelings. All agreed that there was need for investigation; however, there were differences of opinion as to what methods to use.

The label "McCarthyism" had its beginning in a series of speeches delivered by the senator in early February 1950. Specifically, in a speech in Wheeling, West Virginia, Senator McCarthy "launched his charge of card-carrying Communists in the State Department and started playing the numbers game as to just how many there were" (Smith, 1972, p. 6). McCarthy's "'I hold in my hand a photostatic copy' had a most impressive tone and ring of authenticity," Smith recalled (p. 7). In these speeches, protected by senatorial immunity, McCarthy attacked the Democratic administration, maintaining that the State Department and other government agencies had been infiltrated by Communists. Some senators complained that McCarthy, by denying the accused the right to be seen as innocent until proven guilty, was abusing the privilege of congressional immunity, but none spoke out. "McCarthy had created an atmosphere of such political fear that people were not only afraid to talk but they were afraid of whom they might be seen with" (Smith, 1972, p. 9). The occasion for Smith's speech favored its effectiveness. On June 1, 1950, the Senate was conducting debates on the Amerasia Case, which was concerned with security risks, and, as Senator Smith reports in her book, the atmosphere was tense.

What may have appeared as blind courage to those who heard her speak that June day was really quite natural for Margaret Chase Smith. She had shown her determination many times before. For example, it was common for her to travel hundreds of miles over rough terrain in threatening weather to fulfill a promise to her constituents. One time, while on her way to one of these meetings, she fell and broke her arm. With no thought of canceling, she simply had the bone set, and persevered. Therefore, considering her character, it really was not surprising that she would take on Joe McCarthy. To some of her colleagues such a move was tantamount to political suicide. But for Senator Margaret Chase Smith it was simply the right thing to do. Just before noon, in the midst of the Amerasia debates, and with her well-thought-out plans and written speech kept secret from all except her administrative assistant William Lewis, she obtained the floor.

McCarthy somehow got wind of what she was up to. Implying that he could keep her from getting Wisconsin support for the Republican Vice Presidential nomination, he shouted to Senator Smith, "Remember, Margaret, I control Wisconsin's twenty-seven convention votes!" (Smith, 1972, p. 12). However, the lady from Maine was not moved. Her diminutive size and her barely audible voice contrasted sharply with the magnitude of her message. She stood upright and proud, the dignity of her rugged New England heritage punctuating her message in defense of our basic democratic values. There was no indication of apprehension—about her gender, her relative inexperience, or her lack of higher education. Although the powerful McCarthy was seated directly behind her, fear of recrimination did not deter her.

In a situation reminiscent of Joan of Arc and the biblical David, the intrepid Mrs. Smith launched an unerring missile from her slingshot: "Those of us who shout the loudest about Americanism in making character assassinations are all too frequently those who, by our own words and acts, ignore some of the basic principles of Americanism" (Smith, 1972, p. 14). Senator Smith never mentioned McCarthy by name; rather, she used the referent "those of us."

The principles of American democracy were an integral and sacred part of Smith's total being and her perception of every other American. She viewed McCarthy's position as extremism, extremism from the Right, and, therefore, as a threat to our democracy. She firmly believed that extremism left unchecked would lead to repression for all.

The "conscience" the senator referred to in the title of her speech is the national conscience. In the introduction, she declared that she was speaking collectively for all Americans: "I speak as a Republican. I speak as a woman. I speak as a United States Senator. I speak as an American" (Smith, 1972, p. 13). Her speech was different from the type of political speech commonly heard in Congress. She did not promote herself or her political affiliations; instead, she presented herself as a representative of the people pledged to defend democratic principles.

With that identity established, Senator Smith defined the urgency that moved her to speak:

> [T]he character . . . [of] the greatest deliberative body in the world . . . has too often been debased to the level of a forum of hate and character assassination sheltered by the shield of congressional immunity.

I think that it is high time for the United States Senate and its members to do some soul-searching—for us to weigh our consciences—on the manner in which we are performing our duty to the people of America—on the manner in which we are using or abusing our individual powers and privileges.

I think that it is high time that we remembered that we have sworn to uphold and defend the Constitution. I think that it is high time that we remembered that the Constitution, as amended, speaks not only of the freedom of speech but also of trial by jury instead of trial by accusation. (Smith, 1972, pp. 13–14)

In simple, straightforward terms Smith argued that the privilege of congressional immunity had been used undemocratically:

[W]e can verbally attack anyone else without restraint and with full protection and yet we hold ourselves above the same type of criticism here on the Senate Floor. . . . Surely we should be able to take the same kind of character attacks that we "dish out" to outsiders. (Smith, 1972, p. 13)

Pointing her rhetoric directly at the warped sense of patriotism of Senator McCarthy, Senator Smith accused: "Those of us who shout the loudest about Americanism . . . ignore some of the basic principles of Americanism: The right to criticize; The right to hold unpopular beliefs; The right to protest; The right to independent thought" (Smith, 1972, p. 14). Senator Smith then broadened her reprimand to include all present:

The exercise of these rights should not cost one single American citizen his reputation or his right to a livelihood nor should he be in danger of losing his reputation or livelihood merely because he happens to know someone who holds unpopular beliefs. Who of us doesn't? (Smith, 1972, p. 14)

Smith observed that one of the present problems was that "[t]he American people are sick and tired of being afraid to speak their minds lest they be politically smeared as 'Communists' or 'Fascists'" (Smith, p. 14). Then she responded to that problem:

As an American, I condemn a Republican "Fascist" just as much as I condemn a Democrat "Communist." I condemn a Democrat "Fascist" just as much as I condemn a Republican "Communist." They are equally dangerous to you and me and to our country. (Smith, 1972, p. 17)

Senator Smith concluded her speech by reinforcing her purpose: "As an American, I want to see our nation recapture the strength and unity it once had when we fought the enemy instead of ourselves" (Smith, 1972, p. 17).

Known as a woman of few words and stereotyped as a conservative New Englander before this, her first major speech, Mrs. Smith gained the attention of the audience with her forthright message. The contrast of this relatively new, lone female member taking to task this hallowed fraternity of men, to the megalomaniacal Joseph McCarthy was compelling. According to an editorial in the *New Republic,* "In the hushed all-male audience, Mrs. Smith's hardly audible tones had visible effect. It was like another still, small voice saying something to listeners that, in their hearts, they already knew" (Editorial, 1950, p. 3).

"Declaration of Conscience" attracted national attention (Smith, 1972). The *New York Times* ran as a front-page headline: "Mrs. Smith Warns of Repression" ("Mrs. Smith," 1950). *Time* magazine called the speech "an eloquent and pointed appeal to the forces of moderation" ("The Congress," 1950). The June 12, 1950, issue of *Newsweek* featured Senator Smith's photograph on the cover with the caption "Senator Smith: A woman Vice-President?" ("WOMEN," 1950). The accompanying article stated:

> What many a bewildered citizen had waited to hear for a long time was said by a woman last week. After months of shocking charges on one side and evasive alibiing on the other, her precise, restrained phrases worked as neatly as a broom sweeping out a mess. ("WOMEN," 1950, p. 24)

This "politically risky speech" prompted the heaviest mail ever received by Mrs. Smith, running 8-to-1 in favor. The elder statesman Bernard Baruch was quoted, "If a man made [this speech], he would most likely be the next President of the U.S." (Smith, 1972, p. 19). The speech established her as "a national figure to be reckoned with by her own Republican Party and respected by the Democrats" (Manning, 1988, p. 303).

As predicted, Joseph McCarthy retaliated. But each time he attempted to execute his revenge, the feisty Margaret defended herself. He succeeded in getting her kicked out of the Investigations Subcommittee in 1951. In early 1952, McCarthy made his most serious attack on Senator Smith. He had her labeled as a communist sympathizer in *U.S.A. Confidential,* written by Jack Lait and Lee Mortimer. The book stated that she was "a lesson why women should not be in politics" and that she "reacted to all situations as a woman scorned, not as a representative of the people" (Smith,

1972, p. 38). Senator Smith sued both the authors and the publishers for libel.

In 1954, McCarthy plotted to stop her reelection to the Senate by running his own candidate, Robert L. Jones, against her. Maggie beat McCarthy's candidate in the primaries by a record number of votes, a five-to-one margin. The story goes that McCarthy, at a press conference in Portland, Maine, asked if there was anyone more popular than Senator Smith in Maine. A reporter responded "Yes." "Who?" questioned McCarthy hopefully. The reporter responded, "Almighty God" (Smith, 1972, p. 53). In defeating Senator McCarthy's candidate by such a great margin, the lady from Maine also destroyed his power in the United States Senate (Smith, 1972, p. 58). After his failed attempt to get Margaret defeated in the Maine primaries in 1954, McCarthy often found himself riding with Smith on the same little subway train that transports senators from the Senate Office Building to the Senate wing of the Capitol Building. McCarthy remarked, "Margaret, we seem to be following each other and riding together." "Yes, Joe," she smiled. "If you don't watch out, people will say we are fellow travelers" (Smith, 1972, p. 61).

After four and a half years of publicized lies and misrepresentations, on October 17, 1956, Lee Mortimer finally acknowledged that the statements about her in his book were false (Smith, 1972, pp. 40–41). Smith had tenaciously fought Mortimer's style of political smear, as well as every other attempt to defame her for daring to criticize McCarthy publicly. Her victories led to McCarthy's defeat. He once remarked in frustration, "There's too damn many women in the Senate!" (Smith, 1972, p. 45).

McCarthy died in 1957. Senator Smith enjoyed a long and successful career in the Senate, retiring in 1972 at the age of 75.

For Margaret Chase Smith, having the courage to deliver "Declaration of Conscience" in a climate where her seemingly more powerful colleagues remained powerless speaks well for her, for the citizens of Maine, and for all patriotic Americans. She serves as a role model for legislators. This speech became the model for her second "Declaration of Conscience" speech, which was delivered in response to the crucial national situation in 1970, when extremism of the Left threatened our democracy. On the anniversary of the first speech, June 1, Margaret Chase Smith again censured both her colleagues and citizens about the need to preserve that precious democratic principle of freedom of speech, restating her warning that extremism of any kind leads to the repression of fundamental rights for all. At age 72, 20 years after her first major speech, "Declaration of Conscience," the lady from Maine proved again that she was indomitable.

Discussion Questions

1. In what ways do you believe Senator Margaret Chase Smith was successful?

2. What moral lessons does Senator Smith's story demonstrate?

3. Imagine yourself as Senator Smith, the only woman in the Senate in 1950. How would you respond to the situation? Would you speak out while your colleagues sat mute? Were there things Smith could have done to minimize her risk?

4. Smith can be referred to as the model public servant. Explain.

5. The Senate is considered the most powerful deliberative body in the world. In what ways did Senator Smith's actions help her to fit in? How did she utilize the power of the Senate? How did she resist the power of the Senate?

6. What do you know about contemporary female senators? How does Smith compare to the women senators serving in office today?

References

The communist party in the U.S. (1947, June 2). *Newsweek,* pp. 22–26.

The Congress: A woman's conscience. (1950, June 12). *Time,* p. 19.

Douglas, W. O. (1948, August). Our political competence. *Vital Speeches of the Day, 14,* 645–649.

Editorial. (1950, June 12). *New Republic,* p. 3.

Graham, F., Jr. (1964). *Margaret Chase Smith: Woman of courage.* New York: John Day.

Hoover, J. E. (1947, June 9). How to fight communism. *Newsweek,* pp. 30–32.

McCarthy, E. (1952). *McCarthyism: The fight for America.* New York: Devin Adair.

Manning, B. (1988). *We shall be heard: An index to speeches by American women, 1878–1985.* Metuchen, NJ: Scarecrow Press.

Mrs. Smith warns of repression. (1950, June 2). *New York Times,* p. 11.

Smith, M. C. (1972). *Declaration of conscience.* New York: Doubleday.

Vallin, M. B. (1992, June 2). Personal (unpublished) interview with Senator Smith.

WOMEN: The lady from Maine. (1950, June 12). *Newsweek,* pp. 24–26.

Endnotes

1. The author wishes to express appreciation to Penn State University, Berks Campus, for financial support of this project.

2. Margaret Chase Smith delivered two speeches with the same theme—the threat of political extremism to our democracy. She purposely gave them the same title and delivered them 20 years apart on the same day —June 1—in 1950 and 1970. All references to Smith's "Declaration of Conscience" speech in this essay are to the first speech, given June 1, 1950.

6

Tillie Olsen

Catching a Lifetime in a Phrase

Maureen E. Hoffman, M.A.[1]

Department of Developmental Education
Central Community College, Nebraska

Tillie Olsen, 1991

The Controversial Vision

to Spencer Bear Heels

Some things are meant to be remembered
Only in the heart.
Some things are meant to be seen
Only for the first time
With the eyes
And kept in
Memory
In the heart,
In the mind.

They cannot be captured on paper
They cannot be captured on film
They cannot be captured on tape.

And though we read
And though we see in film
And though we hear recordings
And though these things feed our hearts
and our Spirits

It will never replace
Life.
It will never replace
The *living* ritual,
the living of the Spirit.

And so the ways are opened
So that members of all races
And all walks
May learn the ways of the earth

Because it is not enough to read
It is not enough to hear
It is not enough to see on film
and hear on tape
Those things that are needed
To heal the Earth
To heal the Spirit.

      —María Cristina González

*I*n graduate school in 1984, I intentionally sought a "woman's story" to explicate the importance of women authors and, perhaps, to confound a stodgy, traditional, chauvinistic professor. Tillie Olsen's 1961 award-winning short story, "Tell Me a Riddle," was the perfect piece. But I was the one confounded by her sparse, haunting writing style, capable of catching a lifetime in a single phrase, and by the intimate familiarity of her characters and their struggles. The wonder and intimacy of that piece sent me in search of more— more words by and about Olsen. I found four more short stories, a 40-year-old novel, and the astonishing nonfiction piece, Silences. I noted too the erratic publication dates and embarked upon a 7-year search for any reference, review, critique, or interview that could explain these dates, that woman, those words. And then I learned that Tillie Olsen is at once the rule and the exception. Her life proves her heartfelt contention that motherhood is a punitive circumstance for women authors. Motherhood clearly delayed her writing and may well have limited it. Yet, Olsen did publish to critical acclaim, and her fictional content came directly from those life experiences that so delayed her writing. Olsen is a paradox—and no matter how many papers I write, how many resources I acquire, how many book reviews I do, or literature classes I visit, I can never get words around Tillie Olsen.

Paging through an anthology of women's literature, I discovered Tillie Olsen quite by accident—and that is precisely my point. How was it that I had progressed through the Nebraska educational system and only midway through a master of arts in English had I *accidentally* discovered this Nebraska-born, award-winning author? No professor in my experience had ever lectured on or referenced Olsen; her name had never appeared on an assigned or even a recommended reading list. Yet here before me on the page were the haunting words and images of Olsen's "Tell Me a Riddle," winner of the O. Henry award for best short story of 1961. In this profound story, an old Jewish grandmother, dying of cancer, randomly reviews her life: a year of exile in Siberia, the risk of learning to read, the dream of America, the endless lack of money, the constant needs of seven children. And out of remembering who she was and what she might have been, Eva, the dying woman, can no longer acquiesce to her family's wants and needs: she argues bitterly with her husband of 47 years, rejects her newest grandbaby, denies anew her Jewish faith.

Olsen's words moved me. Her squabbling David and Eva might have been my own parents; Eva's remembered poverty came dangerously close to detailing my own growing up. "Never again to be forced to move to the rhythms of others," Eva vowed (Olsen, 1976, p. 68), and I nodded knowingly. Nor was I alone in finding myself in Olsen's words. Sharing a passage orally with a colleague, my own voice hoarse with emotion, I looked up from my reading to see tears streaming down her face. Others, hearing the rhythm of Olsen's words, feeling their tug, would murmur, "My God! That's my in-laws," or simply whisper, "yes . . . yes . . . yes." Returning my tattered copy of the story, a male co-worker, looking uneasy and perplexed, kept repeating, "She wouldn't hold the baby . . . she couldn't hold it." We may not yet have known of Joyce Carol Oates's pronouncement that "Tell Me a Riddle" was "supremely beautiful in its nuances, its voices and small perfect details" (Oates, 1978, p. 32), but we certainly knew what touched us. Who crafted this story? we wondered. How did she seemingly know us so intimately? Who was this Tillie Olsen?

Discovering who Tillie Olsen was proved as fascinating as reading her novella. Indeed, I soon learned that to read Tillie Olsen's works is to read her life—so intricately bound are the two. Thus her *seemingly* sporadic publication dates—*Tell Me a Riddle,* a collection of four short stories published in 1961; *Yonnondio: From the Thirties,* a resurrected novel first started in the 1930s and ultimately published in 1974; and *Silences,* a collection of essays written over a 15-year span and published in 1978—actually mark periods in Olsen's life when family and financial conditions permitted the creative/artistic Olsen to emerge from the roles of mother/wife/worker to write. The *Tell Me* collection, for instance, evolved from two significant, freeing circumstances. First, in 1954 Olsen's youngest daughter started kindergarten. Second, Olsen acquired a Stanford University creative writing fellowship. During this rich period of lessened family responsibilities and relieved financial demands, Olsen wrote the four short stories that comprise the *Tell Me* collection, including the award-winning title story.

In sharp contrast to this burst of writing in the late 1950s and early 1960s, similar circumstances of family and funding constrained rather than freed Olsen at other times and account for the almost 40-year gap between the inception of *Yonnondio* and its publication. Literary circles first heard from Olsen in 1934 when the *Partisan Review* carried "The Iron Throat," the opening chapter of her novel (Lerner, 1934). According to a prefacing page of the novel, the Indian word *yonnondio,* taken from the title of a Walt Whitman poem, means "lament for the aborigines." In his poem, Whitman laments those who are unrecorded, unvoiced, unknown—lost. In her novel, Olsen gives voice to and thereby makes known the Holbrook family: Anna and Jim and their children, 6-year-old Mazie and her younger siblings Will, Ben, Jimmie, and baby Bess. Set in the 1920s, the novel traces the Holbrooks, caught in a world defined by poverty and powerlessness, as they move from a Wyoming mining town to a Dakota tenant farm to an unnamed Midwest city wrapped in packing-house stench. Editor/reviewer Annie Gottlieb termed *Yonnondio: From the Thirties* "a remarkable book for a 19 to 24-year old writer, or for any writer" (Gottlieb, 1974, p. 5).

Remarkable, indeed! When the first chapter appeared, publisher Bennett Cerf found the piece so promising that he eventually contracted to pay Olsen a monthly stipend for a finished chapter every month. Yet little came of the deal, and ultimately this promising young writer ceased writing— which is not to say she ceased to exist. In fact, a closer look at Olsen's life suggests that the surprise is not so much her silence as her survival.

Nineteen-year-old, Nebraska-born Tillie Lerner—already a member of the Young Communist League, political organizer of packinghouse workers, and Depression-era itinerant—started writing her novel in 1932, at approximately the same time she became pregnant with and gave birth to her first daughter. Bennett Cerf's enticing offer prompted Lerner/Olsen to send her daughter to live with relatives and to move from San Francisco to Los Angeles to write. She quickly discovered "that she felt very separated from the kind of human beings she was closest to, and from her own child" (Duncan, 1982, pp. 212–213). Shortly thereafter, Olsen relinquished her contract, retrieved her child, and returned to San Francisco. (Years later in the *Tell Me* collection, Olsen's short story "I Stand Here Ironing" would set the scene for a mother's interior monologue reviewing the circumstantial choices she made raising, alone, her first-born daughter.) In 1936, Tillie Lerner married union organizer Jack Olsen. By 1937, she was pregnant with her second child; the writing stopped. Not until 1974 would *Yonnondio: From the Thirties,* as originally envisioned and written in the 30s, appear in print in its entirety. Olsen herself speaks of that silencing time:

> In the nearly twenty years I bore and reared my children, usually had to work on a paid job as well, the simplest circumstances for creation did not exist. This was the time of festering and congestion. For a few months I was able to shield the writing with which I was so full, against the demands of jobs on which I had to be competent, through the joys and responsibilities and trials of family. For a few months. Always roused by the writing, always denied. "I could not go write it down. It convulsed and died in me. I will pay." (Olsen, 1978, pp. 19–20)

What Olsen names here is achingly familiar to many women: the exhausting struggle to salvage the creative self. How extraordinarily difficult it is for an author, artist, musician, or entrepreneur to emerge from the daily demands of husbands and households, family and finances. From "Iron Throat" to *Yonnondio,* Olsen learned firsthand the cost of coming to words:

> My work died. What demanded to be written, did not. It seethed, bub-
> bled, clamored, peopled me. At last moved into the hours meant for sleep-
> ing, I worked now full time on temporary jobs, a Kelly, a Western Agency
> girl (girl!), wandering from office to office, always hoping to manage two,
> three months ahead. Eventually there was time. (Olsen, 1978, pp. 19–20)

Time, of course, came for Olsen in the mid-50s, when her last child started school and when Olsen acquired not only the creative writing fel-lowship at Stanford but also a 2-year Ford grant in literature (Burkom & Williams, 1976, p. 74). And in that writing time, Olsen wrote the truth of her life. Here were work-worn mothers, confused adolescent daughters, a drunken sailor, a dying Jewish grandmother—all trying to understand the circumstances that both contained and shaped the lives they lived.

The struggle Olsen experienced in getting to her writing, the overcom-ing of job responsibilities and family obligations, the balancing of roles as mother/wife/worker/author, the searching for time, the salvaging of energy not only influenced her various fictional pieces (and dictated her publishing dates) but served as the basis for her 1978 nonfiction publication *Silences.*

Comprising two talks Olsen delivered in 1962 and 1971, an afterword she wrote in 1971 to accompany the reprint of a novel written by Rebecca Harding Davis in 1861, and a "long aftersection," *Silences* explores far more explicitly "the relationship of circumstances—including class, color, sex; the times, climate into which one is born—to the creation of litera-ture" (Olsen, 1978, p. x). She then quotes at length diary entries from the likes of Franz Kafka, Virginia Woolf, and Katherine Mansfield—diary entries that recount financial and family obstructions to writing and that express the ever-present need for *time* to write. She reviews the names (Jane Austen, Willa Cather, Pearl Buck), marital status (usually single), number of children (usually childless, seldom more than one), domestic circumstances ("All had servants.") of those women whose work has endured through the past two centuries.

Olsen wastes little time in getting to that which she knows best—motherhood as a silencing circumstance:

> More than in any other human relationship, overwhelmingly more, moth-
> erhood means being instantly interruptible, responsive, responsible. Chil-

dren need one *now* (and remember, in our society, the family must often try to be the center for love and health the outside world is not). The very fact that these are real needs, that one feels them as one's own (love, not duty); *that there is no one else responsible for these needs,* gives them primacy. It is distraction, not meditation, that becomes habitual; interruption, not continuity; spasmodic, not constant toil. . . . Work interrupted, deferred, relinquished, makes blockage—at best, lesser accomplishment. Unused capacities atrophy, cease to be. . . . Almost no mothers—as almost no part-time, part-self persons—have created enduring literature. (Olsen, 1978, pp.18–19)

Olsen knows whereof she speaks; her own silenced years underscore the clear, sad truth of her words. Motherhood and enduring literature are mutually exclusive terms.

But Olsen would have you know that it is not just *her* experience that gives credence to her words. She argues that a "punitive difference in circumstance" exists between women writers and men writers. Her conviction spills across the pages. She notes, for example, the "predominantly male literature" most women study in college. Presumed universally true by the men who write, read, analyze, and teach it, such literature, with its "restrictively male" perspective, offers women an inaccurate and incomplete truth. Such literature not only separates women from their own content but also denies the validity of that content as well. After reviewing society's words, phrases, attitudes, and beliefs that consistently deny women writers access to the truth as they know and understand it, Olsen observes:

How much it takes to become a writer. Bent (far more common than we assume), circumstances, time, development of craft—but beyond that: how much conviction as to the importance of what one has to say, one's right to say it. And the will, the measureless store of belief in oneself to be able to come to, cleave to, find the form for one's own life comprehensions. Difficult for any male not born into a class that breeds such confidence. Almost impossible for a girl, a woman. (Olsen, 1978, p. 27)

A few pages later, Olsen once more addresses motherhood as a "punitive difference in circumstance." After reciting, again, the names of successful and childless women writers like Katherine Ann Porter, Flannery O'Connor, Jessamyn West, and Joyce Carol Oates, Olsen footnotes:

The old patriarchal injunction: "Woman, this is man's realm. If you insist on invading it, unsex yourself—and expect the road to be made difficult."

> Furthermore, this very unmarriedness and childlessness has been used to discredit women as unfulfilled, inadequate, somehow abnormal. (Olsen, 1978, p. 31)

Thus are women caught in a society that believes men may marry and write, but women must choose, and, as Olsen notes a bit later, however they choose, they pay. She cites then such women as Harriette Arnow, Dorothy Canfield Fisher, Cynthia Ozick, and Alice Walker as examples of women who have successfully combined motherhood and writing, but she cautions:

> I hope and I fear for what will result. I hope (and believe) that complex new richness will come into literature; I fear because almost certainly their work will be impeded, lessened, partial. For the fundamental situation remains unchanged. Unlike men writers who marry, most will not have the societal equivalent of a wife—nor (in a society hostile to growing life) anyone but themselves to mother their children. (Olsen, 1978, p. 32)

Olsen calculates the cost of their choice: "Some wrote before children, some only in the middle or later years. Not many have directly used the material open to them out of motherhood as central source for their work" (Olsen, 1978, p. 41). Olsen builds a strong argument: motherhood hinders literature.

Even as the punitive difference in circumstance between men and women writers tends to limit the number of women writers and curb their respective bodies of work, so too, it contributes to yet another binding restriction to female authors. In *Silences,* Olsen explores how difficult it is for women to "harvest 'art' out of their situations" (See, 1984, p. 77). By this Olsen means that often what women (mothers?) know best—domestic settings, children's relationships, parenting struggles, aging parents—an entire gamut of valid and authentic topics and experiences—seldom appears in literature, and more significantly is seldom deemed valid when it does appear. Thus even when women writers do consider as valid content their own motherhood experiences (or any other distinctively female experience that contradicts male stereotypes of women), they are "still suspect as unnatural if they concern themselves with aspects of their experience, interests, being, beyond the traditionally defined women's sphere" (Olsen, 1978, p. 32).

It is a harsh accusation, these words from 1978, but any reader who has grown up with a diet of "classics" knows full well the usual "token" women included in the field—Austen, Cather, Dickens. And probably these same readers can recall far more readily the themes of "To Build a Fire" or *The Old Man and the Sea* than they can such works as Olive Schriener's *The Story of an African Farm* or Charlotte Perkins Gilman's "The Yellow Wallpaper" or Rebecca Harding Davis's *Life in the Iron Mills*. I remember my own incredulity when I first saw *The Norton Anthology of Literature by Women;* such a thick, rich book with female thought and words haunting back to the 1300s. Why had I not heard of these women before?

Olsen experienced a similar collision with the past when she embarked on an effort to salvage the name and work of Rebecca Harding Davis, author of the 1861 literary landmark *Life in the Iron Mills*. Olsen herself tells the story:

> I first read *Life in the Iron Mills* in one of three water-stained, coverless, bound volumes of the *Atlantic Monthly,* bought for ten cents each in an Omaha junkshop. I was fifteen. Contributions to those old *Atlantics* were published anonymously, and I was ignorant of any process whereby I might find the name of the author of this work which meant increasingly more to me over the years, saying with a few other books, 'Literature can be made out of the lives of despised people,' and 'You, too, must write.' (Olsen, 1978, p. 117)

Years later, in the reference room of the San Francisco Public Library during her lunch hour, Olsen discovered who the author was. She says simply, "It did not surprise me that the author was of my sex" (Olsen, 1978, p. 117). Eventually, through Olsen's efforts, *Life in the Iron Mills* appeared in print again—after 111 years—clearly bearing the author's name and carrying Olsen's own afterword, which later became one complete section of *Silences*.

The parallels between Davis and Olsen are startling: each sparked literary promise with her first, early efforts; each struggled to write in the midst of demanding family responsibilities; each survived society's imposed silences; each stands as a paradoxical sign of cautionary hope for other aspiring women writers. Of the reclamation that brought Olsen so nearly full-circle to her beginnings, essayists Burkom and Williams say, "What is the most significant about the 'Biographical Interpretation' is not that it reflects the experiences of one woman—Davis, Olsen—but that it renders the reality of many" (1976, p. 80).

Olsen values Davis for more than the mere fact that their lives were similar, however. For Olsen, Davis's fiction voices a nearly lost generation: "To those of us, descendants of their class, hungry for any rendering of what our vanished people were like, how they lived . . . [her book] is immeasurably valuable" (Olsen, 1978, p. 114). Like those of us who now find ourselves in Olsen's words, so she too found herself in Davis's. In addition, for Olsen, Davis exemplifies from an earlier time what Olsen exemplifies from her own: the punitive difference in circumstance.

In *Silences*, Olsen details a formidable argument, one she herself both reinforces and contradicts. Clearly, she exemplifies the punitive difference in circumstance she so eloquently documents in *Silences*. Interrupted by the demands (and delights) of mothering, Olsen the author has produced a small body of works. Yet at the same time her small body of works captures and holds a truth many women have known but few have seen in literature. Olsen's fiction and nonfiction (her enduring literature?) validate the female experience and give it credence by expressing it as literature.

On the other hand, by having written all of her slender volumes of fiction about poverty-stricken families, worried mothers, growing children, and aging parents, Olsen contradicts the argument that women still cannot harvest art from their situation. Olsen could not have brought the depth and intensity she did to those stories except for her own experiences. Thus Anna in *Yonnondio*, the unnamed mother in "I Stand Here Ironing," and Eva in "Tell Me a Riddle" all reflect both the character and person of Olsen's own mother, Ida Beber Lerner, who mothered six children in the Depression, as much as they do of Olsen herself, who mothered four in other hard times. Little wonder then that Olsen reveals the kind of demanding life she knew in the plots and settings of both *Yonnondio* and "Tell Me." Little wonder that through the characters of Anna and Eva, she explores what happens when the circumstantial demands of life numb the creative forces within. The issue is not so much *what* these women might have achieved but rather how the roles of wife and mother and how the demands of too many babies, too fast kept them from *ever knowing* what they might have achieved.

Similarly, even as the content of Olsen's writing reflects the "situations" from which she harvested her art, her publication dates, seemingly delayed and erratic, reflect the effort of that harvest. Olsen's arduous struggle to balance the demands of her family with the desire of her art epitomizes feminists' concern for women who are repeatedly "lost" in society's stereotypical expectations. In addition, Olsen's own attentiveness to the "lost" literary voice of Rebecca Harding Davis evidences her commitment to that issue. For feminists, all of Olsen's life, from her own literary silence to her determined efforts to return Davis to print, underscores the daily struggle of women to be heard—whether as creative voices in humanities or as valid, mattering voices in society.

Here is what I most want you to know about Tillie Olsen: she survived! Her eloquent, haunting words were not lost. Amidst babies and bills, her stories surfaced and sang to us. Her truth triumphed. Delayed—but never denied—Tillie Olsen survived! And each time we discover her again, we hold hope.

Discussion Questions

1. What are some "situations" from which women might harvest art? What form might that "art" take?

2. Think of a woman in your life. What is her art? How has she given voice to that art? How has it been silenced?

3. How would you characterize Olsen's voice in her fiction? In *Silences*?

4. How valid today is Olsen's 1978 contention that motherhood impedes the creation of literature?

5. In *Silences,* Olsen argued how difficult it is for women "to harvest 'art' out of their situations." Is that argument as valid now as it was in 1978? Why?

6. How do the other women discussed in this text support Olsen's argument of the punitive difference between men and women? How do they disprove that argument?

7. What women do you know personally who might find their voices in Olsen's fiction? In Olsen's biography?

References

Burkom, S., & Williams, M. (1976, February). De-riddling Tillie Olsen's writing. *San Jose Studies,* 65–83.

Duncan, E. (1982). Coming of age in the thirties: A portrait of Tillie Olsen. *Book Forum, 6,* 207–222.

Gottlieb, A. (1974, March 31). Review of *Yonnondio: From the thirties* by Tillie Olsen. *New York Times Book Review,* p. 5.

Lerner, T. (1934, April-May). The iron throat. *Partisan Review,* pp. 2–9.

Oates, J. C. (1978, July 29). Review of *Silences* by Tillie Olsen. *New Republic,* pp. 32–34.

Olsen, T. (1976). *Tell me a riddle*. New York: Dell.

Olsen, T. (1978). *Silences*. New York: Delacorte.

See, L. (1984, November 23). PW interviews: Tillie Olsen. *Publishers Weekly,* pp. 76–77.

Endnote

1. The author wishes to express appreciation to faculty at the University of Nebraska, Kearney, for fostering the vision of this manuscript.

7

Confinement in the Sexual Wasteland

The Writings of Aphra Behn and Fay Weldon

Cynthia L. Caywood, Ph.D.

Department of English
University of San Diego

Bonnie A. Hain, Ph.D.

Department of English
Southwestern Louisiana University

One Fantasy

I dream of waking up one day
looking like my neighbor Victoria
and my hair would all of a sudden
be golden and my breasts would heave
under sweaters I knitted myself
with silver threads woven into
the yarn. If I were Victoria
I would can summer peas and my voice
would pierce the air like the voices
of angels. I would speak not
from the throat but from the spot
below the chest, the place all men
dream of, rarely find, but if I
were Victoria I would go everywhere—
even the tattoo parlors on Broadway
where men with eyes like prunes
rub hands together as they touch
the hot skin of adolescents
who long to be touched. I would take
the mail boat to Padre Island
and lie there naked until the wind
surrounded me like the silent hands
of Victoria's lovers. I would take
the train to Denver, then come home
and plant a thousand tulips, sip
brandy until they all came up
at once. And in the shade of the oak,
I would be myself
and watch Victoria, dream the dream
that Victoria's dreaming and never waken.

—*Phyllis Kahaney*

$\mathcal{A}$phra Behn has long been a research interest for both of us because of her groundbreaking career as the first woman commercial playwright in England. Fay Weldon has more recently attracted our interest because of her satiric, bitter examinations of contemporary women's lives. More specifically, our interest in the idea that women still do not own their bodies comes from the personal experience of being two attractive, reasonably proportioned, intelligent women of "normal" weight who have had lifelong struggles with body image and the despair, self-abuse, and inferiority that goes along with such feelings. During the course of writing the piece, both of us became pregnant and bore children and came to understand the irony of Weldon's perspective that through pregnancy it becomes possible, on some level, to reclaim one's body for oneself, however transient that moment may be.

Men do like to have women confined. In a million million little suburban houses, women are still confined, by love, loyalty and lace curtains. It is not so terrible a fate. All fates are terrible.   (Weldon, 1982/1990d, p. 103)

$\mathcal{A}$s students of 17th and 18th century British literature and history, it is easy for us to believe that White, Western women have made great progress. The evidence surrounds us. Modern women enter Oxford and Cambridge, an opportunity denied to women 300 years ago. We marry whom we choose and divorce if we must, choices not easily available to our female predecessors. We practice law, buy property, have bank accounts, drive cars, speculate, negotiate, and deal, freedoms unimaginable to women in Charles II's court. Yet, when it comes to our bodies, we are still not free. We still suffer from cultural *confinement,* to use the ancient term, be it literal, emotional, verbal, or physical. We are still defined externally and by the culture-at-large in terms of bipolar sexual oppositions, oppositions that are both physical and psychological.[1] On the physical plane, the potential for pleasure/eroticism found in sexuality and the sexual act has been set against the potential for reproduction; playing across the two on the psychological plane are society's need for confinement of the female versus her individual desire for freedom. We might diagram these oppositions as shown on the following page.

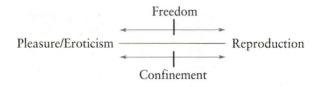

The pleasure/eroticism versus reproduction opposition manifests itself in the traditional roles into which women are cast. Women are either seducers or reproducers, fallen women or angels of the house. The psychological oppositions define the playing field where the physical oppositions may be run out.

The degree to which economies of confinement have and have not changed through history is dramatically illustrated when the work of Aphra Behn (1640–1689), the first British professional woman writer, is set against that of contemporary feminist British author Fay Weldon. Both writers focus on the issue of women's fleshly confinement: recognizing, naming, deconstructing, and reconstructing the terms of confinement. Both challenge their respective culture's appropriation of women's bodies, disrupting the prevailing sexual economy of their respective times. Yet despite this congruence, the two writers come to radically different conclusions. This disparity, which we will discuss in depth, points to a troubling ambiguity about the "gains" made in Weldon's and our postmodern, postindustrial world, which emerges as a sexual wasteland as hostile to women's autonomy as the 17th century Behn's more traditionally constricting patriarchy.

In this essay, then, we will investigate what each writer demonstrates about the terms governing female sexuality, i.e., reproduction, eroticism, confinement, and freedom. In so doing, we will suggest an uncomfortable developmental relationship: Behn envisions a utopian world that defies the patriarchy of her period by freeing women from the burden and threat of pregnancy. Weldon deconstructs that vision, casting doubt upon any notions of women's progress. Instead, she sets about rewriting the female sense of self by returning to the place from which Behn departed.

To set up the comparison, we need to examine the terms of confinement in each writer's historical context. In Behn's period, only a few of the four defining terms were allowed into play. Antonia Fraser, in *The Weaker Vessel*, summarizes the relative lack of playing space women of the 17th century possessed:

Under the common law of England at the accession of King James I, no female had any rights at all (if some were allowed by custom). As an unmarried woman her rights were swallowed up in her father's, and she was his to dispose of in marriage at will. Once she was married her property became absolutely that of her husband.[2] (1984/1985, p. 5)

Fraser documents extensively the degree to which women were forced into unwanted marriages and how married women were bound by numerous pregnancies, few rights, and little claim to their children when a marriage was troubled enough to be ended. When we frame this history through our earlier diagram, we see that, because women's flesh had to be controlled for reproductive purposes, the terms *reproduction* and *confinement* were present, whereas *pleasure/eroticism* and *freedom* were absent. Female value in this system was defined largely in ways that supported the major terms of reproduction and confinement. Virginity and youth were primary determiners of female worth, and passivity and innocence were the most valued traits because all of these qualities better serviced reproduction and confinement.

In contemporary White Western culture, this traditional patriarchal system has been challenged by the advent of the pill, which has freed women from their biological destiny. By and large, young White Western women are no longer measured primarily by reproductive standards. Rather, a new patriarchal system exists that measures women in terms of their sexual/erotic value rather than their reproductive one. Their bodies are still the primary determiners of their worth, but freedom is still absent and confinement is still present. In the new patriarchy, even when women are free to pursue erotic pleasure, they must be confined reproductively and through expending much of their energy on remaining sexually attractive. In short, women are promised sexual pleasure, idealization, and if they desire them, children in exchange for a different kind of confinement: the body itself, not just the reproductive organs.

Against this historical context, our comparison can shift to the first of the primary terms, *reproduction*. It is not surprising that in Behn's new economy of female flesh, she chooses to negate reproduction because it is the term at once most valued by the patriarchy, most antithetical to financial independence, and most threatening to female sexual pleasure. In her fiction and dramas, Behn negates the value of reproduction by either demonstrating the hardship pregnancy must necessitate for the woman who desires to be free or by depicting women who have learned to balance sexual desire against reproductive consequences. For example, in "The Adventures of the Black Lady" (1915/1967e), Bellamora, having been seduced, runs off to London to bear her illegitimate child. There, society conspires to force her into marrying her lover, and she finally succumbs to its pressure, despite her loathing for him. The moral of Behn's story seems to be that to become pregnant is to surrender one's autonomy. By way of contrast, Hellena, the heroine of Behn's comedy "The Rover, Part I" (1915/1967h), demonstrates greater wisdom about the ways of the world. Balancing desire and practicality, she insists that her rakish lover must marry her before they have sex: "And if you do not lose, what shall I get? A Cradle full of Noise and Mischief, with a Pack of Repentance at my Back?" (p. 101). In Behn's plays and novellas, sexually free characters either manipulate the system, entertaining their lovers within the protective circle of marriage, or are courtesans and are thus already stigmatized.

In her love poetry, Behn negates the reproductive term more dramatically. She follows the pastoral convention of transcending the threat of pregnancy altogether; her lovers copulate freely and guiltlessly, and the only hazards are unreciprocated love or abandonment. She creates, in other words, a utopian vision of women, simultaneously confined and free, who can indulge their libido without reproductive consequences. Suppressing or negating the term *reproduction* allows Behn, then, to go on to restructure the other terms in interesting and, for her time, liberating ways, as we shall see.

Informed by the freedoms afforded by modern birth control devices, Fay Weldon deals very differently with the issue of reproduction. She suggests that the cornerstone of Behn's system, negating reproduction, is not without serious consequences. The means by which reproduction is negated may indeed mean freedom from pregnancy but often at enormous cost. Taking birth control pills disrupts and tames women's natural physical and psychological cycles. Liffey, in *Puffball,* goes off the pill and reverts to a more natural state. Her "pituitary gland was once more its own master and stimulated the production of oestrogen and progesterone, as it saw fit" (Weldon, 1980/1990b, p. 28). More destructive is abortion. Helen, in *The Hearts and Lives of Men,* comes close to aborting her first pregnancy, prompting Weldon's narrator to speak of abortion's toll: "Abortion is sometimes necessary, sometimes not, always sad. It is to the woman as war is to the man—a living sacrifice in a cause justified or not justified, as the observer may decide" (Weldon, 1987/1989c, p. 66). However, if a woman chooses to avoid pregnancy, she will be forever haunted by those lives that did not happen. In *Leader of the Band,* Starlady Sandra, proud of her lithe but barren body, also says: "Sometimes I am pursued by the pattering of little feet, and know they are the ghosts of my dead children" (1988/1990a, p. 50). And, of course, a woman who remains childless risks having no value, no visibility in the world, particularly as she grows older. In *The*

Rules of Life, the narrator writes of Gabriella Sumpter, the dead woman whose voice he is transcribing, "Poor Gabriella, I thought. The only one in the world to take herself seriously—but that, no doubt, is the fate of women who do not marry and do not have children, for whatever reason" (1987/1988, p. 80).

Despite her doubts about the freedom offered by barrenness, Weldon does not offer easy alternatives. If denying reproduction means containing a natural function, motherhood means containing oneself. Starlady Sandra mocks the commonly held sentiment that women find their true fulfillment in motherhood: "Nature sets traps to lure us into motherhood, that I'd agree; but once the trap is sprung she offers precious few rewards" (Weldon, 1988/1990a, p. 52). The children that inhabit Weldon's novels can be as unattractive and complex as they can be in the world of the living. Ruth, in *Lives and Loves of a She-Devil,* labels her children a "pigeon pair," given to "complaints," and "voicing vindictiveness" (Weldon, 1983/1989d, p. 12). In addition, the comfort that motherhood supposedly affords is tenuous, often leaving one vulnerable to Fate. The narrator of *Female Friends* warns: "Give birth and you give others the power to destroy you, to multiply your hurts a thousand times, to make you suffer with them" (Weldon, 1975, p. 204). And the identity and place in culture motherhood affords one can be equally illusory. Esther, in *The Fat Woman's Joke,* declares: "I had my child. . . . Now the child is grown up and . . . the drive is finished in me. I am dried up. I am useless. I am a burden" (1967/1986, p. 185). For Weldon, then, negating reproduction is not a simple, clean choice. In Weldon's world and in our world, reproduction is a frighteningly ambiguous term in and of itself that defines women in a way from which there is no escape.

Another point of contrast between the two writers that also under-scores the nature of modern women's confinement is their consideration of the value of erotic pleasure for women. In Behn's poetry, because repro-duction is absent, sexuality is defined solely in terms of the erotic pleasure that it affords. Behn's eroticism is centered in the self, with the female a willing, equal participant—a revolutionary choice, given her historical context. Her understanding of female sexual pleasure is surprisingly mod-ern. It is both physical and psychological, residing, specifically, in the geni-talia and in the imagination.

One of Behn's frankest poems, "The Disappointment," takes up directly the precise physical character of female erotic pleasure. Initially hesitant to give in to her desire, the poem's Cloris at last succumbs to Lysander's skillful caresses. The narrator, describing graphically but gracefully their progress, refers directly to the vulva in mythic and universal terms.

[Lysander's] daring Hand that Altar seiz'd
Where Gods of Love do sacrifice:
That Awful Throne, that Paradice
Where Rage is calm'd and Anger pleas'd;
That Fountain where Delight still flows,
And gives the Universal World Repose. (Behn, 1915/1967f, p. 179)

Behn's choice of words here is telling. The vulva is, variously, an Altar, upon which Gods sacrifice, an Awful Throne, a Fountain from which delight flows. Although this language may seem objectifying, Behn nullifies such a reading by referring to the penis in relational terms. She describes it as "Nature's Support" (Behn, 1915/1967f, p. 180), and when Lysander loses his erection, it is named an "Insensible" that falls "weeping" (p. 181). In these and other examples, Behn reverses the traditional hierarchy and makes the vulva the ascendant term, while the penis is the "other." Thus, the vulva is first a center of female pleasure and second an object of male desire (because it will allow the male pleasure).

Behn also focuses on the psychological side of female sexual pleasure when she eroticizes male voices and language. For example, in "A Ballad on Mr. J.H. to Amoret, asking why I was so sad," the abandoned narrator reminisces: "His Wit was such it cou'd controul / The Resolutions of a Soul" (1915/1967a, p. 155). Interesting also are those moments in Behn's poetry when the woman speaker falls into desire through written words alone. In "On a Copy of Verses made in a Dream," a male lover sends a woman his poetry, the reading of which causes sexual arousal (Behn, 1915/1967b). Most playful, perhaps, is Behn's wholehearted acknowledgment of male beauty; she often gives as elaborate a description of male beauty as male writers do of female beauty, pointedly using the same language and lingering over the same features as they would. In "Our Cabal," Behn lusciously details the charms of the handsome Philocles, justifying the desire so many women feel for him (Behn, 1915/1967d). In these ways, Behn demonstrates that eroticism should be genderless and self-affirming.

In opening up the playing field of sexual "other" and allowing females to objectify, Behn succeeds in legitimizing the female libido. This legitimacy is an open challenge to the traditional patriarchy that surrounded her, which controlled female desire by denying or denigrating it. Her society's position is dramatized in the poem discussed earlier, "The Disappointment," when Cloris of that poem matches Lysander in desire, a response that makes him impotent (Behn, 1915/1967f). By contrast, in "On a Juniper Tree," Behn rewrites this story by having the initially reluctant Cloris match her lover's desires and join him in marathon lovemaking

(Behn, 1915/1967c). In other words, Behn suggests that denying women their libido compromises male pleasure and emasculates them, whereas accepting it enriches and invigorates men. To invoke her own words, "the gain is Universal" (1915/1967f, p. 181).

Yet despite the attractiveness, even the rightness of Behn's vision, it seems naive, even idyllic, when compared with our and Weldon's more jaded perspective. Weldon is considerably more realistic about the liberating possibilities of women and society embracing their erotic potential. First of all, reflecting the modern perspective, Weldon does not need to privilege erotic pleasure at all. She simply accords erotic fulfillment to women as a natural right. So common is erotic fulfillment that it often serves as the origin rather than the end of Weldon's stories. *Leader of the Band,* for example, opens with Starlady Sandra running off to France with the provocative saxophone player Mad Jack, "zonked out of [her] wits by sex" (Weldon, 1988/1990a, p. 1). Rather than the self-liberating end that Behn envisions, Weldon seems to suggest that erotic power and pleasure, at least as it is conventionally discovered—through connection to a man—is a place where women get stuck. Starlady Sandra's passion for Jack leaves her mired in the egocentricity of her own desire. If she is to have any hope of living humanely, she must extract herself from it. Praxis, in the novel of the same name, finds as she ages greater and greater erotic pleasure and less and less of herself. It is only when she becomes older and less erotically valuable, when she goes "down among the women," as Weldon sardonically names it, that she begins to claim an identity and purpose (Weldon, 1978).

In Weldon's world, the danger of erotic pleasure is twofold. First, it may lie in the completeness that sexual connection seems to offer, a feeling that is ultimately deceptive. The narrator of *The Heart of the Country* (1987/1990c) comments: "Sex with a man gives you such a stunning sense of safety . . . as long as it lasts. It's an illusion, isn't it? It stops: it presents you with perfection and then snatches it away" (p. 130). The second danger of erotic pleasure may lie in the separation erotic power affords beautiful women. Grace, in *Female Friends* (1975), is sexually irresistible and monumentally selfish; she delights in tormenting her lover and her children with her emotional unavailability. As such women age, their aloofness leads to abandonment and death. Moreover, female overvaluation of the self as a sexual being leads to erotic enslavement. Women who allow themselves to be destroyed by the desiring male gaze figure largely in Weldon's fiction. In *Little Sisters,* Weldon tells the bizarre story of two beautiful women whose bonds of sisterhood are forged through the sexual abuse they experience at the hands of the men who desire them. The elder, crippled, embittered Gemma tells her figurative "little sister," the sexy Elsa,

"To be wanton . . . with your life, your sexuality, your future—is a dangerous matter. You . . . have made yourself a hundred times more stupid than you need be. Women . . . have to, if they are determined that men shall be their masters" (1977/1985, *Words of Advice,* p. 19). Thus, although Weldon would agree with Behn that erotic pleasure is a gift, to center oneself in desire leads not to Behn's Golden Age but to a gilded cage where wholeness and self-knowledge cannot exist.

Again, as before, Weldon refuses to offer easy alternatives. If eroticism is confining, so too is asexuality. Housewifery, a retreat from "the wide erotic world" (Weldon, 1988/1990a, p. 55), is for Weldon one of the most appalling of traps. "What we have here, ladies and gentlemen," says the sneering narrator in *Little Sisters,* "is not a woman, but a housewife" (1977/1985, *Words of Advice,* p. 129). "Who dreams of kitchens," asks Gemma in the same novel, "except those who have given up dreams of love?" (p. 90). Nor is there any escape to be found in falling outside the system of erotic valuation. Women who are sexually unattractive, and thus denied erotic pleasure, are similarly monstrous as those who understand themselves only as sexual beings. In *The Lives and Loves of a She-Devil* (1983/1989d), Ruth, an ungainly, unloved woman, sets off on a hideous *bildungsroman* of revenge against her husband, his mistress, and herself. Determined to dethrone Mary Fisher, the mistress, Ruth liberates herself from duty and earns the capital for her vengeance by descending more and more deeply into self-degradation. Her journey culminates in a plastic surgery clinic, where she is systematically and painfully disassembled and reconstructed into a clone of Mary Fisher.

Thus, Weldon's examination of the term *eroticism* is also paradoxical and confusing when compared with Behn's open-hearted and celebratory enthusiasm. Informed, perhaps, by the post-60s experience of *Playgirl,* Chippendale's, and other signposts of women's greater erotic freedom, Weldon has considerable doubts that such "freedom" really liberates women from objectification and self-hatred.

A final point of comparison between the two writers is found in the end to which their explorations of the terms led them. Having negated reproduction and reconstructed eroticism, Behn takes on the psychological terms that define female sexuality and renegotiates them in such a way that they are no longer in opposition to each other but rather, exist harmoniously. Not surprisingly, given her erotic aesthetic, Behn releases "freedom" from its prior bonds, in which freedom means a dangerous disregard for the strict rules of moral and sexual conduct. Rather, she redefines freedom to mean women's freedom to transcend, to cut through, those sexual constraints and to enjoy giving and receiving erotic pleasure.

Ironically, Behn's freedom can thrive only in confinement. It may be the confinement of a happy marriage, or more interestingly, it takes the form of a mutually agreed upon constancy, which legitimizes all forms of sexual intimacy. Immorality is to be found only in broken promises and vows. In *The Golden Age* (1915/1967g), a poem that describes Behn's utopian vision of life before the patriarchal structures we label "civilization" were in place (kings, religion, honor, etc.), she describes the form love took as one in which no inhibitions existed and constancy was natural:

> The Lovers thus, uncontroul'd did meet,
> Thus all their Joyes and Vows of Love repeat:
> Joyes which were everlasting, ever new
> And every Vow inviolably true:
> Nor kept in fear of Gods, no fond Religious cause,
> Nor in obedience to the duller Laws.

In short, what creates war between men and women is infidelity. What creates pleasure, and the freedom to enjoy it, is constancy, women's only requirement for sexual exchange.

In contrast to the clarity and optimism of Behn's reconstruction of the rules governing women's eroticism, the only redemption for women in Weldon's postmodern world is found in seeking and understanding the inevitability of confinement and learning simply how "to be." Ironically, Weldon's path toward that knowledge takes women through the very place that Behn has abandoned, the womb. And, given the dispiriting ambiguity of her larger examinations of female sexuality, this theme has an astonishing clarity. For Weldon, the heart of femaleness seems to lie in the female capacity for giving life and the organs that make this possible. Weldon does not say that all women should exercise that potential. Rather, she is interested in the *capacity* for giving life, what it is, what it means, and how it shapes and controls lives.

In almost everything that Weldon writes, the central decision of her characters' lives is whether or not to have children; they define themselves through this wonderful and terrible choice. What is most important is that the choice be made in full awareness of what it means to make it: that one is negotiating with the primary biological reason for possessing life. Each time one makes love is a monumental act because in it resides the very purpose of our being. Consequently the organs for giving life, especially those organs overlooked in the new patriarchy's obsession with externals, are at the heart of female identity, so much so that to lose them may mean to lose oneself. In "And Then Turn Out the Light," 47-year-old Tandy Watson undergoes an involuntary hysterectomy. When the surgeon argues that the organs had served their purpose, she laments, "Those organs are *me*. I am nothing now. You have taken it upon yourself to turn out the light of my life" (Weldon, 1985/1989a, p. 117).

Given the power that she accords the reproductive organs, it is not surprising that Weldon accords to pregnancy (as opposed to the term *reproduction*) a singular status. She mythologizes it into a process by which women move from innocence to experience. For Starlady Sandra, it represents her path to personal redemption and self-reclamation. Having spent a lifetime indulging her own desire and ridding herself of unwanted fetuses, she finds herself at age 42 pregnant by her irresponsible lover. She chooses the child over a life with him, even though she is fully aware that there may be no tangible point in doing so. That is, it is not important that she reproduce herself or him. What is important is the choice, and the awareness of herself as conduit between the past and the future: "I am the fulcrum where the past and the future balance, in which I am like anyone else. But I am also the point where the mad, the bad and the infamous meet; the possessed and obsessed. I had better get it right—this infinitesimal spark of moral decision which is apparently required of me" (Weldon, 1988/1990a, p. 155).

Similarly, in *Puffball,* Weldon documents Liffey's violent journey toward physical and spiritual maturity through the agency of a pregnancy. After she has borne the child, she returns to her cottage and the formerly vain, self-centered yuppie gazes at herself in the mirror. "She thought she seemed a very average person: no longer pretty, or elfin or silly, or anything particularly definite, anymore. She was much like anyone else" (1980/1990b, p. 271). In this sense of her ordinariness lies Liffey's redemption, for in Weldon's cosmology, separateness or the primacy of the I is the source of most human sorrow. It is also for this reason that pregnancy, the ultimate connectedness of one human being to another, becomes an event and choice of mythic significance in Weldon's world. In that connectedness lies a kind of ultimate confinement. Historically, as in Behn's period, women were literally confined during pregnancy. More aptly for modern women, they are confined by it, in that their erotic potential for creating life is confined in the act of creating it. They contain life; they are containers for life; they are confinement itself. In the being of confinement, Weldon argues, women find the only freedom there is, that of simply being.

In negating reproduction and redefining the other terms that contain female sexuality, Aphra Behn creates a utopian vision of possibility for women, both confined and freed, who can indulge their libido without reproductive consequences. Marriage is not necessary because reproduction is not the aim or result of sexual intimacy, and constancy is founded upon the bedrock of one's word. By making this new Golden Age her subject, she is able to transcend the sexual constraints that would contain her self-identification as writer. In other words, by writing her gender's way out of those terms of definition, she writes her own way out and makes a space for herself in the patriarchal economy that would otherwise leave her in the cold.

Yet, despite Behn's daring and success, her vision is an innocent one. Her solution is bound by the period in which she wrote. We celebrate her frank eroticism; we agree with her legitimizing the female libido; we honor her call for constancy. But we know from experience that freedom from reproduction does not necessarily mean freedom from containment. Divorced from their connection to the now-absent womb and ovaries, the breasts, hips, and external genitalia of modern women become the object of fetishist, pornographic worship. Women are no longer baby machines, they are sex machines.

Like Behn, Weldon recognizes the prevailing terms that define and contain women. Like Behn, she takes on those terms, but she goes further than Behn. As a modern woman who has lived through the sexual and women's revolutions, a journey she recounts again and again in her novels, Weldon has knowledge denied to Behn, and she deconstructs her solution. She knows that as long as women's sexuality is conceived of in dichotomous terms, wholeness and ownership are impossible. Therefore, she realizes that she must set the terms into a dizzying, ambiguous dance of irresolution. All movements lead to confinement, yet she mythologizes confinement in the transcendency of pregnancy. There women find the freedom of "being," the only freedom there is, and in that state, where there is no subject or object, no self or other, no absent or present, women can escape from the containment posed by polarities into eroticized feminine wholeness.

Discussion Questions

1. What challenges do you think the first woman writing for the 17th century stage, a largely male institution, would have faced?

2. What obstacles do women in general face when they want to write honestly and openly about eroticism and sexual expression?

3. In what ways do you think your own sense of beauty in general and your attractiveness in particular is culturally defined and controlled?

4. Into what roles do you think women are cast, either by themselves or by the culture? How does identification with one role limit wholeness or total integration of the self?

5. Does Weldon's perspective, that through an understanding of women's reproductive capacity some kind of autonomous self-definition can be reached, seem reductive or old-fashioned?

6. What would a modern woman say to Aphra Behn about her hopes for women as they are described in this reading?

References

Behn, A. (1967a). A ballad *on Mr.* J.H. *to* Amoret. In M. Summers (Ed.), *The works of Aphra Behn* (vol. VI) (pp. 153–155). New York: Phaeton Press. (Original work published 1915)

Behn, A. (1967b). On a copy of verses made in a dream. In M. Summers (Ed.), *The works of Aphra Behn* (vol. VI) (pp. 174–175). New York: Phaeton Press. (Original work published 1915)

Behn, A. (1967c). On a juniper tree. In M. Summers (Ed.), *The works of Aphra Behn* (vol. VI) (pp. 148–151). New York: Phaeton Press. (Original work published 1915)

Behn, A. (1967d). Our cabal. In M. Summers (Ed.), *The works of Aphra Behn* (vol. VI) (pp. 156–162). New York: Phaeton Press. (Original work published 1915)

Behn, A. (1967e). The adventures of the black lady. In M. Summers (Ed.), *The works of Aphra Behn* (vol. V) (pp. 1–11). New York: Phaeton Press. (Original work published 1915)

Behn, A. (1967f). The disappointment. In M. Summers (Ed.), *The works of Aphra Behn* (vol. VI) (pp. 178–182). New York: Phaeton Press. (Original work published 1915)

Behn, A. (1967g). The golden age. In M. Summers (Ed.), *The works of Aphra Behn* (vol. VI) (pp. 138–144). New York: Phaeton Press. (Original work published 1915)

Behn, A. (1967h). The rover, Part I; or The banished cavaliers. In M. Summers (Ed.), *The works of Aphra Behn* (vol. I) (pp. 1–107). New York: Phaeton Press. (Original work published 1915)

Fraser, A. (1985). *The weaker vessel*. New York: Vintage Books. (Original work published 1984)

Weldon, F. (1975). *Female friends*. London: Heinemann.

Weldon, F. (1978). *Praxis*. New York: Summit Books.

Weldon, F. (1985). *Words of advice*. New York: Random House. (Original work published as *Little sisters,* 1977, New York: Random House)

Weldon, F. (1986). *The fat woman's joke*. Chicago: Academy Chicago Publishers. (Original work published 1967)

Weldon, F. (1988). *The rules of life*. New York: Harper & Row. (Original work published 1987)

Weldon, F. (1989a). And then turn out the light. In F. Weldon, *Polaris and other stories*. New York: Penguin. (Original work published 1985)

Weldon, F. (1989b). *Polaris and other stories*. New York: Penguin. (Original work published 1985)

Weldon, F. (1989c). *The hearts and lives of men*. New York: Dell. (Original work published 1987)

Weldon, F. (1989d). *The lives and loves of a she-devil*. New York: Random House. (Original work published 1983)

Weldon, F. (1990a). *Leader of the band*. New York: Penguin. (Original work published 1988)

Weldon, F. (1990b). *Puffball*. New York: Penguin. (Original work published 1980)

Weldon, F. (1990c). *The heart of the country*. New York: Penguin. (Original work published 1987)

Weldon, F. (1990d). *The president's child*. London: Hodder and Stoughton. (Original work published 1982)

Weldon, F. (1991). *Down among women*. Chicago: Academy Chicago Publishers. (Original work published 1971)

Endnotes

1. We recognize that Western culture has imposed on the male form as well, but in this essay we limit our focus to the cultural containment of the female body.

2. Although this quote refers to the early part of the 17th century, Fraser (1985) argues that little had shifted legally for women by the end of the century.

8

In My Shoes for Life

A Disabled Woman's Journey

Thuy-Phuong Do, M.A.

*School of Communication
San Diego State University*

Thuy and her mother

*S*ilenced; for so many years of my childhood, I felt angry and misunderstood. Isolated; I was different from the others, they did not know enough to accommodate me. I played by their rules. Crippled; I was mentally and not just physically. No one could give me answers because those who surrounded me did not have my experience nor did they understand. Now, I am a woman in my early twenties. I have developed confidence and undying will only through years of experience and intense ponderance, day in and day out. Ironically though, what I find is that I have worked hard to build myself into an adaptive person only to find that the world has not done enough to adapt to my situation. I am still isolated, silenced, and crippled as many disabled women are. There is always someone out there in the world who will remind us exactly how disabled and helpless we are. I cannot rest until my silent rage is calmed by bringing understanding to others that goes beyond the facts. By understanding what it is like to walk in my shoes for life, I feel that the able bodied would never think or say the harmful things they often do.

Three Days

It started when I was 2 years of age. I was living in Vietnam. I do not remember much about my country. I was too young when I left to have memories. In fact, I rely heavily on the stories my parents told me about when I was growing up and have learned to appreciate those times. One story my mother would frequently tell me was about the visits to my grandmother's house. She had a large backyard with a pond and ducks. Whenever I would go over there, sure enough, I would be near the pond, chasing the ducks. "Trying to grab their tails," as my mother always said. She used this story to contrast the story that would follow about the major turning point in my life.

That day, my mother had taken me to the hospital to receive a vaccination against polio. It was 1974. The medical care was very poor in the country at the time because of the war. Soon after I received my first polio vaccine, my mother was called back to the hospital so that I could receive my second polio shot. My mother recalls arguing with the nurse, telling her that it was too soon for a second immunization, but the overly aggressive nurse insisted it was time.

The day after, I woke and was not able to move from the neck down. I was paralyzed. I had contracted polio from the vaccine. I remember my mother describing me as limp. My parents did not know what was wrong. They thought I would die as many children did at the time. Days after, my grandmother, who was a nurse, came to see me. She touched my burning forehead and told my parents that I had contracted polio. I was rushed to the hospital. I was put on an ice bed to quickly bring down my near-lethal temperature. My mother recalls seeing my body turn purple from the cold ice and hearing my screams, "Ma con muon di ve!" (I want to go home). That image stuck out from the experience for her. Nothing else mattered besides the pain she felt to see her child so young, so scared.

I spent the next 2 weeks at a well-known French hospital in Saigon. The doctors there gave up and said they could not help me. My mother, however, would not give up. She contacted a local acupuncturist who volunteered his services to help those in need. My mother took me there and in a matter of weeks, I began to wiggle my toes. Eventually, I began to regain most of my movement, except in several places on my legs. I am thankful for what the acupuncturist did.

The irony came as I learned, at the age of 7, that if I had been taken to the acupuncturist just *three* days earlier, I would have been able to walk again. Three days; I cried. I could not help the disgust and anger I felt knowing that piece of information. Three days; I would have rather not known. But I had told my parents I didn't want to be kept in the dark about what had happened to me. Three days; how could life be so cruel to me? I was so young. Three days; I felt God was punishing me for something a relative of mine did.

It took me a long time to tell people about my story without getting teary-eyed. I am now 23 years old, and I have been physically disabled for 21 years. I have (post) polio, a disease that attacks the nerves throughout the body. I use crutches to help me walk. Throughout the times of extreme pain and joy growing up, I have discovered many meanings about life through my own unique perspective. I want to share these understandings with you.

I'm Not a Stereotype

There is a large body of literature that deals with being a woman and disabled. Two major concepts that are discussed in most of the literature are beauty standards and self-concept. Women become double minorities because of their sex and their disability (Deegan & Brooks, 1985; Lonsdale, 1990; Vash, 1981). This leads to a low self-concept. According to Lonsdale, disabled women become double minorities because of the culturally accepted ideal image of a woman. This unobtainable standard of beauty (i.e., unrealistic body proportions such as a small waist and big breasts) is used to judge other qualities of all women, such as their intelligence, credibility, and character. In fact, many women suffer both psychologically, through low self-esteem, and physically, through diseases such as bulimia, because of these unattainable beauty standards (Deegan & Brooks, 1985; Lonsdale, 1990; Vash, 1981). For disabled women, the pressure to be attractive is even more intense because they have very visible abnormalities that do not fit the standard of beauty.

To make the situation worse, stereotypes—such as that the disabled aren't entitled to an attractive partner or that they are asexual—weigh heavy on the self-concepts of disabled women. For example, Lonsdale (1990) describes women who could increase their mobility by walking on crutches or canes but instead opt to use a wheelchair to avoid limping ungracefully. Lonsdale states that a woman's self-image suffers the further she perceives herself to be from the standard of beauty. Also, disabled women are more likely than able-bodied women not to marry and also not to divorce (Deegan & Brooks, 1985). Since the disabled woman internalizes rejection more than disabled men or able-bodied women, her self-concept becomes lower. It is unfortunate that a woman who is disabled must face these stereotypes when her value as a mate is by no means relative to her physical attributes.

I'm a Story: Walking in My Shoes, My Story

Kindergarten. I was beginning to use my crutches and I was clumsy as kids often are at that age. It was difficult adjusting, I fell every single day. But the falls aren't what I remember the most.

The most vivid memory I have is of my teacher, Mrs. Austin. She did something for me that was a key event in shaping my attitude of myself and my disability. It happened during break time, when we would get a snack of graham crackers and a carton of milk. We had to form a line, pick up a carton of milk from a bucket, and grab two graham crackers. I always tried to be first in line because every time I was last, the milk would be at the bottom of the bucket and I would have to ask one of the students to bend down and grab it for me. One day, the teacher observed this and told me that I could get the milk myself. She told me to lean on one of my crutches and put the other one against the wall, freeing one hand so I could grab the milk. I hated her for this. I cried. I hated the fact that she made me do it myself in front of all the other kids. But I thank her for it now. That was the first day I learned to get an attitude about my difference. She showed me that I may have been different, but my difference did not limit me, only *I* limited me. God bless her.

A typical day in 1996. My eyes opened and I looked at the clock. Eight-fifty-four. Time for me to get up. I walked to the bathroom, grabbing the walls along the way. I brushed my teeth and washed my face. I then went into my room to get dressed. I put on the shirt, my leg braces, and then the jeans. I always put on leg braces when I am about to go out into the public. They give me support, especially when I need to walk long distances, which I always find myself doing while I'm at school.

Mental note: where am I headed? Will there be a lot of stairs? Is there an elevator? Are these shoes comfortable enough for the environment I am going into? If it's raining, is the concrete the slippery kind? Are there waxed floors in the building that are slippery when wet? Where is the disabled parking? Are the building's doors hard to open? These are questions that I always ask myself before I go into any setting.

Today, I am headed to the computer lab to do an assignment for one of my graduate classes. There are no stairs, and the elevator is usually working. I do not need to do a lot of walking, so any shoes will be fine. It's cloudy, but no rain is anticipated, so the concrete and floors do not matter. The disabled parking is very close. The doors are easy to open.

I grab my backpack and my crutches and I'm off! I get into my car and start the engine. I push in the hand control for the brake and gas, and grab onto the "suicide ball" that I steer with. I move my left hand down and in to control the gas and brake, and I move my right hand in a circular motion to steer.

I get to campus and park in the disabled parking next to the building. I walk in and take the elevator down to the basement. It's a little stuffy down there. There is a muddle of noise coming from the open doors of the professors' offices. I sign in at the front desk where the two lab helpers are seated. Neither of them even acknowledges me. No eye contact. They just sit and stare at the monitor in front of them.

I get lucky when I walk into the lab and find a computer in the aisle of the last of four rows of tables. Walking between rows gets difficult when you have to move four feet instead of two. Try it with a backpack that keeps getting caught on computer cables or chairs. I could break a sweat just trying not to peg anyone sitting at a terminal. As I sit, a woman working one computer over from me stares at my leg braces and gradually becomes aware that I notice her stare. She then looks me in the eye and smiles.

There is the constant noise of keyboards and computer beeps that one learns to block out in the lab. Frustration hits; I don't know how to do the assignment. I get up and go to the front desk and ask one of the helpers dressed in maroon jackets for help. No one was helping, no one was courteous. I get more frustrated and decide I'm on my own. Eventually, I figure it out. I leave the building, get in my car, and drive home. I feel good for the accomplishment because nothing is too simple to take for granted.

Elementary school, it's time for recess. The kids' playground was a sandy dirt field. The field was very large back then, like a desert, because the world of an elementary school student was so small then. I hated recess. I can hear the kids screaming and laughing. It sounds like they are having so much fun. Every day, for half an hour, while the other kids played tether ball and kick ball on the dirt field, I stayed upstairs, sitting on a bench, alone. I was an outsider to my classmates. I was separated by what seemed like a hundred stairs. Even if I got downstairs in 15 minutes, recess would be half over and I would never get asked to play on a kick ball team or to play tether ball. I was a voyeur, longing for a chance to fit in with the crowd. One day, another girl in my class sprained her ankle and could no longer play with the other kids at recess. So she sat on the outdoor cafeteria benches and talked to me. I was so happy. I actually had a friend. I finally knew someone was aware of my existence during recess besides my teachers. It's easy to forget that you exist when others do not interact with you or when they treat you like a disease. It's like when someone you really like ignores you when you are in the same room as they are. It really hurts.

Elementary school was my time of sadness. I had a lot of time to think of my difference. I was physically and mentally separated from the other kids. I felt so much like a hindrance that I would get stressed out about the smallest detail. I remember how I used to be afraid that I would hold up the class when we walked in a line to an assembly so I would ask to leave early so that I wouldn't hold that class up. I remember my teacher, Mrs. Ross, saying to me, "We will wait for you. You are part of the class too." I remember getting upset once again, thinking that the teacher did not understand, but she did. She let me know I was as beautiful if not more beautiful than the rest. I think she could see the mental anguish I was facing at such a young age. The other kids could never understand me. Mrs. Ross's concern again showed me that I needed to develop an attitude about my disability.

The music is loud, and the room is packed full of people like sardines. The dance club is casual and located near the beach, which means that the crowd is of college age. There is ego in this room. A shy person would not do well in this aggressive environment. I walk in and manage to find a seat away from the dance floor. I enjoy going to clubs every once in a while to dance and hang out with my friends. I like watching the characters in the club, too. I spot a guy who looks like he's in the military looking at me. He sees my crutches so he's afraid to ask for a dance. A song comes on that I like, and I ask one of my friends to dance. The minute I sit down, the military guy comes up to me, "Wanna dance?" I look hesitant. He quickly replies, "Come on, I saw you out there, so don't use your crutches as an excuse."

This is typical. Someone will spot me and be hesitant until they see me out on the dance floor. In fact, I've had many able-bodied people approach me and compliment me for having "soul" or "great motivation." If they're surprised I'm out on the floor dancing, I think they'd have cardiac arrest if they saw me playing tennis or giving a speech! Is it really complimentary to have someone say that you have a lot of soul or motivation for being able to dance? I could understand if I was sky diving. I think I'm constantly underestimated. I'm not surprised, though; most able-bodied people do not even think they can utter the words *walk* or *dance* without upsetting me.

The doctor explained the operation, step by step. Nothing could go wrong. I was 12 years old at the time. How could I have any less than 100 percent confidence in my doctor? After all, he knew everything. He had an authoritative and definite tone: "We'll be performing a triple orthodesis. I've done this procedure many times before and it's been very successful."

"Okay," I replied in a soft and passive tone.

The doctor went on explaining in his most simplified manner: "We'll go in and cut a triangular piece of bone out of the ankle. This way, the foot will not be turned inward as it is right now. We'll also take a vein and wrap it around the big toe to pull the foot up. Any questions?"

I tried to think my hardest of any questions. "No, not right now."

The doctor felt an uncertainty in my voice. "How do you feel about surgery?"

"If it'll help me, then it's okay," I answered.

The doctor was right, though; I was depressed. "Haven't I been through enough?" I thought. I'd been in and out of hospitals very early in my life. I thought it had stopped. At this point, it felt like it never would. "God help me, I don't want to lie in the hospital alone and in pain. I feel helpless. Why am I so helpless?"

I counted the days until the surgery. I came to the hospital in the morning. My mother was with me. The rest of the family was at school or work. I was put in a uniformly white and sterile hospital room to await my doctor's pre-examination. You can always tell when you're in a hospital; the smell of alcohol, no matter where you walk, is inescapable. I was given two hospital gowns, one to cover my front side and one to cover my backside that the first did not cover. After a few minutes, my doctor came into my room. My feet and hands had started sweating. I could feel my heart beat through my neck at the jugular. He looked at my foot and asked me if I had eaten anything in the last 24 hours. I said no.

I was then wheeled to the entrance of the operating room. My mother followed. My anesthesiologist met me at the entrance. He was wonderful. He was about 5 feet 4 inches and weighed approximately 150 pounds. He was wearing a pink dress shirt with a very large tie. He was so funny and sweet that I soon forgot I was scared. He talked and talked up until the moment I was ready to be wheeled into the operating room. Then it hit. All of a sudden there was a silence. My anesthesiologist got serious for the first time. He started gently stroking my forearm.

"So how are you feeling?" he said.

"Fine," I said with confidence.

My shield of courage did not hold up because my mother started crying. I could not see her, but I could feel the tears rolling down her face. This prompted the anesthesiologist to change the mood by returning to his sweet clownlike posture and vocal intonations. As they began moving me into the operating room, my anesthesiologist turned to my mother and caringly asked her if she'd be okay.

I knew she'd be fine. I also knew that she was crying out of sorrow for what I've had to endure as a child. She was there at every painful moment of my childhood. I can honestly say that she felt and carried my pain. Perhaps she internalized my pain as somehow being her fault. I just thank God she was my mother.

In the operating room, my anesthesiologist and his assistant were dressed in the standard off-green operating uniforms. The room was white and smelled like alcohol. Above me the operating light shined brightly. I was asked if I preferred rock or Beethoven or no music at all. I said Beethoven. My anesthesiologist then asked, "Do you want bubble gum or regular laughing gas?"

I answered quickly, "Bubble gum."

The mask went over my face. I breathed in the gas and immediately felt sick. I then quickly tried to push the mask off my face because the smell was so hideous. It smelled like a combination of toxic gases.

"No! No!" my anesthesiologist said gently.

My arms were restrained and I started to scream and cry simultaneously. My forehead was stroked as I lay on the operating table. I began to feel the loss of my senses. Fear of the loss of control of my bodily functions, one by one, possessed me. I was scared. I wanted to be knocked out quickly. Slowly, my hearing faded. I could not hear my own crying. It was like watching a silent movie. Then I saw the operating light above start to blur. It was so overwhelming, my olfactory senses and the touch of my anesthesiologist no longer mattered. My eyes closed. I was out.

Four hours later, two hours after the time I was supposed to be done, I woke up in the recovery room and immediately threw up. A nurse rushed to me. I was so disoriented, I didn't even feel embarrassed that I had thrown up in a room full of people. Yet, as I looked around me, I quickly closed my eyes because the others around me looked worse than I felt.

I can't imagine how the surgery took 2 hours longer than it was supposed to, because the doctor was so sure of himself. After all, he had done the procedure before. According to my mother, what happened was that when the doctors were done, my foot had bent the total opposite of the way it was bent before, so they had to go in and straighten my foot. Doctors are not gods. They can be questioned, and science is only theoretical.

I opened my eyes and realized I was in my hospital room. Boy, I just wanted to sleep. The next two days were very lonely and physically painful. I was given morphine, which helped the pain but also kept me very drowsy. All I wanted to do was sleep. I did not want to eat at all. I was embarrassed to have a nurse help me to use a bedpan. Every time my mom would come visit after work, I would cry. She thought it was out of pain. To me, I was just so happy to see a familiar face. My mother would always cry when I cried, in empathy, in sorrow.

Day three, my best friend finally got her mom to let her bike to the hospital to see me. I was so happy. I cried the second she walked in. She started to cry and asked me why I was crying. I told her it was because of the pain. It was really because of the loneliness. I never slept well in the hospital at night. Even with the morphine. The reasons were many. Every 30 minutes, no doubt, my IV would have to be adjusted, or a nurse would come squeeze my toes so painfully tight to see if there was proper circulation that my eyes would fill with tears, or a doctor would examine me, or an X-ray technician would have to take an X ray. As I was almost getting used to the constant interruptions, it came time for me to go home.

I spent the next 3 months in a cast and a wheelchair. I missed the first month of middle school. I felt I'd missed out on the whole year. I was so excited to finally get to school. But when I got there, everyone had paired up with best friends. It seemed like there was no chance for me. I wanted to stay home for the rest of the year. However, I did end up making lots of friends and doing very well academically.

"Mom, look at this!" My mother comes over to check out the bargain I had just found on the clearance rack at Nordstrom. Within the next 10 minutes, my mom and I are swimming in a pile of clothes we have picked out to try on. The salesperson approaches, looking only at my mom and addressing her, "Would you like a dressing room?" But my mom looks to me to answer because her English isn't very good. I answer, "Yes, we would." This usually forces the salesperson to acknowledge my existence. However, there are those instances when I could be on the ground having a heart attack and the clerk would still ask my mom if I was okay. It is a very common experience for the disabled to be shopping and have the salesperson ask their attendant what the disabled individual wants. For example, in Sonny Kleinfield's book, *The Hidden Minority,* he interviews a disabled professor, Bruce Hillam. Bruce is paralyzed from the chest down. At the age of 15, he dove into a 15-foot pool and broke his spinal cord. Bruce requires the assistance of an attendant to get dressed. Often, he will take his attendant shopping with him to avoid the need to ask an unwilling salesperson to assist him. Bruce says, "When I go clothes shopping, I need someone to help me get things on. The salesperson will always address questions to that person: What size does he wear? Could he use some suspenders, too? As if I were a pet" (Kleinfield, 1977, p. 13).

I've had my share of experience with stereotypes. Shopping is just one of them. I am now in the parking lot of the university where I got my bachelor's degree. A young man with blond hair and preppie clothes is walking with his girlfriend. They have just gotten out of a Mercedes. I have just gotten out of a nondisabled parking space. The young man clearly sees my crutches. He remarks, "There are too many damn gimps at this school!" His facial features are aggressive and mean. I am deeply offended; my thoughts go crazy in my mind: "I can't believe I just heard that. God, I feel sick to my stomach. How could he say that so directly but yet not have the decency to say it to my face. What an asshole! Doesn't he realize that he could be in my shoes tomorrow? Does he think that he is invincible?"

A harmful nonverbal communication cue that outsiders use is the stare. Eye contact is very important in our daily interactions. However, I have received many intensely rude stares that, as a kid, made me feel handicapped. At this point, I have learned to ignore stares; I just assume that people do not realize they are being rude and that they are curious. I'm with my boyfriend in a restaurant. As the hostess leads us through the restaurant to our table, I am in my own world and not concerned about the people around me. I pay no attention to them. However, I hear my boyfriend, who is walking behind me, say, "Don't let your eyes fall out!" Oh boy, I'm cued in that someone was giving me the "handicapped" stare. They looked at me as if they were staring at the freak at the carnival show. It happens. My boyfriend is very sensitive about this, whereas I am indifferent. People can approach me and ask me what happened, as most do. But the ones who stare in ignorance are the ones who will never approach and never learn I am more like them than different. Stereotypes still exist. For any minority.

In junior high, I was put in advanced or gifted classes. This meant I would be in the classes with the most intelligent students and the most challenging curriculum—although I know that my friends in regular classes could do just as well as the advanced students. In both 7th and 8th grades, something happened that surprised and frustrated me. When my counselors would see that I had advanced classes on my schedule, they would automatically put me in regular P.E. (physical education). And if they saw adaptive P.E. on my schedule, they would put me in regular academic classes, even though I would request advanced classes and adaptive P.E.

The myth that the physically disabled are mentally disabled sickens me. In my adaptive P.E. class, although there were students who needed special education, the majority of the students could have done well in regular or advanced classes because their disability was *only physical*. I firmly believe that teacher expectations affect student performance. A student's being in special education classes lowers the teacher's expectations dramatically.

Using examples from other disabled individuals helps. Bruce Hillam says it best when he states, "A really deflating thing is that many people equate serious physical limitation with mental incompetence. They see my chair and assume I'm a dumbo" (Kleinfield, 1977, p. 13). The stereotype must be broken because it is disempowering and causes low self-esteem and lowered expectations for the disabled individual. Disabled individuals feel as though they have to prove themselves, and the able-bodied seem ignorant to the disabled. Referring back to Bruce, "You don't need feet to think" (Kleinfield, 1977, p. 10).

Un-covering the Story

The literature that uses experimental methodology to look at the lives of the disabled does little justice to those it tries to explain. Reducing a very personal and unique experience for each individual into a statistic is unfair. Being disabled, I am very concerned about what information is being disseminated about our culture. Every time I read a book with statistics, I experience a numbness. The numbers begin to blur: "The U.S. National Health Interview Survey conducted from July 1, 1957, to June 30, 1961, indicated that 7.3 percent of the noninstitutionalized U.S. population was seriously limited in such major activities as working, keeping house, or going to school" (Albrecht, 1976, p. 4); *this is not me.* "10.4 percent was seriously limited if recreational, social and civic activities were included" (Albrecht, 1976, p. 5); *this is not me.* I begin to remove myself because I have no way of understanding what the process of the phenomenon is. I have only the numbers that explain and generalize something I am supposed to be. However, my experience differs from what the numbers tell me.

I would argue that one could not have knowledge about the disabled unless one asked me about my own experience and talked to other individuals about their experiences. Having knowledge about the disabled requires knowing about the feelings and specific experiences of each person. A scientific study can only dissect an experience and explain only one of the many different phenomena contained in that experience. Not knowing all the details of a very personal experience makes it easy for the able-bodied to say, "It didn't happen to me—why should I care?" Or the able-bodied can conclude that they know the statistics and therefore understand what's going on. I have found myself in the former position. If I read statistics about a group, I said to myself, "This is not me, so I see no reason to know this." If I read individual narratives, however, I became intensely engaged. I don't ignore things that do not pertain to my experience just because they didn't happen to me. These experiences did happen to someone, and I may meet that someone someday.

Narratives help us not only to understand and experience what the author experienced but also to reflect on and make sense of our own lives. The strength of the narratives of those around us in connection to our own

I am not a stereotype.

should not be underestimated as a means of achieving meaning and knowl-edge (Bochner, Ellis, & Tillmann, 1996; Ellis, 1997). Moreover, it is hard to get emotional about a statistic unless it is very powerful and common to one's experience. Otherwise, it is meaningless.

Re-living the Story

I invite you to collect your thoughts. In the beginning, I talked of stereo-types with which disabled women are faced and the fragile self-concepts we have because of the power of those stereotypes. We have a need to compare our successes with those of the able-bodied. Stereotypes of the disabled have caused me and others great pain—we are not the stereotype. In presenting my stories and the literature on stereotypes and myths, it is clear that prejudice is still alive and thriving. Much of what is stereotypical is so implicit that there is little awareness of its effects on the self-image of the disabled. If the disabled have such a bad image as to be thought of as subhuman, it is necessary to reverse these harmful stereotypes. The world is full of misunderstood differences. The disabled are treated as a minority.

Unfortunately, this large minority has been silent for too long. Only recently have the voices of the disabled been heard. Our fears of physical difference must be confronted and de-mystified.

I leave you now with a challenge. Although you may have a sense of what the life of one disabled woman looks like beyond the mere snapshot we are given in everyday life, it might be better to think of my story as a book—a book of which you have been able to read the first and last few chapters. There is much left out; there is much to be written. Understanding the phenomenon of being disabled takes more than one narrative. You must continue the dialogue with others, disabled and able-bodied, and listen to each other's voices.

References

Albrecht, G. L. (Ed.). (1976). *The sociology of physical disability and rehabilitation.* Pittsburgh, PA: University of Pittsburgh Press.

Bochner, A. P., Ellis, C., & Tillmann, L. M. (1996). Relationships as stories. In S. Duck (Ed.), *Handbook of personal relationships* (pp. 307–324). Sussex, England: Wiley.

Deegan, M. J., & Brooks, N. A. (Eds.). (1985). *Women and disability: The double handicap.* New Brunswick, NJ: Transaction.

Ellis, C. (in press). Evocative autoethnography: Writing emotionally about our lives. In Y. Lincoln & W. Tierney (Eds.), *Voice in text: Reframing the narrative.* New York: SUNY.

Kleinfield, S. (1977). *The hidden minority: A profile of handicapped Americans.* Boston: Little, Brown.

Lonsdale, S. (1990). *Women and disability: The experience of physical disability among women.* London: Macmillan Education.

Vash, C. L. (1981). *The psychology of disability* (vol. 3). New York: Springer.

9

Singing Along

The Self-Reflective Power of Carly Simon's Musical Diaries

Thomas Endres, Ph.D.

Department of Communication
University of Saint Thomas

Carly Simon, 1994

*W*hen I was 15 years old, the Carly Simon song "Embrace me, you child," from her No Secrets *album, in which Simon sang of her feelings of abandonment following the death of her father, touched me. I had just lost my father, and it was then that I first learned of the amazing self-reflective and cathartic powers of music. I have followed Simon's music, as well as her life and career, ever since. In many respects, I feel that I owe Carly Simon this essay; it is my way of repaying her for providing the music that took me through the toughest phases of my life (e.g., high school, college, graduate school, marriage, and parenthood) and gave me symbolic insight into the frustrations of women's muteness. Of course, Carly Simon's work has not helped me artistically—I can't sing, dance, or play an instrument—but communicatively. When I listen to the life experiences of my mother, my wife, and my daughters, I know I am better equipped to hear their voices.*

However much I tell myself that I'm strong and free and brave,
I'm just another woman raised to be a slave.   (Simon & Brackman, 1975)

$\mathcal{I}$n her 1975 album *Playing Possum,* pop artist Carly Simon laments the frustration she feels being a "slave" in a dependent relationship. She is certainly not the first woman to experience this frustration (Simon, 1975). What makes Carly's situation unique is that she was able to give voice to her feelings through her music. Singing of her anger over being a slave helped loosen the shackles of her muteness. It is possible that she gave voice to other women's muteness as well. As pointed out in the preface to photographer Peter Simon's 1975 photo essay about his sister Carly:

> At first glance you might see them [the photographs] as a study of one girl —Carly Simon—in the act of growing up; then you might see the collection as portraying the archetypical American girl, going through the process of acculturation, and view the physiological as well as the stylistic changes a human being undergoes through the evolution of time, regardless of who she turns out to be. (*Carly Simon Complete,* 1975, p. 8)

Although Simon's may be a single voice in her recordings, there is an unrecorded but undeniable chorus of female voices who have experienced the same frustration, outrage, and muteness. Many may even have traveled the same path as Carly as she gained voice and as the focus of her lyrics changed over the years.

To fully understand Carly Simon the singer, one must first understand her life before her fame. Carly was born in 1945. Her father, Richard Simon, was co-founder of Simon and Schuster Publishing Company. She was not close to her domineering father, a frustrated pianist who would criticize her playing during piano practice, sit down to demonstrate the proper method, and remain at the piano for hours while ignoring his daughter.

Her family was wealthy, living in New York during the school year and summering in Martha's Vineyard. The Simon household was often frequented by famous individuals such as publisher Bennett Cerf, musical writers Richard Rodgers and Oscar Hammerstein, and classical pianist Arthur Rubinstein. Carly's older sisters, Joanna and Lucy, were beautiful, confident, and poised, and she always felt the least attractive of the three. This feeling was enforced when Sloan Wilson, author of *The Man in the Gray Flannel Suit* (1955), noted in his memoirs that all of the Simon family was strikingly attractive, except Carly.

These insecurities led young Carly to speak with a stammer (Jerome, 1978), because she suffered from anxiety and agoraphobia. Her first visit to a psychiatrist was at age 9. In her attempt to win her father's affection and compete with her sisters, Carly became the clown of the family. Richard Simon became ill in the late 1950s and died in 1960, despite daughter Carly's superstitious habit of knocking on wood 500 times every night for several years to protect him.

After high school, Carly attended Sarah Lawrence for two years as a Russian Literature major. She then teamed briefly with sister Lucy to sing children's songs during the mid-60s. When that ended, she worked odd jobs for a while, and then pursued an individual singing career. That step was quite a challenge because Carly's childhood anxieties manifested themselves as severe stage fright. It is here that Carly Simon first began to sing her diaries and began to give voice to her muteness.

There are three stages through which Carly passed as she moved from being "mute" to having a "voice." In the 1970s she went through her *Amorphous Period,* during which she was trapped and defined by those around her. As her life's story began to change in the early 1980s, her protagonist entered a *Transition Period,* which moved her away from her previous downtrodden imagery. Finally, from the mid-1980s on, Carly's lyrics have recounted stories of a woman taking control of her life, a woman ascending into an *Actualization Period.* As Cheris Kramarae (1981), a noted scholar in the area of female/male communication, explains, a metamorphosis such as Carly Simon's transforms herself, her protagonist, and her listeners from members of a "muted group" to women with a voice.[1]

The Amorphous Period

Carly's first big break, her rise to fame, and the release of her first eight albums between 1971 and 1978 all came during a time when she was experiencing a great deal of inner turmoil and confusion. "Carly Simon's most repeated public statement about who she is: 'I have no definite image of myself'" (Shapiro, 1977, p. 53). In her personal life, Carly seemed to define herself mostly by whom she was involved with at the time; that is, she was an amorphous figure. Rumors circulated about her romantic connections with celebrities such as Mick Jagger, Warren Beatty, Kris Kristofferson, and Cat Stevens.

This amorphous sense of self manifested itself in Carly's first two albums, *Carly Simon* (1971a) and *Anticipation* (1971b). Many of Carly's songs have a similar central protagonist in a repeated plot: an unnamed woman who has a desire to be strong and autonomous but is unable to do so because of forces outside of her control. Other characters often hold her down. Although these characters are sometimes relatives or female friends, most often the antagonist is a male significant other. The woman of the songs is continually motivated to succumb to the wishes of more powerful others even though doing so creates dissonance for her.

Carly's first hit, "That's the way I've always heard it should be" (Simon & Brackman, 1971a), exemplifies this. The story revolves around a young woman who is in turmoil because her boyfriend is coercing her to get married:

> You say that we can keep our love alive. Babe, all I know is what I see. The couples cling and claw, and drown in love's debris. You say we'll soar like two birds through the clouds, but soon you'll cage me on your shelf. I'll never learn to be just me first, by myself.

Though the woman seems to have a good sense of independence and survival at this point, she eventually submits by the end of the song: "Well, O.K., it's time we moved in together, and raised a family of our own, you and me. Well, that's the way I've always heard it should be. You want to marry me, we'll marry."

The amorphous perspective is emphasized on Carly's next album in the song "The girl you think you see" (Simon & Brackman, 1971b), which begins, "Tell me who you long for in your secret dreams. Go on and tell me who you wish I was instead of me." A later verse, representative of the messages throughout the song, demonstrates the woman's lack of self-definition: "I'm not necessarily the girl you think you see. Whoever you want is exactly who I'm more than willing to be. I'll be carefree, a Peace Corps trainee, your Gypsy Rose Lee, to please you."

In 1972, Carly married rock/folk singer James Taylor. Taylor was addicted to heroin at the time. Carly's amorphous imagery continues, as she now defines herself in terms of her rocky marriage. In Carly's 1972 album, *No Secrets,* the main female character in the song "It was so easy," laments: "And now we are grown, with debts and regrets. And broken hearts and sentimental schemes. Now every day just fairly seems to over-throw old dreams. Love can drive a normal woman to extremes" (Simon, 1972a).

It is not just male significant others that add to the feeling of form-lessness and frustration for the woman of Carly's amorphous period. In the song "Embrace me, you child" (Simon, 1972b), we hear of the woman's father, who sings whiskey tunes, and how he harmonizes with God, who sings lullabies. She is enamored of the father and is devastated when he dies:

> Then one night daddy died and went to heaven. And God came down to earth and slipped away. I pretended not to know I'd been abandoned, but no one sang the night into the day. And later nighttime songs came back again, but the singers don't compare with those I knew. And I never fig-ured out where God and daddy went, but there was nothing those two couldn't do.

The imagery of abandonment in these lyrics is merely Carly's dramatic expression of the muted feelings she felt toward her father. Even in death, he defines her.

Carly's jealously of her sisters also manifests itself during this period. In a 1972 interview, Carly said of her sister Lucy: "I emulated her life. I wanted to be her . . . I was Lucy for a number of years" (Rosin, 1972, p. 111). This feeling was given dramatic form in Carly's song "Older sister": "She turns everybody's heads, while I wear her last year's threads, with patches and stitches and a turned up hem. Oh but to be, oh but to be, oh but to be, I'd like to be, just once to be, my older sister" (Simon, 1974b).

Things became increasingly complex for Carly in 1974, with the birth of her first child, Sarah Maria. In her song "I think I'm going to have a baby," the woman discovers she is pregnant and becomes concerned with the way she is being treated: "So you pick me up, and you tune me up. And you wind me up and you play me. You talk about heart and you say you know soul, and the way to treat a lady. You're putting out too many phonograph records. I think I'm gonna have a baby" (Simon, 1974a).

Later, in the song "Slave," although the protagonist woman hopes to go it alone without the significant other, she finds she has been socialized otherwise:

Gotta stop these thoughts about you. Gotta learn to live without you. Gotta find some freedom for this weary slave. I worship your opinions. I imitate your ways. I try to make you grace me with a word of praise. I find I gave away the soul that I wanted you to save. I'm just another woman raised to be a slave. (Simon & Brackman, 1975)

In the song "Cow town," a woman from France named Simone marries a Texas millionaire named Donald Swan, who takes her from Paris and moves her to his ranch. The lyrics show Simon's loss of self:

Now she thinks about France and the night life there. And its cafes and bistros. Donald, a hard-working, simple man, likes to see the livestock shows. And when he's not off on business, he's out checkin' out cows and pigs. And she gets weary on a twelve mile prairie, starin' at the drilling rigs. (Simon, 1976a)

A final external force that defines the amorphous woman's character is that of children. Carly's second child, Ben, was born in 1977 with a malfunctioning kidney. Although Carly has expressed nothing but love for her offspring, she admits that the pressures of a two-career family, coupled with Taylor's lack of parenting time, put stress on their relationship. In her musical diaries, the children themselves may not be the source of tension, but circumstances related to them serve to confound and delimit the choices of the protagonist woman.

In "Fairweather father" the woman reflects upon the sacrifices she has made for her family and the compensation she must provide for the lack of paternal support:

But the mother advertised as a bargain wife. She'd make things easy for the rest of his life. And to make herself more appealing, she'd think only of him and forget her own feelings. . . . Fairweather father, doesn't like to hear the baby cry. Doesn't like to know of the aches and pains of the day gone by. (Simon, 1976b)

In 1978, Carly stated, "Most of my songs are about my relationship with James, so much so that sometimes I'm hesitant to reveal them to the public. . . . I do try to change the extraneous circumstances a bit, so they won't look like an exposé" (Young, 1978, p. 42). Thus, many thought the song "Tranquillo (Melt my heart)" was a love song about James, but it was actually about a woman trying to get her son to go to sleep. "I wanted to go out dancin', but you got me dancin' round and round Your momma's never gonna get to town. These plans of mine, better put 'em on hold" (Simon, Taylor, & Mardin, 1978).

The woman of Carly's amorphous period is characterized by frustration brought about by the realization that one's self is being defined by others. She is not necessarily powerless, but she chooses to remain formless and flexible. In the same way, many women of that time found themselves defined by their spouses, lovers, jobs, children, or other outside force. This can leave women angry but muted, having no way to express their frustration at such treatment. Carly Simon felt that frustration and, although she was not able to escape it during this period of her career, she was able to vent it through her lyrics. That helped her to make a transition in her life and lyrics.

The Transitional Period

Beginning in approximately 1979, when public knowledge about problems in the Simon-Taylor household began to grow, Carly's lyrics started to shift to narratives of greater autonomy. The three albums she released from 1979 to 1981 contain stories of women who vacillate between amorphousness and independence.

In some scenarios, the woman protagonist starts out strong and then backslides. In Carly's 1980 hit song "Jesse" the woman has refused the advances of an old love who has hurt her in the past. She relents, however, by the end of the song, as she sings: "Jesse, I'll always cut fresh flowers for you. Jesse, I'll always make the wine cold for you. Jesse, I can easily change my mind about you. And put on cologne, and sit by the phone for you" (Simon, 1980a).

In the final verse, the woman ironically asks Jesse to open the wine and "drink to the heart that has a will of its own" (Simon, 1980a). More often, however, the scenario is reversed during the transitional period, with the woman starting out weak and gaining strength by the song's end. One such example occurs in "Vengeance" (Simon, 1979b), in which the woman has been stopped by her policeman lover and threatened because he suspects she is seeing another man. Rather than submit, the woman responds with the following words.

Just because you are stronger and you hold it over me, I'll put the pedal to the floor and prove to you that I'm free. Though you've stopped me once again, it's not the end of the war. It's vengeance, she said. That's the law.

A similar scenario is enacted in the song "Take me as I am," where the woman's significant other has just seen the woman of his dreams pass by in a car. The protagonist laments:

> Once you said you were in love with me, and maybe you still are. But the passion you once showed me now is lost among the stars. And you fancy some new fancy girl will come and change your life around, but she just turned the corner in her car. (Simon, 1980b)

Unlike the woman of the amorphous songs, the woman of the transitional period then defines herself in the scene. "While for some other dreamin' driver, I am that romantic stranger. Lookin' better than I am, more mysterious by far. Speeding through his dreams, while I'm drivin' in my car" (Simon, 1980b).

Even the title of this song reflects a new character developing. This new woman is willing to take charge of the scenes. For example, in "Coming to get you" (Simon, 1979a) the woman answers a phone call from her child, who has been taken away by her spouse, his lawyer, and her in-laws. Rather than resign herself to this fate, she assures the child, "I'm coming to get you, let there be no mistaking."

The driving force behind the transitional changes during this period is the fact that Carly has identified and named the aggressor. She can distinguish between the heroes and villains of her narratives, and she has begun to opt for the hero. Not surprisingly, the most common antagonist turns out to be a man. This is clearly portrayed as she sings about "Them": "I know that them we are not. I have loved them a lot and I have loved a lot of them. You could say that I'm experienced enough to know that they are aliens" (Simon, 1980c).

The vibrancy of the narrative is enhanced in the chorus: "What do they want? What shall we do about them?" A female backup group sings all of the words except "them." That single word is sung by a male backup group, including James Taylor.

In 1981, Carly released her *Torch* album (Simon, 1981), a collection of nonoriginal torch music from the 1930s and 40s.[2] The romantic ballads and heartbreaking blues characterize the transitional period when examined in light of Carly's biography. Her marriage to James Taylor ended that year. Her son Ben underwent a kidney transplant. To top it off, during a rare live performance in Pittsburgh, Carly suffered a nervous collapse on stage. *Torch* in many ways seems to pay mournful tribute to the sorrows of the time. Holden (1990) described the album as "an epitaph for Simon's failed marriage" (p. 64). With the mourning, however, came a purging of the spirit. When asked about the timing of *Torch*, Carly answered, "It seemed like a coincidence at the time that I was singing these songs of heartbreak just when James and I were in quite a lot of pain. But I also believe—as Freud did—that there are no coincidences" (West, 1982, p. 8). *Torch* was the final cleansing that carried Carly through her transitional period to self-actualization.

The Actualization Period

From 1982 on, Carly's musical diaries are filled with stories of women reaching for self-actualization. In her real life, Carly came out of the self-imposed seclusion of the transitional period and returned to the public eye. Tabloids and periodicals covered her new dating scene with the likes of actors Al Corley and Albert Finney and drummer Russ Kunkel.

The protagonist woman in Carly's songs became more internally guided. She is motivated to forget the past and look ahead to a happy and fulfilling life. We hear this as the woman reflects upon a failed relationship in "It happens every day" (Simon, 1983c):

> After you break up, you say these words to your friends: "How could I have loved that boy? He was so bad to me in the end." Well, you make him a liar. Turn him into a robber. Well, it happens every day. But I don't regret that I loved you. How I loved you I will never forget. And in time I'll look back and remember the boy that I knew when we first met.

Some scenarios go so far as to rewrite the negative entries from the amorphous period. The title song from Carly's 1983 album, "Hello Big Man," refers to the line Carly's diminutive mother Andrea spoke upon first meeting the imposing Richard Simon (Simon, 1983a, 1983b). Carly details their romance in the song and concludes with the verse: "You keep expecting something to go wrong, and nothing does. They still live in the house where we were born. Pictures of us kids hanging all over the walls." After all the heartache and tension, the woman in the lyrics has a happy ending with her father.

The woman of the actualization songs can think for herself, even if she was oppressed in the past. Though Carly did not write the following song,

"Tired of being blonde," she included it in her 1985 *Spoiled Girl* album, and it presents a clear narrative that mirrors Carly's sense of self:

> She left the credit cards under her goodbye note. "All of these are yours, goodbye" and that was all she wrote. Keys to the Porsche she dropped on the floor in the den. Left in the '70 Dodge that he drove her in. She wasn't angry, she wasn't sad. She was just leaving a life that a lot of women wish they had. She was tired of being blonde (chorus). Tired of living a life that had only been planned by one. Tired of coping with the desperation. Tired of fighting back the feeling inside that told her to run. Tired of hiding her own inclinations. (Raspberry, 1985)

In December of 1987, Carly announced her marriage to writer Jim Hart ("On Martha's Vineyard," 1988). Said Carly, "I'm about the happiest I've ever been in my life" (Hall, 1987, p. 38). Her newfound contentment became manifest in her lyrics.

The actualization narratives are staged in typical, simple settings: homes, restaurants, nightclubs. They serve as a tangential backdrop to the protagonist woman in "Give Me All Night," who has become empowered with the ability to ask for what she wants.

> I have no need of half of anything. No half time, no half a man's attention. Give me all of the earth and sky, and at the same time, add a new dimension. Half the truth is of no good. Give it all, give it all to me. I can stand it. I am strong that way. (Simon & McMahon, 1987)

In 1989, Carly won an Academy Award, as well as a Grammy and a Golden Globe, for her song "Let the river run" (Simon, 1989) from the soundtrack to the movie *Working Girl* (Lamanna, 1990). This was a milestone in her career, as it marks a major step away from her diary-focus to a more universal appeal to seek the "New Jerusalem." Just as Carly's life was undergoing transcendent change, so were the characters in her songs. The protagonist woman gains voice and emerges as victor. This is quite evident in Carly's song "Don't wrap it up":

> I ain't nobody's princess, stuck in Sunday school. I ain't nobody's fool. So I'll help myself to love, and I'll have the whole career. Don't wrap it up, I'll eat it here. Just look at you now, the ultimate guy. Class, and wit, and style. Once I might have pretended to be someone else, attracting you with guile. But now I'm not about to dress up in some other woman's shoes. I've got nothing to lose. (Simon, 1990a)

These lyrics are a far cry from the slave dramas during the amorphous period.

During this same year, Carly released a second album of nonoriginal songs. *My Romance* (Simon, 1990b), with its accompanying video, is a collection of happy-spirited romance songs from the 1950s and 60s. There is not the angst of the analogous *Torch* (1981) album. The tone is playful and upbeat; it is Carly singing what she wants because it makes her happy.

More telling are Carly's latest works. In 1992 Carly released the ultimate quasi-biographical set of songs in her original soundtrack to the aptly named movie, *This Is My Life* (Simon, 1992d). Director Nora Ephron called Carly and asked her to write the score for a comedy/drama about a single mother raising her children while trying to maintain a career. Carly's response: "From the night of Nora's first phone call, I couldn't wait to start writing the score" (liner notes). Carly's muse for the work was the memory of her late Uncle Peter "Snakehips" Dean, who taught her to sing scat and play the ukelele.

The first song Carly wrote for the movie, "Love of my life," was one expressing her love for her children, Sarah and Ben: "From the moment I first saw you, the second that you were born, I knew that you were the love of my life" (Simon, 1992b). The score's most upbeat tune, "The show must go on," is a tongue-in-cheek stab at her stage fright (Simon, 1992c). Detailing a variety of excuses for backing out of a performance—e.g., "sick with butterflies," "lose my voice," "split my gown," and even "You want to watch the end of 'Cheers'" and "You find out there's no Santa Claus"—the woman perseveres. She concludes, "But when I'm in the spotlight, it's got to be a hot night."

In the movie, the mother, Dottie, reflects upon how boring her life was before Hollywood and Las Vegas. The song "Back the way" captures this and also is a metaphor for Carly's evolution from amorphousness to actualization:

> Back the way it was before, I was always waiting. Everyone thought I was okay, but now I'm scintillating. Back the way it used to be, some people thought I was pretty. But not many passes were made at me. Back the way it was before. But now my prayers are answered, and my star is on the rise. Flashbulbs popping, traffic stopping. Everyone's my best friend. (Simon, 1992a)

Where does one go after self-actualization? Carly's work in the past three or four years can only be described as reaching a level of transcendence, a point beyond the search for voice and beyond the market-driven expectations of commercial production. Now that Carly has found her voice, she uses it in a justifiably self-indulgent series of vocalizations. In 1993, Carly released *Romulus Hunt,* a "family opera" about the trials and tribulations of a 12-year-old boy's quest to reunite his divorced parents. One does not write an opera with the goal of commercial success in the pop/rock market foremost in mind. It was written because Carly had an opera inside her to write.

Following this, Carly released a collection that she describes as "the most personal album, in a sea of personal albums, I have ever made" (Carly Simon Online). The collection, *Letters Never Sent* (Simon, 1994), is just as the title implies: a musical tribute to a series of unmailed letters Carly found in the top of her closet. What is important to note is that all but one of the songs are glances backward. They are thoughts relived, not present frustrations expressed. The only "current" selection, "Like a river," is Carly's memorial song to her mother, Andrea, who had just passed away.

A fitting summation of Carly's three-decade career was released in December of 1995 (Simon, 1995a). The three-CD collection, *Clouds in my Coffee, 1965–1995*, is a retrospective including Carly's original demo tape, numerous hit singles, and reworked earlier selections. Finally, Carly tapped into the video market as Lifetime Productions released their taping of Carly's performance *Live at Grand Central* (1995b). Her unannounced performance at one of the world's largest transit stations during rush hour literally stopped traffic. In this performance, we clearly see a woman riding the wave of self-actualization. Unencumbered by defining antagonists and unfettered by market demands, Carly Simon has done more than find a voice—she incarnates the articulate.

Conclusion

Adapting a social anthropology model created by Edwin and Shirley Ardener, Kramarae (1981) developed the "muted group" theory to explain discrepancies between men's and women's communication. The theory assumes that men, as our society's historically dominant sex, have developed the words and norms for language usage. Because men's and women's experiences differ, women find it difficult to express themselves using a linguistic code that does not fit their world view. They are muted. As a result, females attempt to express themselves via nontraditional mediums such as letter writing, conversation groups, collective essays, artwork using household materials, and diaries.

Examination of Carly Simon's lyrics indicates that her songs are her personal diaries set to music—an "autobiographical songbook" (Hall, 1987, p. 38). "She pulls her songs out of her own experiences and gives them the feeling of real life" (Morse & Morse, 1975, p. 8). Diary writing is a communicative form consistent with the experiences of women:

> The form has been an important outlet for women, partly because it is an analogue to their lives: emotional, fragmentary, interrupted, modest, not to be taken seriously, private, restricted, daily, trivial, formless, concerned with self, and endless as their tasks. (Moffat, cited in Kramarae, 1981, p. 13)

Comparing her writing style with that of her ex-husband, singer James Taylor, Carly describes Taylor as a "poet" and herself as a "reporter" (White, 1981, p. 23). She adds, "I've always felt that a lot of my songs deal with spying on myself" (p. 26). In fact, according to muted group theory, Carly's lyrics can be viewed as a diary—a tactical approach for expressing her experiences outside the traditional male language code. However, Carly's product, her recordings, end up looking different than the typical diary entry. She takes her personal experiences, translates them into a quasi-fictional format, and sets them to music. The private element is removed or strongly masked within a dramatic narrative filled with heroes, villains, social backdrops, and legitimizing forces. Carly provides the following story, which explains her personal approach to writing:

> In my seventh grade English class, a certain rather imposing Mrs. Townsend said that when you write fiction write about what you know best. Draw from your own experience; there is enough of a world inside yourself. So I switched from writing stories about kangaroo children who were too large for their mother's pouches (not realizing, of course, that was me) to more obviously autobiographical material, where only my name was changed. . . . I gave myself some artistic license: shapelier curves and fewer blemishes in general, but the family set-up was usually identical. I still tend to write about my most intimate relationships. (*Carly Simon Complete*, 1975, p. 11)

Most often, it has been those things that hurt Carly that manifested themselves in her songs. As Carly admits, "We write more often out of pain and frustration than exuberance" (Arrington, 1980, p. 102). This is consistent with the tenets of muted group theory, which say that women search for ways to express themselves in unique fashions. Carly sums it up when she states, "Frustration, above all else, makes me write because I can really work things out on paper. Plus, there are a lot of things I can say in a song that I can't say in person" ("Keep Your Eye," 1982, p. 106).

In overcoming her muteness, Carly is actively engaging in a creative use of communication that allows both a release of tension and the production of musical art. It was pointed out in *Redbook* that "[i]f the dark side of Simon's soul has caused her problems, it has also helped fuel her creative drive and make her one of the most compelling and durable singers and composers of the rock era" (Holden, 1990, p. 64).

Carly Simon has spent the past three decades translating her personal diary into lyrical form as a way of giving voice to her muteness. At first, her narratives served primarily as a release valve for her inner turmoil, lack of locus of control, and amorphous sense of self. As tension was released and the primary antagonists were identified and confronted, Carly's life and music metamorphosed through her transitional period. And now, for more than a decade, Carly and her lyrical protagonist counterpart have become more actualized: an inspired series of narratives linking one woman's experiences in dramatic form to the social consciousness of all women.

By using a communicative form typical to women's experiences, the diary, Carly freed herself from her muteness. But her impact goes far beyond the expression of one woman's struggle. Carly's ability to take her personal experiences as a woman and translate them into a universal dramatic narrative understandable to both men and women is what gives her music its forceful persuasiveness. Dramatic narrative is not a sex-based phenomenon, as other linguistic forms, such as humor, may be (see Kramarae, 1981). As a result, men should better be able to understand women's experiences by listening to these narrative diaries than if they were listening to a woman express her experiences through a muted and derivative language system. This is especially noteworthy given Carly's latest works, where the sexes are no longer placed at such odds with one another. Women and men alike are invited to share in the self-actualization.

Giving voice to her angst has allowed Carly to move on to different and more varied accomplishments; there is less need to disclose her life musically through her diaries. Her energies have turned to movie themes, children's books, her first opera, and, for the first time in more than a decade and a half, public appearances.

As one music reviewer noted during the actualization period, Carly's songs "probably say more about the way life is lived in the eighties by an attractive, intelligent woman than any three weighty sociological treatises ever could" (Reilly, 1983, p. 83). And Carly's Oscar, Grammy, and Golden Globe, along with her four gold and two platinum albums, prove that not only has she found her voice, but that people are indeed listening.

Carly Simon is an innovator and a role model for women. She has demonstrated that alternative modes of expression outside the traditional male domain (e.g., public speeches, books) are appropriate avenues for reducing women's muteness. As the muteness diminishes, even more avenues for creative language use by women are opened up. Carly herself seems to address this in her song "Life is eternal" (Simon & Gohl, 1990) as she croons, "And the horizon is nothing, save the limit of our sight."

Discussion Questions

1. To what extent do Carly Simon's experiences mirror, or fail to mirror, the experiences of contemporary American women?

2. How is Simon's voice, expressed through the medium of popular music, different from the voice of other women discussed in this book? Does being a singer/songwriter differ from being an orator, a poet, a political figure, or an author? In what ways do their audiences and their responses differ?

3. Compare Carly Simon with other popular female recording artists. Is her work analogous to that of her early contemporaries such as Joni Mitchell, Janis Joplin, or Carole King? To that of recent artists such as Alanis Morrisette, Tori Amos, or Ani DeFranco? How does Simon's "voice" compare with that of history's most popular female recording star, Madonna?

4. This reading portrays diary-writing as a unique form of female communication, a way of finding voice outside of the male idiom. Do you agree? Is a female "diary" different from a male "log" or "journal"? Discuss the extent to which you believe the following are uniquely female forms of voice: letter-writing, collaborative essays, conversation groups, modern art or dance. Provide examples.

5. Many rhetorical scholars criticize the focus on "biography" in the analysis of a communicator's work. In contrast, this essay places great emphasis on biography, linking Simon's childhood and life experiences to the transitional phases of her lyrics. How important is it to know the history and background of an individual when you are studying the impact of their words and works at a given place in time? Does the importance differ based on the gender of the person being studied?

References

Arrington, C. (1980, October 6). No nukers Carly Simon and James Taylor have a new cause: Stopping fission at home. *People Weekly,* pp. 102–107.

Bormann, E. G. (1972). Fantasy and rhetorical vision: The rhetorical criticism of social reality. *The Quarterly Journal of Speech, 58,* 396–407.

Bormann, E. G. (1982). Fantasy and rhetorical vision: Ten years later. *The Quarterly Journal of Speech, 68,* 288–305.

Bormann, E. G. (1985). *The force of fantasy: Restoring the American dream.* Carbondale: Southern Illinois University Press.

Carly Simon Complete. (1975). New York: Knopf; Warner Brothers Publications.

Carly Simon Online. http://www.ziva.com/carly/

Endres, T. G. (1989). *Coming around again: Carly Simon and the dramatistic representation of women's experience.* Paper presented at the annual meeting of the Central States Communication Association, Kansas City, MO.

Hall, J. (1987, August 17). After an onstage collapse and a six-year battle with stage fright, Carly Simon braves a comeback. *People Weekly,* pp. 38–40.

Holden, S. (1990, July). Carly Simon: I've stopped running from problems. *Redbook,* pp. 62, 64.

Jerome, J. (1978, July 17). With stage fright behind her, Carly Simon is a working mom whose road hang-up is Pampers. *People Weekly,* pp. 88–91.

Keep your eye on Carly. (1982, June). *Harper's Bazaar,* pp. 104–107.

Kramarae, C. (1981). *Women and men speaking.* Rowley, MA: Newbury House.

Lamanna, D. (1990, June). Carly Simon back in the groove. *Ladies' Home Journal,* pp. 44, 46.

Morse, C., & Morse, A. (1975). *Carly Simon.* Mankato, MN: Creative Education Society.

On Martha's Vineyard, Carly Simon comes around again and quietly weds another writer named James. (1988, January 11). *People Weekly,* p. 38.

Raspberry, L. (1985). Tired of being blonde [Recorded by C. Simon]. On *Spoiled girl* [Album]. New York: Epic Records/CBS.

Reilly, P. (1983, December). Carly Simon's "Hello Big Man": Sensuality, wit, and pop-music art. *Stereo Review,* pp. 83–84.

Rosin, M. (1972, November). Carly Simon letting her mind flow. *Harper's Bazaar*, pp. 111, 145.

Shapiro, J. (1977, February). The extraordinary Simon women. *Ms.*, pp. 49–53, 84.

Simon, C. (1971a). *Carly Simon* [Album]. New York: Elektra Records.

Simon, C. (1971b). *Anticipation* [Album]. New York: Elektra Records.

Simon, C. (1972a). *No secrets* [Album]. New York: Elektra Records.

Simon, C. (1972b). Embrace me, you child. On *No secrets* [Album]. New York: Elektra Records.

Simon, C. (1974a). I think I'm going to have a baby. On *Hotcakes* [Album]. New York: Elektra/Asylum/Nonesuch Records.

Simon, C. (1974b). Older sister. On *Hotcakes* [Album]. New York: Elektra/Asylum/Nonesuch Records.

Simon, C. (1975). *Playing possum* [Album]. New York: Elektra Records.

Simon, C. (1976a). Cow town. On *Another passenger* [Album]. New York: Elektra/Asylum, WEA Records.

Simon, C. (1976b). Fairweather father. On *Another passenger* [Album]. New York: Elektra/Asylum, WEA Records.

Simon, C. (1979a). Coming to get you. On *Spy* [Album]. New York: Elektra/Asylum Records.

Simon, C. (1979b). Vengeance. On *Spy* [Album]. New York: Elektra/Asylum Records.

Simon, C. (1980a). Jesse. On *Come upstairs* [Album]. New York: Warner Brothers Records.

Simon, C. (1980b). Take me as I am. On *Come upstairs* [Album]. New York: Warner Brothers Records.

Simon, C. (1980c). Them. On *Come upstairs* [Album]. New York: Warner Brothers Records.

Simon, C. (1981). *Torch* [Album]. New York: Warner Brothers Records.

Simon, C. (1983a). *Hello big man* [Album]. New York: Warner Brothers Records.

Simon, C. (1983b). Hello big man. On *Hello big man* [Album]. New York: Warner Brothers Records.

Simon, C. (1983c). It happens every day. On *Hello big man* [Album]. New York: Warner Brothers Records.

Simon, C. (1985). *Spoiled girl* [Album]. New York: Epic Records/CBS.

Simon, C. (1989). Let the river run. On *Working girl: Original soundtrack album* [Album]. New York: Arista Records.

Simon, C. (1990a). Don't wrap it up. On *Have you seen me lately?* [Album]. New York: Arista Records.

Simon, C. (1990b). *My romance* [Album]. New York: Arista Records.

Simon, C. (1992a). Back the way. On *This is my life* [Cassette]. New York: Qwest Records.

Simon, C. (1992b). Love of my life. On *This is my life* [Cassette]. New York: Qwest Records.

Simon, C. (1992c). The show must go on. On *This is my life* [Cassette]. New York: Qwest Records.

Simon, C. (1992d). *This is my life* [Cassette]. New York: Qwest Records.

Simon, C. (1993). *Romulus hunt* [CD]. New York: Angel Records.

Simon, C. (1994). *Letters never sent* [CD]. New York: Arista Records.

Simon, C. (1995a). *Clouds in my coffee, 1965–1995* [CD]. New York: Arista Records.

Simon, C. (1995b). *Live at Grand Central* [Video]. New York: Lifetime Productions.

Simon, C., & Brackman, J. (1971a). That's the way I've always heard it should be [Recorded by C. Simon]. On *Anticipation* [Album]. New York: Elektra Records.

Simon, C., & Brackman, J. (1971b). The girl you think you see [Recorded by C. Simon]. On *Anticipation* [Album]. New York: Elektra Records.

Simon, C., & Brackman, J. (1975). Slave [Recorded by C. Simon]. On *Playing possum* [Album]. New York: Elektra Records.

Simon, C., & Gohl, T. (1990). Life is eternal [Recorded by C. Simon]. On *Have you seen me lately?* [Album]. New York: Arista Records.

Simon, C., & McMahon, J. (1987). Give me all night [Recorded by C. Simon]. On *Coming around again* [Album]. New York: Arista Records.

Simon, C., Taylor, J., & Mardin, A. (1978). Tranquillo (Melt my heart) [Recorded by C. Simon]. On *Boys in the trees* [Album]. New York: Elektra/Asylum Records.

West, C. (1982, March). Talking with Carly Simon. *Redbook,* pp. 8–10.

White, T. (1981, December 10). Fathers and lovers: Carly Simon learns how to say goodbye. *Rolling Stone,* pp. 23–26.

Wilson, S. (1955). *The man in the gray flannel suit.* New York: Simon & Schuster.

Young, C. M. (1978, June 1). Carly Simon: Life, liberty and the pursuit of roast beef hash. *Rolling Stone,* pp. 42–46.

Endnotes

1. An earlier version of this essay (Endres, 1989) used Ernest Bormann's Fantasy Theme Analysis (FTA) as a theoretical framework. FTA interprets dramatic narratives created by groups or individuals. One goal of FTA is to identify rhetorical visions, or unified scripts of dramatis personae, settings, plot lines, and sanctioning agents that converge to form a broad view of reality. In the original analysis, the three periods —Amorphous, Transitional, and Actualization—were labeled rhetorical visions. For further information on FTA, see Bormann (1972, 1982, 1985).

2. Excluding her 1981 *Torch* and 1990 *My romance* albums, which consisted of nonoriginal lyrics written by the likes of Hoagy Carmichael, Duke Ellington, and Rodgers and Hart, Carly has solo-authored approximately 70% of her recorded material and co-written an additional 25%.

Part Two

Women's Wisdom

Part Two of this volume, Women's Wisdom, focuses on women's contemporary life experiences. These accounts evolved from each author's direct dialogue with groups of women who face a variety of circumstances. Highlighted are the ways in which cultural mores continue to restrain women and restrict their voices. These restrictions are achieved by confining women's expression of emotion, by narrowly defining their roles, by labeling certain topics taboo, by limiting their opportunities to write, by muting their attempts to speak, by stigmatizing their health conditions, and by subjecting them to daily attacks on their self-images, identities, and safety.

The essays in Part Two: Women's Wisdom reveal the extent to which women's roles are changing and how their life experiences are beginning to be recognized as important and distinct from male experience. The women who speak out in these essays poignantly reveal women's efforts to reconnect heart, body, and soul whether in childlessness, motherhood, education, religion, health, or illness or in overcoming the divisions that separate women from whom and what they are and want to become.

10

Elation and Devastation

Women's Journeys Through Pregnancy and Miscarriage

Julie L. Ross, M.A.

Human Resources
ACCEL Technologies, Inc.

Patricia Geist, Ph.D.

School of Communication
San Diego State University

There must have been a place
deep within
that held the oceans of my love for you
and when you died
it burst.

how else explains the endless tears?

—*María Cristina González*

*T*his chapter gives voice to a group of women who have often been silenced and who have silenced themselves. Many women who experience miscarriage feel constrained, inhibited, and hesitant to communicate the emotions surrounding the loss. Family and friends may intend to provide support, but often instead communicate in ways that do not validate a woman's experience or do not allow her to express emotions and grieve the loss. This project was especially difficult to research and write because Patricia had experienced three miscarriages previously and was pregnant during the course of the writing. The women interviewed for this article gave voice to their painfully real and personally important losses. This written account has become a vehicle for these women to tell their families and others what they need most in the way of support, as they continue the journey to transform the losses into their memories or their hopes.

Each of these
my three babies
I will carry with me
in my soul, my blood and my bones.
The face on you, the smell of you
will always be with me.   (O'Connor, 1990)

Hearing the lyrics of Sinead O'Connor's song replayed again and again, I open my diary to reflect on what now seems like a distant past.

My Diary

February 28, 1991

Got the news today. My heart pumped rapidly as I waited to hear.
    "Emily O'Donnell, let me see here, positive."
    "Are you sure? Are you sure?"
    "O'Donnell, right? Yes, it's positive," the nurse, Adriana, confirmed.
    "Is there any way there could be a mistake? How sensitive are the tests?" I'm starting to cry now, barely able to talk.
    "You're gonna make me cry. Is this your first?"
    "Yes, I'm so excited. I'm 37 and this is my first."

"How long have you been trying?"

"We just started. A month. I can't believe it! I'm so happy!" In the rest of the conversation, in between my tears and rapidly beating heart, I learned that next week I would meet with the midwife, who would give me information about diet, expected birth date, birthing classes, caring for myself. I also scheduled an amnio class for the following week. Adriana recommended that David, my husband, attend the class with me.

I can't help myself. I walk quickly, almost skipping, to my supervisor Jennifer's office; she's the only one I can tell. She's in. "Jennifer, I have to talk to you right away." She picks up on the anxiousness in my voice and immediately walks back to her office. I shut the door behind us and stand there for a few moments, unable to speak, unable to contain my elation.

"What is it?" she asks, a bit sternly. She thinks I'm upset.

"I'm pregnant!" She jumps two steps to me and I to her and we embrace and laugh, almost giggle, hugging tightly, slapping and tapping each other's backs. I can't remember what was said now. Something like "just one month," "fertile Myrtle," or the like. I just remember feeling so full of emotion, hers and mine, sharing this news and the things to come.

I wanted David to be the first to know, but I also wanted to tell him in person. I told Jennifer I planned to buy him a bottle of Calvados, with a baby bottle nipple on it just like Kathy did for my brother, Bill.

After my lunch appointment, I'm sitting with friends when David calls.

"Did you find out?" he asks anxiously.

"No" I lie, crossing my fingers under the desk. "I'll call you when I do."

As soon as I'm alone I call David.

"How would you like to be a father?"

"Really? That's great, that's great!" He sounds like he's feeling a mixture of excitement and nervousness. "Look, I've got a client in my office. I'll call you back."

When he calls back, we talk about the doctor's phone call. I have to say, in retrospect, I wish I had waited to tell David in person. It was so difficult with people in his office and mine to truly celebrate and feel the occasion.

March 13, 1991

Two weeks later already. I've gone to my first appointment with Nurse Hudson, the midwife. She felt my uterus and said she could tell it was changing. Getting puffier. She told me to quit caffeine and not to jog. I didn't want to hear that. I quit caffeine, cold turkey, and I was shocked. The jogging was something else. I decided the psychological harm was greater than the physical harm. I jogged yesterday and today. It felt so, so good. I still don't believe I'm pregnant. Other than bigger breasts, nothing feels different, probably because it's still a secret. I'm realizing that so much of who we are is based on our communication with others.

David and I went to the amnio class. It was interesting. We decided to go with the CVS, an early test where they send a catheter through the vagina and take a sample of the placenta and test for abnormal chromosomes. In two weeks I will go in for a sonogram, and they will know more about how far along I am and my due date. I can't wait! After that, we schedule the CVS.

Friday, March 22, 1991

I have a ravenous appetite. I never really feel full. I have been craving pasta, breads, and most interesting, all the foods I grew up on, bologna sandwiches, tomato soup and toasted cheese, peanut butter and jelly, chicken noodle soup. But I don't want to gain too much weight, so starting today I'm going to weigh myself and keep tabs on what is happening.

I'm getting more and more anxious to talk to people about the pregnancy. A month from now seems too long to wait.

Thursday, March 28, 1991

Sonogram today. I had to drink 24 ounces of water and hold my bladder for 2 hours. The pain of holding all of the water actually made me cry. Finally I was sent in.

I felt warm gel on my lower stomach, a flat metal device and this fluid over my stomach. All they could see was the genetic sac.

"Are you sure about the first day of your last period?"

"Are your periods regular?"

Lots of pictures taken. The baby looks like a black spot on the monitor. Then they use a vaginal monitor.

"Do you always use this method also?"

"Only if we can't get a good reading on the others," comes the vague reply.

"Why would you not get a good reading?"

"If it were smaller, it's harder to get a good reading."

I'm getting nervous. They give short, general answers, not alleviating my growing tension.

"They're developing the film now, and then the doctor and the genetics person will talk with you." I hope they will alleviate my fears. I wish David were here. He would know what questions to ask.

Bad news. No heartbeat. D and C tomorrow. It's over.

December 1991

It's been almost a year since I've been able to write. After the first, I couldn't write anything about the second miscarriage. I almost felt jinxed in some ways. I couldn't write like I did for the first pregnancy. I couldn't write with the same kind of excitement. I was so hesitant. It was so hard.

I was home one day and as I stood up I gushed blood. A total flood down my legs, through everything. It was all over the floor. I ran to the bathroom. Sitting on the toilet, I heard something drop, splashing into the blood-filled toilet bowl. I assumed it was the baby. I called Emergency.

"You've got to take out what is in the toilet, put it in a bag, and bring it in."

I was crying hysterically, that's all I could do. I put it in the sack and just sat there, looking at the sack, crying and crying and crying. It was this big, big, bloody thing. I called David at work. He came home and took me to the Emergency ward. We sat. The thing in the toilet turned out not to be the baby. It turned out to be a big blood clot. We had to sit for a long time waiting. We finally got in and they examined me.

"This is threatened miscarriage," the Doctor said. "There is a good chance you will miscarry this child. On the other hand, people do this all the time and still keep the child." We were just devastated.

So that was it. I miscarried late in August. I actually went in for my sonogram and there was no heartbeat. It was the same. I mean the story is identical: Bad news, no heartbeat, D and C tomorrow. It was just horrible.

January 7, 1992

Here we are again, pregnant. Third time is a charm. January 6th was the sonogram, vaginal. Every sonogram since losing the first two babies, my heart beats a mile a minute.

"Is that the heartbeat? Is that the heartbeat? Is that the heartbeat?"

"Yeah, that's the heartbeat, that's the heartbeat." They look at me strangely.

"Are you sure that's the heartbeat? Tell me."

The baby had a strong heartbeat, this one's a keeper. I love him or her already.

January 22, 1992

One week ago today we found out our baby's heart had stopped beating. Third time wasn't a charm. Only moments, hours alone on Monday, have helped me face my grief, walk through it, as my friend Marion says. Today Marion talked about the grief of loss of all kinds. David and I now realize that we must gather strength and do this a fourth time after the loss of three children, 7, 8, and 9 weeks old.

Sharing Our Lives

After losing that third baby, I decided that it was time to talk to someone. I had to say to myself, "Emily, you need help." I have come to a support group for women who have lost children through miscarriage. I hesitated to come here, but my friends treat me as if I'm crazy for still being in so much pain. Sometimes I wonder if I am.

Curious, I look around the room at the women who have assembled here. Will I be talking to crazy women or to clinical professionals? These women look normal, like this could be a group of friends meeting for coffee. I look at the name tags as if that will give me some clue about these women's personalities. Monique, Alexandra, Brenda, Janet, Stephanie, Melissa, Tera, Carol, and Diedra. The names reveal nothing. Some of the women are younger than me, some are older. All are drawn here by a common thread, the loss of a baby through miscarriage.

"Hi, my name is Monique. I am your group facilitator for this meeting. I'd like to begin by going around the group and each of us telling our stories."

The woman sitting to Monique's right speaks up first. "I guess I'll begin. My name is Alexandra. My husband and I had planned our pregnancy. We wanted to have a specific age difference between our children. When I found out the baby had died, it was sheer disbelief because everything had been going perfectly. I had never felt that way before. I thought I was losing my mind. I had a D and C the next day. I found out later that the doctor had told my husband that I was overreacting and high-strung, that he'd better watch me. My husband was mad at the doctor for saying that, but he still believed it. One of the most important things that this group has done for me is to let me know that what I'm feeling is normal, even though the doctor told my husband that it wasn't."

I'm relieved to hear that someone else wondered if she was normal. She looks as if she's got it all together. I would never have known that we felt the same.

"My name is Brenda. I've had four miscarriages. The thing I think I've realized the most is how much I've had to look at my whole life. Losing my babies affected everything. It's not just the one thing, and you grieve through the baby and that's the end of it. I feel like time is slipping away. You know, every month that goes by is traumatic. I not only have to deal with the losses, but I have to deal with my own expectations for my life. How I planned my life, and how that will never be. One important point that I have realized is that you don't just grieve for the span from when you know you are pregnant until you miscarry. The span is from before you know you are pregnant, when you start planning and thinking about how your family is going to be."

We are all silent, thinking of the lost dreams and plans in our own lives. Brenda has voiced, for all of us, the monumental impact our miscarriages have had on our lives.

"It was a bit different for me," Janet began. "I never thought I'd be married before 30, and I never wanted children. When I met my then-future husband, I realized that my life was changing. We waited for a while before deciding to have a baby. About 8 weeks after I got pregnant, I started bleeding and having weird pains, not really cramping. I just felt miserable. We went to the hospital for our first ultrasound the next day. The doctor, who was very nice, started checking for the heartbeat and he was looking, looking, looking, and he said, "There's no heartbeat." My husband lost it. I have never seen him cry like that. While I was waiting for the D and C, I began having horrible pains. The doctor came in and said that the baby had already come out. They had to do a D and C anyway to remove the placenta and everything. I remember feeling as if my hopes had been crushed, that something was taken away against my will. You put yourself in the care of the medical experts and you take their advice, you try to be healthy, but you realize that it would be the same thing as trying to fight gravity. You could get the best plan you want and it's not going to work because there are forces that you don't have any control over."

I know firsthand about the losing battle with gravity. I fought and fought for my three babies to no end. If fighting were enough, I would have my children. But more often than not, it is a losing battle from the start.

"My name is Stephanie. I had a miscarriage 5 years ago. It was my first pregnancy with my husband. I have a daughter from a previous marriage. We were going in to hear the heartbeat for the first time. Both my husband and the doctor were joking around, and then the doctor stopped joking. We realized something was going on. The doctor said that he couldn't find the heartbeat, that I'd had a missed abortion, which I had not heard of at that time. I had a D and C two days later. I was crazy. I was wild, and I thought I was totally nuts because I couldn't stop crying. Now because of everything I've done, I know that I was in deep, deep grief, but at that point I thought I was nuts."

Looking around the group, I see heads nodding, eyes reflecting agreement. It is comforting to hear that I am not the only one to wonder about my sanity. We can't all be crazy, can we? Maybe what I am feeling is normal after all.

"I'm Melissa. On my first miscarriage, the fetal tissue started reabsorbing at 10 weeks. After the D and C, I experienced the same kind of high and crash as I did after my two children were born. My body also produced milk, as if I'd had a baby. I had never imagined that I could lose my baby. Nothing in the pregnancy packet I had received prepared me for this. Only one line, 'If something goes wrong, contact your health provider.' Nothing about what could go wrong. Nothing about the effect of the hormones on you, about producing milk. I got pregnant again right away. Around 9 weeks, I started bleeding very heavily. I found out later that I had lost twins. The miscarriages shocked me. It had never happened to anyone I had known, and I didn't think it could happen to me. Losing these babies has taken away my naïveté. Bad things can and do happen to me."

I could feel Melissa's pain, the pain of losing her babies and the pain of losing that innocence we all began with. We began invincible, and suddenly, tragedy was thrust upon our lives. No longer were we immune to the dangers of the world. If this could happen to us, what could be next?

"My name is Tera. I had a miscarriage about a year ago. There are times when I feel like I have a good handle on this and I don't need to talk about it anymore. But at other times I really feel like maybe I could really use therapy and don't realize it. So I thought talking about it might help. Losing the baby was incredibly painful and traumatic. The pain began on the same day that I officially found out I was pregnant. I was in constant, excruciating pain for 3 days before having emergency surgery. It was an ectopic pregnancy that was so far along that the surgeon had to remove the tube; the remaining tube was in bad shape as well. This was supposed to be a joyous occasion, to be pregnant, and yet here I was. Things couldn't be worse, and I just knew, I already knew at that point that it was going to be bad news. The feeling of defeat and failure, and just feeling very pathetic. I got very depressed and started sobbing there in the waiting room. Then I felt humiliated because I was sobbing in a room full of strangers. Between the shock of being pregnant and 3 days of constant pain, I didn't know what was what."

It's my turn now. I can feel my heart pounding. I hope I don't cry. "My name is Emily. I just had my third miscarriage. I really thought that I would be able to keep this last baby. But here I am, a jumble of emotions. Yesterday, my husband asked me to describe what I'm feeling. It's so hard to sort through. I feel angry because it seems so easy for other people. I see all these other women who are pregnant. I see people in the world who abuse their children, children who don't have parents who care. I just feel angry that I know I will be a good mother and I don't get that opportunity. I feel sad about what we lost. There was this little baby in us, in me. That was our baby. I remember all the excitement of thinking about what we were going to buy, what we were going to do, and how we were going to spend our time. I've tried not to blame myself, but it's hard not to think it's because I'm 38. I waited this long and now I'm getting my due. Thinking, 'Well, you made your choice and here you are.' Jogging, eating, aging, having been a crazy college student. It's all very complicated. The biggest change I think I have made is that I used to think I wanted a girl. But I've started to think about a boy in a different light. Now it's just important that I have a baby, a healthy baby, no matter what."

I can't believe I got through it. My voice choked and my eyes teared up, but I didn't cry. I feel as if my load has been lightened by sharing, talking it out with others in the group. We work in unison to bear each other's sorrow.

"My name is Carol. I feel a bit strange about being here because I had my miscarriage over 30 years ago. But then again, it is something that affects you for the rest of your life. When I got married, the doctor told us that we would probably never have children, so when I got pregnant 6 months later, it was quite a surprise. Between 2 and 3 months later, I woke up bleeding. The doctor told me I was definitely having a miscarriage and sent me to the hospital. After the D and C, I remember saying, 'What should I do? Should I stay home from work tomorrow?' and the doctor said, 'Oh, you can go to work tomorrow.' I very clearly remember thinking, 'This is not right. I mean, this is terrible.' I felt terrible."

Carol paused, and I realize that just 3 years ago, I didn't even know what a D and C was. Yet almost all of the women here have been through it at least once, that sterile, cold procedure that robs us of our children.

Carol continued, "Having a miscarriage is something you never forget. Every so often, I think about what my life would have been like if that first baby had lived. I think, 'There could have been four children, instead of three. How would that have changed my life?' Certain health forms ask you how many pregnancies you have had. Well, all my life I've said I have three kids, and suddenly the number is four. The death of a baby, regardless of its size, definitely makes an imprint on your life. It's gone and you have to deal with that, you have to grieve."

Diedra was the last to speak. "I've been pregnant seven times in 5 years. I have four children, but I lost three babies. Each miscarriage was different. The first was like a heavy period. I had the second while I was out of state visiting my parents. I basically went into labor, giving birth at 8 weeks. The third was very dramatic because the baby lived to 14 weeks. I thought I was past the danger. I was devastated. I was so excited about being pregnant, I shared it with everyone. I felt like such a fool afterwards. You are looking 9 months ahead and further, and that is all taken away. It's over. You're not pregnant anymore. It's like I know that, but I need to keep talking about it. People don't want to talk about it. They feel uncomfortable."

The group sat silently as Monique began to speak again. "I appreciate the experiences each of you have shared. I think Diedra brought up a good point about how others react. I'd like each of you to think about the kind of support you received from other people, what they said to you and how you felt about that, and share that with the group. I feel that being able to explore what was helpful and what wasn't is an important part of learning about ourselves and our losses."

After a moment, Alexandra spoke up. "I remember people saying that I was young and could have more children. People said that something was wrong with the baby. One friend even said, 'Your kids would have been too close together in age and it would have been too hard on you.' All I wanted to hear was that they were sorry and that they were there for me. It made me feel like this baby didn't matter. Like this baby was just a process and not a person. Even the doctor, when I asked him whether it was a boy or a girl that I had lost, looked at me like 'What the hell is wrong with you? Have you lost your mind?' He made me feel so stupid, like 'What difference does it make? It's gone.'"

Brenda seemed hesitant to speak, but after a pause said: "After my second loss, people were taken back, like 'Oh my gosh, she's had another one.' People were supportive initially, but there wasn't a lot of continued support. I think it's one of those things where people see it as 'You know, it happens' and a couple of weeks later, 'It's over and you should be over it.'

I never had people say to me, 'You should be over it,' but people don't need to say that in their words. It's just by how they respond to you. Most people think that infertility is when you can't get pregnant, not that you can't carry a pregnancy. They don't even realize that I wonder if I'll ever have a child."

Melissa's face showed her disgust. "A woman at work came to me and said, 'You're over 40. You have two kids anyway. It's for the best.' That seemed to be a recurring theme, 'Two kids and it's for the best.'"

I had experienced this sort of reaction also. Everyone was afraid to be excited when I announced I was pregnant after my miscarriage. My fear registered on their faces when they'd say, "That's great." I know they were thinking, "Why are you putting yourself through this?"

Melissa agreed: "People would say, 'You have two beautiful children and a wonderful husband. You should be thankful.' In and of itself, that's true. But that hurts so much. You don't understand that there's a loss here. I tried to hide it, trying to be what everybody wanted me to be. I was saying I was fine, but inside, my heart was aching. I felt like I was lying all the time and I couldn't show my true self because people didn't want to hear it. It was so hurtful. Now I've learned to express myself. I just tell people, 'I'm not doing well' if I'm not."

Looking appalled, Carol exclaimed, "I can't believe that things haven't changed. I would have expected things to have changed since my miscarriage 30 years ago. I remember my boss, who was a woman, and other women in the office saying, 'What's the big deal? Why are you crying?' I remember thinking, 'Is there something wrong with me that they should not be the least bit sympathetic?' After that week I never talked about it with anybody. I mean, I didn't want to bring it up again because I had been rejected."

"Things haven't changed that much," Janet agreed. "Even the people who don't know about our miscarriages say things that hurt. I've had people say that we love dogs more than children because we raise dogs. They say we're on the 'fast track' or that we don't have time for children. They have no idea that we're trying desperately to have children. Trying desperately to keep our children alive."

"And you blame yourself so much for not being able to. I remember going in for the D and C and the doctor coming in and saying, 'Stephanie, is there anything I can do for you? Do you have any questions?' I said, 'What did I do to cause this?' And he said, 'I've already told you. You didn't do anything. You didn't cause this.' The last thing I said before I went in was, 'I don't believe you.'"

Monique spoke up for the first time. "After my second miscarriage, my daughter asked me, 'Mom, how come you only have dead babies?'"

Alexandra said quietly, "I found out that in my miscarriage, the baby was fully developed but it died. It was a rare type of miscarriage. That made it harder because I know that my body attacked the baby. I want to have another baby, and I wonder if it will happen again." The group sat still, feeling the pain and the guilt we had all kept locked inside. Finally Diedra broke the silence.

"After my third miscarriage, I heard something that I had never heard before. A dear lady said, 'Diedra, God made that baby and he wanted you to bear that baby, but he wanted that baby in heaven for himself. He made this beautiful child and he wants to raise the baby himself. You can see the child when you get to heaven.' It was such a positive outlook because so many people had been telling me, 'Oh, it was a boy and you can't carry boys' or 'Oh, it was probably good because it would have been deformed.' So I felt like I was always making bad babies. There's something wrong with me or there's something wrong with this baby, and 'it's a really good thing that it didn't get born.' Very few people said, 'It was a perfect baby and it's in heaven because God wanted that baby.' I grasped onto that one. After going through it three times, I liked that. I liked that a lot."

Tera looked thoughtful. "The best support I received was from a woman in the waiting room when I broke down. I was sobbing, and this woman came to me and seemed to be very comfortable despite the fact that she didn't know me. She put her arm around me and just comforted me and babied me like my own mother would have. She understood that I was in a lot of pain, but she told me not to worry, that God was with me and that I was going to be all right. Very soon, my crying subsided. On the other hand, my family tried to minimize everything. They had good intentions, but they wanted so much for me to get over this. Their way of comforting was, 'Oh, don't worry, so-and-so had an eighth of a tube left and she has five children now,' or 'You're young. I know you'll be pregnant in no time. Don't worry about it.' So, there was no chance for me to get this out. It's like you're not allowed to feel bad about this."

"You just want someone to listen and be there for you," Alexandra added.

I completely agree. "For my first two D and C's, my in-laws sent beautiful bouquets of flowers. They were wonderful, just wonderful. My husband's mother even offered to come down and help out. It was such a wonderful surprise that she could understand. It said to me, 'You have a right to grieve, to be in pain.' On the last miscarriage, we didn't tell anyone. So I came home and there were no flowers, no phone call. By not sharing, we cut ourselves off from our support."

I knew that this group was fulfilling part of that need for sharing, for support. Although our experiences are unique, we share many of the same feelings. Maybe, by talking, each of us could gather strength from each other and from ourselves, to grieve for our babies and heal our wounds.

As a group we talked for a bit longer, sharing memorial ideas. Many of the women have named their babies. Some have released balloons, planted trees, bought special items, all to help them remember and love their lost children. I file these ideas away to sort through later, searching for the right memorial for my three little ones. Monique concludes the group session for the evening. "Thank you all for coming, for sharing. Talking to others about your feelings, about your babies is very important. I appreciate the comfort you have been to each other."

I feel a little better. I know now that I'm not crazy, that what I'm feeling is normal. Even though this is painful, I will live through it. Maybe, I will have the strength to try for another baby soon.

Emily's Baby

And I did gain the strength. Just 14 months after my third miscarriage, Brenna Nicole was born. Yet I feel a deep sorrow amidst my elation, thinking back to the women who voiced their losses. I wish for them the miracle I hold in my arms.

The emotions and events related here reflect the experiences of women who have had miscarriages. In an effort to present women's voices in a unique and moving dialogue, we have used their words to tell their stories. Their stories include voices at different societal levels: the voices of society on motherhood and miscarriage, the voices of the medical community, the voices of friends and family. Most important, the voices of the women tell their stories, of elation, of devastation, and of their search for meaning. In doing so, they fight to overcome the overwhelming lack of support from research, friends, family, and society.

People, even those close to the mother, rarely provide the support and sympathy she needs. All too often, others diminish the significance of the loss (Bansen & Stevens, 1992) and minimize the emotional effect of the miscarriage (Elkin, 1990). Stories like Carol's, where co-workers think that the loss is "no big deal," are still all too common today. The women discussed the pain of receiving messages such as "get over it," "you're young," and "it's for the best." These kinds of communication experiences complicate rather than ease the pain of miscarriage.

In some cases, even the literature on miscarriage delegitimizes the grief of the parents. Although research on miscarriage is abundant, clinical articles describe the physical aspects of miscarriage, scarcely acknowledging that a death has occurred. Libraries and bookstores carry few books addressing the emotional issues involved in miscarriage (Allen & Marks, 1993). DeFrain (1991) cites some researchers who go so far as to support the mistaken reasoning (Theut, Zaslow, Rabinovich, Bartko, & Morihisa, 1990) that later infant losses are worse than earlier losses. Under this reasoning, women who have lost an infant 3 or 4 months after birth to SIDS (sudden infant death syndrome) have more of a right to grieve than women who have experienced stillbirth or miscarriage. According to this rationale, women such as Emily, who miscarry early in their pregnancies, have less right to grieve than women who miscarry later in their pregnancies. This type of reasoning robs women who have miscarried of the right to their emotions as well as valuable resources of support (DeFrain, 1991). It must be recognized that although grief is different, the grief of losing a baby at 7 weeks in a pregnancy can be just as intense for some women as the grief of losing a 2-month-old child. Women may vary in their grieving and in the support they need, but a loss, no matter when it occurs, deserves to be acknowledged.

Acknowledgement is further denied because our society has no mourning rituals for parents or burial rituals for miscarried babies and rarely is there a funeral (Elkin, 1990). Many times, parents mistakenly believe that their only option is for the hospital to take care of the body, or they may be pressured to make a hasty decision about the disposal of the body (Borg & Lasker, 1988). Hospital release of the body may be complicated and is generally not encouraged by hospital staff (Leroy, 1988). These are examples of the ways society does not recognize miscarriage as the loss of a child, denying the legitimate right of the mother to grieve.

Only recently have researchers begun to address the personal aspects of miscarriage, such as women's feelings of grief and bereavement (Allen & Marks, 1993; Bansen & Stevens, 1992; DeFrain, 1991). Bansen and Stevens (1992), however, assert that although miscarriage is experienced by a significant number of women, to this day only a few researchers have attempted to capture these "women's lived experiences." Of the issues addressed by these researchers, some have focused on enhancing the ability

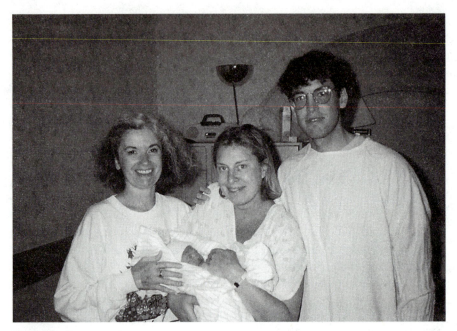

The birth-day

of nursing professionals to address women's needs during and after miscarriage (Bansen & Stevens, 1992). Others, such as Allen and Marks (1993), have used interviews with women to explore such emotional issues as love and attachment, grieving, and relationships with partners and living children. Although these studies make a valuable first step toward privileging women's voices through the use of interview data, there is a great need to explore aspects of a woman's miscarriage experiences, especially those created through her communication, or lack thereof, with others. Perhaps someday women will not be left to their silence, to their internalized loss and pain, but instead be supported in the sharing of their voices in a process that acknowledges and ritualizes their loss and dignifies their lived experiences.

Discussion Questions

1. This essay does not address issues of race and class in relation to women's experiences of miscarriage. Do you think women of different races or income levels would have similar responses to miscarriage?

Why or why not? Would their cultural backgrounds mandate different responses?

2. How did the experience of miscarriage affect the women's views of themselves? their goals? their dreams? their view of their roles in life? their self-blame? From where or whom does this blame originate (e.g., society, family, friends, self)?

3. What kinds of messages from medical professionals would seem to help or hinder the emotional healing process for women who have miscarried?

4. At one point in her diary Emily writes, "Other than bigger breasts, nothing feels different, probably because it's still a secret. I'm realizing that so much of who we are is based on our communication with others." What significance does this have on Emily's ability to grieve and seek support from others?

5. The women in this reading assigned "personhood" to the fetuses they were carrying. How do issues of abortion rights, the right to choose, and the right to life play into the women's experiences? For example, if people do not believe that a 7-week-old fetus is a baby, would the support they provide a woman who has miscarried be any different from the support offered by people who believe that at any point of development a fetus is a baby?

6. What experiences have you had with miscarriage (e.g., your own, a family member's, a friend's, etc.)? How did you and others respond?

7. Your sister has a friend who has just had a miscarriage and your sister is wondering how she can help her friend. Based on the voices of the women in this essay, what advice would you give your sister?

References

Allen, M., & Marks, S. (1993). *Miscarriage: Women sharing from the heart.* New York: Wiley.

Bansen, S. S., & Stevens, H. A. (1992). Women's experiences of miscarriage in early pregnancy. *Journal of Nurse-Midwifery, 35,* 84–90.

Borg, S., & Lasker, J. (1988). *When pregnancy fails.* New York: Bantam Books.

DeFrain, J. (1991). Learning about grief from normal families: SIDS, still-birth, and miscarriage. *Journal of Marital and Family Therapy, 17,* 215–232.

Elkin, E. F. (1990). When a patient miscarries: Implications for treatment. *Psychotherapy, 27,* 600–606.

Leroy, M. (1988). *Miscarriage.* London: Macdonald & Co.

O'Connor, S. (1990). Three babies. On *I do not want what I haven't got* [CD]. New York: Chrysalis Records.

Theut, S. K., Zaslow, M. J., Rabinovich, B. A., Bartko, J. J., & Morihisa, J. M. (1990). Resolution of parental bereavement after a perinatal loss. *Journal of American Academy of Child Adolescence Psychiatry, 29,* 521–525.

11

The Mystery and Mystique of Natural Childbirth

Lisa Rose Gates, Ph.D.

School of Communication
San Diego State University

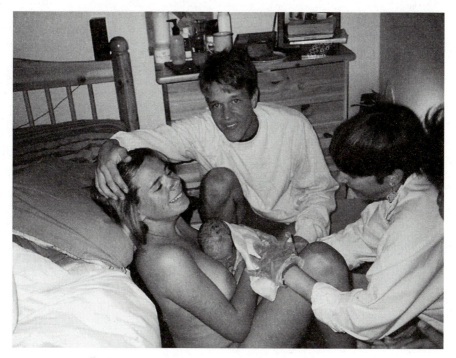

Ecstacy

Tales of childbirth, like male "war stories," stay with women their entire lives. Birth is not a discrete process beginning with the onset of labor and ending with the delivery of a baby. As the women's stories that follow reveal, the process begins long before conception. In this piece are my own birthing experiences. My first birth involved numerous interventions: narcotic drugs, an epidural, an internal fetal monitor, an ultimate cesarean section, and more pain medication after the birth. To this day, I still ask myself why I didn't say no to the proffered medication, and why I didn't request a longer trial of labor. When my husband and I decided to have a second baby, I opted for a natural approach. I labored without medication for approximately 8 hours, when the doctor finally said that he needed to use forceps. I agreed to the use of a Sufenta spinal, which is similar to an epidural, but not as long lasting. Still, my goal of achieving a completely natural childbirth goes unrealized. In this essay, I recount my own experiences along with the voices of other women to provide views of natural childbirth, why we want to do it, how we feel about our birthing experiences, and how we believe others see us based on our "radical" views. As I and the other participants reveal, the desire to birth naturally is about women's efforts to reconnect heart, body, and soul as we make the transition into motherhood.

    Mystery.
Where is she found?
In the subtle details of detective novels
In the developing baby within my womb
In soft whispers into a best friend's ear
In the stuff of everyday?
Where is Mystery?
Where does she reside?
I shall not find her.
I dare not stop my search.
    —LISA GATES

Reflections on Natural Childbirth

While driving to a Bradley method[1] class reunion at the home of my natural birthing instructor, Nancy, I reflected on a number of things. Since Cameron was born, I had been with him constantly. I realized also that it had been 3 months since I gave birth and yet I was still feeling some soreness from the episiotomy.[2] In short, I was still adjusting to having a new baby and being the mother of two boys. I also knew that I would have to tell the other two women from my childbirth class about my labor and delivery. I knew that in telling the story, I would relive the disappointment I felt in not having a completely natural childbirth.

The profound and mysterious connection between a mother and her baby in pregnancy occurs in so many ways: physically, as the baby is nourished by its mother's body; emotionally, as the bonding between mother and baby begins even before the two actually "see" each other; and socially, as the mother considers her changing societal role and as the baby is introduced to social life. Despite this connection that epitomizes both pregnancy and childbirth, the "best" way to give birth remains a controversy that alienates and separates all of the participants involved in the birthing process. Indeed, the voices of those supporting "natural" childbirth have been largely suppressed, and some staunch supporters of natural childbirth have been persecuted. Many feminist authors have argued that medicine has robbed women of the experience of natural childbirth (Arms, 1994; Martin, 1992; Rothman, 1982, 1989). In response to routine medical practices in childbirth, some women choose to give birth naturally—without the use of narcotics, anesthesia, or "unnecessary" procedures.

When I arrived at the reunion, Nancy embraced me and kissed my baby softly. She said, "Oh, Cameron, it is *so* good to meet you!" "And how are *you*?" she asked, as she escorted me into the house. "I'm all right," I replied with something of a forced smile. Entering her country-style home brought back warm memories of the nights my husband, John, and I spent sitting on her living room floor practicing relaxation techniques and learning how to manage my labor. Nancy is a wonderful instructor. A former nurse-midwife, she is an ardent supporter of natural childbirth. She was completely honest with us about the fact that labor would be painful (although she claimed that one woman she knew actually had an orgasm during delivery!), but, as she used to say, "If *I* can do it, *anyone* can do it."

After having two children of her own naturally, she felt the need to share her passion about natural birth with others. She offered us many emotional, practical, and medical reasons to support natural childbirth, a process she believes is safe—even without most medical intervention. When a class member asked her to distinguish between a medical birth and a natural birth, I recall her saying, "The medical approach to birthing has a totally different mindset from natural childbirth. It's a model of 'we will deliver for you.' See, natural childbirth is aligned with midwifery, which maintains that the more you do for yourself, the better. There's really nothing about birth that has to do with anybody else but you."

But now Nancy stood next to me and I knew that I would have to tell her about what happened to me in the labor and delivery room. I was, however, momentarily distracted by the joy I felt in seeing the other women. After all, we had spent 12 Mondays together, revealing some of our deepest concerns about facing one of our most significant life events. One woman, Kyle, whose belly barely showed during her ninth month of pregnancy, was actually wearing jeans with a *belt* and had her blouse tucked in. She looked great. She was the most athletic among us. The others: Marisa, the energetic, lively one, and me, Lisa, the analytical and skeptical one, dressed to cover up the excess weight we retained from pregnancy. I was happy about simply being with these women but I was curious to see what we would all look like *after* birth—I'd known these women only with full bellies.

I was again reminded of my own feelings of disappointment as Marisa told the story of her "totally natural" birth. It is an understatement to say that Marisa was terrified of childbirth. She swore that if it became too painful, she would choose drugs. Although she strongly believed that a natural birth would be best for her and her baby, she didn't believe in her own ability to give birth without anesthesia. When she shared this with the group, I felt that she was speaking for the rest of us. After all, how can *anybody* be *certain* about whether she can do it or not until she has actually experienced a contraction.

Contraction. The word doesn't begin to describe the overwhelming feeling of pressure and pain, the mystery of the wavelike nature of the pain, the often sharp pains felt in the vagina as it stretches open for the baby's debut, and the "double peak" contractions that begin to subside only to increase suddenly with great vigor. As with other forms of pain, there is truly no way to describe to someone else what the pain feels like. When I try explaining to other friends who have not birthed a child what my contractions felt like, I realize the limitations of language. Perhaps that's why we can't remember our pain very well—we can't articulate it. Fortunately, though, for Marisa, her pain was brief. She had the shortest labor of the four of us. Only 2 hours.

After we all exchanged hugs and admired each others' babies, Nancy ensured that we each had a tall glass of water (which is important for nursing mothers). We told our birthing stories once we were all seated on the floor. Within these stories are the voices of mothers, midwives, and nurse-midwives who support natural birthing. The political, social, and emotional struggles that have been fought to maintain natural birth as a viable option for women are revealed in the telling of these birthing tales. Nancy began by asking Marisa to use one word to describe her labor.

Marisa's Birthing Tale

"Fast. The labor was really rapid. I was vacuuming at 5 o'clock. It was probably at about 6:30 that it started to get really hard." Nancy asked what techniques Marisa had used to help manage the pain. "We used deep breathing for relaxation. My husband attempted to use imagery such as the floating on the ocean but I told him, 'Cut that out because you're making me seasick.'" We all laughed. "And that's about all we had time for—and then, of course, the good pressure on the back."

I asked Marisa whether she'd had any medical intervention at all. She said, "No. There wasn't enough time—except for the episiotomy attempt. My husband actually stopped them from giving me an episiotomy. When I saw my sister have a baby and an episiotomy, I just about passed out. I thought to myself, 'That's not going to happen to me.' I saw the Susan Powter Show. They had three horrifying births. One woman said she ripped past her anus! And when I saw what happened to my sister . . . they say the episiotomy is little, but it's like a 3-inch gouge. Anyway, they were going to use some injection to numb my vaginal area so they could give me the episiotomy. Well, I guess my husband saw them pick up a needle, but I had said that I wanted a pressure episiotomy only if I *had* to have one.[3] My husband asked the doctor what he was doing, and the doctor says, 'We're going to have to give her an episiotomy.' And my husband says, 'No, I don't *think* so.' The doctor asked if we were sure, and my husband says, 'Yes.' So, the doctor put the needle down. Meanwhile the nurse was saying, 'But she *has* to have one.' But the doctor very willingly put it down. And the doctor also offered to have one of the monitors put on the baby's scalp because of how fast my labor was, and I refused. He says, 'You don't have to.' I said, 'I'd prefer not to.' I think the doctor felt, you know, we'll give it a couple more pushes and if the baby comes out, fine, and if I tore a little bit, no big deal. They were really cool. But I wasn't going to get so adversarial that I wouldn't let them do the best thing for my child."

As I nursed Cameron, who was falling into a gentle sleep, I was surprised by the courage of Marisa and her husband, especially in standing up to the doctor. It is very difficult to challenge society's so-called experts, especially when the experts band together in resistance (Giddens, 1992).

I sensed that Marisa was truly satisfied with her birthing experience. There didn't seem to be any regrets on her part. As if to confirm her own

experience, Kyle asked, "Did anything happen that disappointed you during the birth?" Marisa said that, actually, there was one thing about the
process that was disappointing. "When Elizabeth was born, they had to
whisk her away, which, you know, was kind of distressing. But because she
had been in some distress and the pace of the delivery was so stressful, they
wanted to check her out. So, you know, they just pulled her over there and
just kind of did their thing. I asked them, 'Please don't wipe all the vernix
off.'[4] But, when I got her she was pretty cleaned off. But then, we got to
snuggle for a good half hour right after that. So that was good."

Nancy explained that in hospitals nurses are supposed to do an immediate assessment of the baby to ensure its health. She explained that, unless
a woman has her baby in a birthing center or at home, there is no way to
ensure any significant bonding time for the family.[5] But Nancy was curious
whether Marisa would change anything if she decided to have another
baby. Marisa responded by saying, "There's nothing I would do differently. I guess my reasons for having Elizabeth naturally are stronger now
than before. What I mean is that through the classes and through my experience, I found that our bodies are designed to do something in a given
course of time if we just allow it. I want my body to do what it's supposed
to do. Unless, of course, you get to the point where the baby is in trouble;
then something else maybe needs to be done. And knowing this (gesturing
toward Elizabeth, who was asleep in her arms) is just the greatest gift in
the world. I knew that I wanted to have a natural childbirth and that we
wanted to make choices about it from start to finish. That's really what I
wanted."

When Marisa finished sharing her story, Nancy served a light lunch.
She couldn't resist reminding us to keep drinking lots of water as long as
we were nursing. Nancy is also a supporter of La Leche League, an advocacy organization supporting women who breast-feed. She talked for a
while about the importance of healthy eating during breast-feeding. We all
happily ate and talked about our recoveries and how long it took us to get
used to nursing.

I wondered if we were making too much of our births. I had the fleeting thought that if the *outcome* was okay, then the *process* wasn't all that
important, that if our babies were healthy and whole, why should we pay
so much attention to the labor and delivery part of it? Part of me fears that
natural childbirth may become another challenge women have to meet to
prove something to themselves and to others. My own reasons for choosing to birth naturally had to do with what happened to me during the birth
of my first son, Tyler. My labor began intensely. The contractions were
severe from the get-go. The nurse offered me a narcotic drug, which only

made me feel sleepy. Then, as the contractions worsened, I was too out of it to cope so I agreed to an epidural,[6] which also meant that I received pitocin.[7] After I had pushed for 2 hours, the baby still was not positioned properly to be delivered vaginally, and I wound up with a C-section—something I desperately wanted to avoid. I was determined to not have any of that happen to me again.

Nancy had encouraged us to consider having a home birth or delivering at a birthing center where, she claimed, we would be more likely to have a natural childbirth. "By being in the hospital," she said, "you won't be as able to tune in to your inner selves. You'll get too concerned with your outer selves, on defense, like an animal. In natural childbirth, the child and the mother are one. Anesthesia blocks the mother's experience, her transformation to motherhood. It's absolutely essential to go through and to feel that process. But we block our relationship. And yet mothers keep on using anesthesia because they don't have a consciousness that natural childbirth works, that they are well designed to do this." My insurance system didn't offer me the opportunity to use a birthing center, and I felt too uncertain about a home birth.

What Nancy said is what many feminist authors have written about birth, which is that women have been duped into believing that pregnancy and birth are about being sick (Arms, 1994; Martin, 1992; Rothman, 1982). And when we are sick, there is a need to be treated by a care provider. It is only when we view birth as a *natural* part of life that we can fully participate in life and not fear it.

Despite tremendous obstacles, Kyle managed to have a natural birth. Nothing, however, could have prepared us for Kyle's story.

Kyle's Birthing Tale

"My labor and delivery story is more like a nightmare. Even though we are so happy to have Jessica, we came close to filing a lawsuit over our experience. Our nurse—'Nurse Ratchet,' we called her. Well, that's not her *real* name! She had to be in control. And she came in and the first thing she wanted to do was give me drugs. Well, I told her, 'No, I'm going to do natural childbirth.' And she said, 'Well, you know that if you don't take them now'—'cause I was 8 centimeters—'you won't be able to have them.' And I have to say that even this woman's tone of voice was objectionable from the beginning."

"Then I said, 'This monitor is really uncomfortable, can't we remove it?' And she goes, 'Well, no.' So I said, 'Well, what about our birth plan?' And she storms out, and she comes back in, and I said something else about the monitor, and she is going on about how I can't take it off. And, finally, I said, 'You know what? My mother had four children without a monitor and I think I can probably do the same thing. And besides, you just told me it was picking up *my* heartbeat instead of the baby's.' So, she stormed out."

I recalled one night when Nancy talked about how nurses are really at the mercy of the physicians who give them their orders. That's why the physician's attitude toward natural birth is so important, especially for women who want natural childbirth in a hospital. As a former nurse, Nancy knew quite well the attitude nurses held about natural birthers. She said, "When someone who wanted to have natural childbirth came in, all the nurses went: 'Who's gonna take 'em?' Cause they're the people who are gonna cause trouble. 'If I can't give you an epidural, if I can't monitor the baby continuously, then what is my job?' And then there's the baby. 'If I can't put eye drops in the eyes, do an assessment, how can I be paid $25 an hour?' Y'know, the reality is that when nurses work under physicians in the hospital they are disempowered. They make very few decisions without 'doctor's orders.' They don't get power where they come from so they get it from the patient. So when I can tell *you* how to have your baby, I can have power in a system that doesn't give me any power." When Nancy said this, I originally thought it was a bit extreme. But Kyle's experience seemed to support what Nancy had been saying.

"Then the doctor gets there. And we thought, well, at least we know *him*. And we thought our *nurse* had an attitude! The doctor made her look like a saint. He came in and checked me and said I could start pushing. And—remember the videotape we watched where they showed the husbands sitting behind the wives during labor while they were pushing? Well, Sam starts to get behind me on the bed—and the nurse looks at me and goes, 'What are you doing? You can't do that. The germs.' And so I go, 'He's going to hold my legs for me.' I mean, I could have had a bowel movement, and she's worried about him sitting behind me? And so I looked at her and I said, 'Go get me another nurse.' Well, the doctor comes in a couple minutes later and says, 'You can't do that here. You can't just ask for another nurse. There aren't a bunch of nurses running around here.' He's yelling at me for asking for another nurse. Here I am—ready to deliver—and they're yelling at me. And Sam gets up and approaches the doctor. And so the doctor goes, 'Step back or I'll have you thrown out of here.'" Marisa gasped. We all looked at Kyle in amazement. Kyle said, "All of this is true, I swear! And Sam says, 'I don't really appreciate your holier-than-thou, God-like attitude.' So, they all left the room. Now, I'm in the room by myself. And I'm pushing. And this doctor's yelling at Sam, and then I hear the doctor say, 'I'll just have you thrown out of the hospital. I'll call security.' Then Sam came back in and they left us alone for 45 minutes. Then we got a new nurse. And then the doctor came back in. And he is still trying to pick a fight with Sam while he's delivering the baby."

I was incredulous. The complete lack of comprehension about the connection between the mother's mind, emotions, and body by the care providers was astonishing to me. When the philosophy of the hospital was threatened, all concern for the patient went out the window. Emily Martin (1992) says that

> we are still a long way from seeing quintessentially female functions as acts women *do* with body, mind, and emotional states working together or at least affecting one another. The day has not come when instead of speaking of . . . "nonprogressive labor" that has to be treated by chemical or operative intervention, we will say that "the woman has stopped her contractions" and focus on alleviating the fear and anxiety which have probably, in the majority of cases, led her to do so. (p. 89)

None of us knew what to say to Kyle. Even Nancy didn't have a whole lot to say about Kyle and Sam's experience. Although Nancy had acknowledged that many physicians are opposed to natural childbirth, much of our course focused on building good rapport with the obstetrician, who was chosen based on his or her support of natural birthing. Since Kyle's doctor knew she wanted a natural birth, his behavior didn't make any sense. Marisa asked Nancy if she had ever heard of anything like this happening before, to which Nancy replied, "It sometimes is the case that the couples I work with have some pretty significant conflict with their care providers—especially when there hasn't been explicit communication with them about what they want. This is why the birth plan is so important. Although a birth plan isn't a legal document, it is a contract between the obstetrician and the birthing couple that lists those things the couple do and do not want for the delivery. It spells out precisely what the couple is trying to do. But, as I told all of you, the birth plan must be discussed with the physician well in advance of the delivery. I do think the conflict arises in the difference between a typical hospital birth and what the couple is requesting. The farther apart those two things are, the more conflict." Turning to Kyle, Nancy said, "I am so sorry, Kyle. It sounds like your birth was a letdown in many ways."

"It's all right," Kyle responded. "We have actually been able to laugh about our experience. We decided not to file charges against the physician because we want to spend our time with Jesse, not in court fighting these people. But, in spite of all the turmoil, we were able to have a natural childbirth."

We were reeling from Kyle's story. It seemed like something out of a movie. I couldn't believe the drama in these stories. There was a surreal sense in being with these women—these mothers—who just a few weeks ago were pregnant women. Through their transformation into motherhood, they seemed much wiser now. But it was now my turn to share my experience. I looked at Nancy, then I looked at Cameron. And I told my story.

My Birthing Tale

"My story has a little bit of everyone's story in it. I labored for about 5 hours and pushed for about 2½ hours. But I have to say that I'm a bit embarrassed by what happened to me. While I labored all that time without any drugs—and, by the way, Marisa, the visualization of floating on the water really worked for me; when the waves broke, my contraction broke and it gave me the optimism I needed to get through each one. But I nearly broke John's fingers during each contraction." I turned to Nancy and smiled. "I know, Nancy, even my *fingers* should have been relaxed, but I needed to convey to someone how much pain I was feeling, and that was my way of sharing my experience with John." Everyone laughed.

"Anyway, as I labored, I didn't want to move from my position. I was completely comfortable lying on my right side. In fact, I was reluctant to change positions once my hard labor began."

Nancy interrupted, "Why? What were you concerned about?"

"I'm not really sure," I said. "I think I was afraid that in another position it would hurt much worse than it did. I felt like everything was working and I didn't want to mess with that."

Nancy said, "That's one of those things that you can figure out only in the moment of labor—only you know how you feel, only you know what's happening with your body. That's why natural childbirth works—you can feel what is happening to your body and what it's doing to help you get your baby out."

I said, "But I couldn't push very well, even though I didn't use anesthesia. You know, when the nurse said that I was completely dilated and that it was time to push, I couldn't believe it. In everything I've read and in class, Nancy, you talked about how we would *know* when it was time to push—that the urge would be undeniably strong. But I never got the urge to push. I pushed anyway. But my pushing wasn't effective. My doctor showed up shortly after I began pushing and was there for about 2½ hours. My eyes were closed almost the entire time I labored—even during pushing. With each pushing contraction, everyone in the room was yelling 'push,' including the doctor, John, and the nurse, who had just finished smoking a cigarette, which made me somewhat nauseous. But I remember opening my eyes at one point and looking at my doctor and he was just sort of staring at the wall, almost dazed. Since it was around 5 o'clock, I knew that he would have rather been asleep than waiting for me to push my baby out."

"I decided that I wasn't going to be able to push Cameron out when I saw my doctor shake his head after one of my contractions. He said we had a couple of options: we could use the vacuum extractor[8] or forceps.[9] I feared the use of forceps because of their link to infant death and disability. So we tried the vacuum. But Cameron was still pretty high up in the birth canal, which caused the vacuum to pop off his head. Finally, the doctor said that the vacuum was not going to work and that we would need to try forceps. At that point, I just wanted it to be over. My doctor said that it would be extremely painful to use forceps without anesthesia. So, I agreed to a Sufenta spinal, which is a shot in the spine that numbs you from the waist to the knees. When Cameron was born, he had a broken collarbone. So, like Marisa, I watched as they whisked my baby off to the nursery. He had to stay in the infant intensive care unit for 3 days. But, for me, the worst part about it was that I think I could have avoided all of this if someone would have just said, 'Before we try the Sufenta spinal, just try getting up out of bed and letting gravity work with you.' I keep thinking that if I'd just gotten up out of bed, I would have pushed Cameron out, without him being harmed by the forceps."

Nancy was upset about my feelings about keeping the doctor awake. She said that the reason she recommends that women try a home birth is so that they can labor according to *their* own schedule. She said, "With a home birth, what would happen if a woman didn't get the urge to push? She would eventually get the urge to push and she would push her baby out. But, physicians don't come to *manage* the labor, they come to catch the baby—if it happens to come out. But when they arrive to *catch* the baby, then something's supposed to happen. Right? And if it doesn't, then that's when intervention happens. It's a mindset of 'Hey, I'm here and you're not completely dilated. What are you doing, honey?' It's a matter of 'It's 12 o'clock, completely dilated. One o'clock completely dilated—the head's in the same place. 'Oh! she hasn't had the urge to push! Well, get the baby out. The doctor's here.' What happened to Cameron probably could have been avoided if you had had the time to wait until you got the urge to push properly. Cameron was probably in the process of turning so that he could be delivered."

"But *my* sadness," I said to Nancy, "in addition to Cameron's injury, is that my body didn't do what it was supposed to do." Nancy said that no one knows whether my body would have done that whether I'd been at home or not. She continued, "I just tell women who want a natural childbirth in a hospital to realize that where you are going isn't set up for what you want to do. See, if you're lying around your own home, or soaking in your own bathtub, then you're going to get a lot more oxygen to your body than if you're in a foreign place. Part of natural childbirth is taking responsibility for your own body. It's knowing that '*I* am going to do it. Someone else is not going to do it for me.' Therefore, the whole body experience changes."

Nancy asked me what surprised me the most about my labor and delivery. After thinking about it, I answered, "I have to say that my ability to work through the contractions was most surprising to me. I have a pretty good tolerance for pain. But I never dreamed that I would have been able to labor like that for so long without anesthesia. It was painful. But it wasn't unbearable." Nancy then spoke about pain, saying, "The whole belief that the pain is bad and at all costs to be avoided is, I think, detrimental to women. People often ask me: 'Why would you choose to experience pain in labor when you could avoid it?' and it's because I don't feel that pain is necessarily a bad thing and that you come out stronger in the end having gone through it. The tragedy is that women believe they can't do something they are designed to do."

Nancy said that however we birthed, our babies were beautiful and we should be proud that we attempted to do what we thought was best for them. She said that there's an emotional healing that takes place after the birth and that if a woman is at peace with it all she definitely heals faster and she's ready to go on. She said that having a reunion was an important exercise in that healing process.

Conclusion

Pregnancy and the related processes of labor, delivery, and recovery are a large part of women's *social* lives. The transforming effects of motherhood affect every part of a woman's identity in the sense that women view their bodies, their social roles, and their overall purpose differently after having given birth to a child (Gates, 1995). The current structures of medicine, so the argument goes, are not welcoming to women's social, spiritual, emotional, or psychological needs. Todd (1989) wryly claims that:

> Women go to their doctors today in the wake of the women's movement and the so-called sexual revolution to seek help with their sexuality as well as with the explosive decisions of whether or not to have babies. Women run up against a medical system that is not organized around these questions but instead focuses on the technical and the diseased to the exclusion of the social context and on the individual to the exclusion of the familial or interactive. (pp. 5–6)

Indeed, most physicians view pregnancy as a medical condition that requires managing, leading them to give fluids intravenously, to regularly use electronic fetal monitors, and to do routine episiotomies.

Despite the dominance of the medical model in childbirth, the midwifery model is currently being practiced through many natural childbirth methods. The model embraces the physiological, emotional, and spiritual changes associated with pregnancy, labor, delivery, and breast-feeding. The midwifery model views women as "inherently strong, courageous, and competent in birth. This view is different from that of the mainstream because it does not focus on pain, fear, and suffering, and does not cause women to think of themselves as helpless or as victims of a faulty process" (Arms, 1994, p. 26). The midwife's role is to be a noninterventionist and to identify problems when they occur so that the woman can be referred to a specialist if necessary.

The women's health revival in the feminist movement can lead us to view the issue of natural childbirth in a new light. Specifically, it focuses our attention on three issues. First, it calls women to be more responsible for their health care choices. Second, it means that women need a better understanding of their options in childbirth through education. Finally, it calls for ideological changes within medical institutions to allow for multiple interpretations and enactments of the birth experience (Gates, 1995). Indeed, it calls into question the competing structures and counterclaims women must reckon with in the process of birth.

There is a dichotomy in operation. On the one hand, women can adopt a contemporary method of birth—a method grounded in science, technology, patriarchy, and institutions (called the "technocratic model of birth" by Davis-Floyd, 1994). On the other hand, women can choose a more painful approach but one that honors nature and women's strength. Unfortunately, there is little room in today's existing practices for negotiating something in-between. We can hope that the voices of the courageous women who defy the contemporary medical model of birth by choosing natural childbirth will be heard and a negotiation between both birthing worlds can begin.

Discussion Questions

1. What was your opinion about natural childbirth before reading this essay? How are women who give birth naturally viewed by others (e.g., friends, family, care providers)? Why are they perceived that way? Has your opinion changed?

2. What are the mechanisms that silence the voices of women who choose natural childbirth, and how are they similar to/different from those that silence women who experience miscarriage?

3. What are the barriers preventing women from achieving natural childbirth?

4. What can be done to begin to open up a space for women's ability to choose their birthing approach without condemnation?

5. Women who choose natural childbirth seem to operate "underground." How can we begin to move the dialogue about birth out in the open?

6. What are the advantages and/or disadvantages of viewing birth as an opportunity for growth, connection, and self-determination?

References

Arms, S. (1994). *Immaculate deception II: A fresh look at childbirth*. Berkeley, CA: Celestial Arts.

Davis-Floyd, R. E. (1994). The technocratic body: American childbirth as cultural expression. *Social Science and Medicine, 38*, 1125–1140.

Gates, L. R. (1995). *Reproducing selves: Contradiction, control, and identity in natural childbirth*. Unpublished doctoral dissertation. University of Southern California, Los Angeles.

Giddens, A. (1992). *Modernity and self-identity: Self and society in the late modern age*. Stanford, CA: Stanford University Press.

Martin, E. (1992). *The woman in the body: A cultural analysis of reproduction*. Boston: Beacon Press.

Rothman, B. K. (1982). *In labor: Women and power in the birthplace*. New York: Norton.

Rothman, B. K. (1989). *Recreating motherhood: Ideology and technology in a patriarchal society*. New York: Norton.

Todd, A. D. (1989). *Intimate adversaries: Cultural conflict between doctors and women patients.* Philadelphia: University of Pennsylvania Press.

Endnotes

1. The Bradley method of birthing supports women's ability to birth without the use of narcotics, anesthesia, or any unnecessary medical procedures. It advocates relaxation, education, and exercise as ways of managing the process of pregnancy and childbirth.

2. An episiotomy is an incision made between the vagina and the anus to open the birth canal for the delivery of a baby.

3. A pressure episiotomy is used to avoid an injection that numbs a woman's vaginal area, or perineum, before the incision is made. When the baby's head is about to emerge, there is a natural numbing effect on the vaginal area so the incision cannot be felt.

4. Vernix, also called vernix caseosa, is the white, lotionlike coating covering babies at birth.

5. Birthing centers seek to create a homelike environment, encourage natural childbirth, minimize the likelihood of medical intervention, and use nurse-midwives to deliver babies.

6. Epidural anesthesia is frequently used in hospitals as a method of pain relief for women in labor. It is administered by injecting a numbing drug into the lower back through a tube, which is left in place so that more anesthesia can be given.

7. Pitocin is a hormone therapy used to cause the uterus to contract with greater regularity and vigor.

8. A vacuum extractor is a device that attaches to the baby's scalp through the use of suction and facilitates the delivery of a baby.

9. A forceps is a spoonlike instrument that is positioned around the baby's head to facilitate delivery. It is criticized for causing injuries to the head and brain.

12

Mobilizing Motherhood

Women's Experiences of Visiting Their Children

Deborah L. Eicher-Catt, Ph.D.

Department of Communication
West Chester University

Homecoming

You can never go back home.
Witty, wise and vacuous platitude
Stimulating heads to nod
Rationalizing discomfort
As we search backwards
For the peace inwards—

Why do we always think
We had it
"Back then"
Like a memory from another lifetime
Or perhaps from before life
We seek the past in our present
Recreating nothing
We can never go back home
Because home is not back.
With years we are given clues
Of that which fulfills
Yearnings
Emptiness
Glimpses
Why do we think it's something
New?
Maybe they're really just signs
Not that we've lost anything
But that we're ready to find something
Ready to move forward
Ready to go home
For the first time.

  —María Cristina González

I remember the exact moment this project was born. *I was sitting at a truck stop somewhere in middle America sipping on some hot coffee after spending yet another long day in the car. I was en route to California to see my two young sons, who were temporarily living with their dad. Although I silently continued to declare myself their mother, I looked across the counter into the mirror behind. My sole reflection made me take pause and question the irony my silent declaration revealed. How could I continue to call myself their mother when we were reduced to sharing time in a "visit," a communicative practice typically framed by its brevity and limited shared space and, what is more important, a practice that is primarily reserved for less intimate relationships? A consolatory thought crossed my mind. I must not be alone in what appeared to be a desperately lonely and ambiguous circumstance known as noncustodial motherhood. Contradicting my prior tendencies to bury the reality of my status (thus not giving "voice" to my experience), upon my return to the Midwest I embarked on a journey to explore this new practice of motherhood. I decided it was time to give voice to this changing situation in many women's lives. I placed an advertisement in a local newspaper asking other noncustodial mothers to contact me. It did not take long to create a chorus of women's voices that reverberated mostly confusion and hardship. As difficult as many of the interviews were as women repeatedly told of their painful struggle to mother, I believe the dialogue we shared helped us all immensely. Through our dialogue we have begun to understand that, although the normative parameters of motherhood appear rigid, we have begun to understand that mobilizing the discourse is a necessary step in our attempts to re-construct what being a mother means.*

As I begin this writing, it is my youngest son's 9th birthday and he is 2,500 miles away, as usual. Although I will reach him by telephone to wish him a happy birthday, I cannot see his elated face when he unwraps my gifts. Our situation is not an easy one to bare. He and his older brother temporarily live with my ex-husband. I am designated the "noncustodial parent." I am able to visit my sons on holidays and during some portion of their summer vacation. Being noncustodial essentially means that I am no longer the primary caregiver on a daily basis, nor am I the final authority regarding the general welfare of my children. Every day I ask myself how can I call myself a mother under these circumstances. The following dialogues with other noncustodial mothers like myself begin to address this essential question.

Disclosing the Experience of Noncustodial Mothering

Many women throughout America are reluctantly finding themselves in the situation of being unable to continue to assume the role of primary care provider for their children as a result of divorce and/or financial instability. The numbers are, indeed, growing.[1] Traditionally, women were granted primary custody of the children in cases of divorce, but this is rapidly changing. Courts are now awarding physical and legal custody to the parent who, regardless of sex, is better able to provide for the children. As evidenced by statistics compiled during a 10-year period in California, fathers' success rates in winning custody increased from 33% to 63% (Greif & Pabst, 1988). Not unlike the challenges posed by America's adaptation to modern life, the current social and cultural trends are making the institutions of motherhood and fatherhood problematic as both men and women are finding themselves in new positions as custodial or noncustodial parents.[2]

Unfortunately, when a woman is a noncustodial mother, *all* her experiences with her children are constrained within the structure of the occasioned "visit." A telephone call, a letter in the mail, and spending a day together are all forms visitation can take. However, no matter the form the visit assumes, the structure of the visit also structures the experience of mothering. Visits, after all, are "fleeting moments" in which we attempt to bridge the gap between times shared together in the past and future times that will be spent apart.

In my case, the hardest aspect of this situation is that the children and I go for months at a time without seeing one another. As the time between visits elapses, the experience for me takes on an almost ineffable quality. The traditional images of what it means to be a "mother" are ghosts that haunt my mind. The uneasiness of past assumptions and future expectations continually undermines my efforts to *move forward* in creating a new definition of what it means to mother. Motherhood speaks to me like a worn tape recording continually reminding me that "mothers are not supposed to visit their children—they live with them and tuck them into bed every night."

In exploring the issue of noncustody I do not assume that fathers who are noncustodial do not experience similar pangs of guilt and pain at being separated on a regular basis from their children. However, the traditional social role expectations of fatherhood permit fathers more latitude in fulfilling the noncustodial role. The everyday care and nurturance of children is not typically designated a father's sole responsibility. A woman, on the other hand, may not only suffer emotional distress similar to that fathers feel at being separated from their children, but they must reckon with their perceived status as "deviant" because they are not adhering to the role expectations of traditional motherhood.[3] In essence, noncustodial mothers' distress is compounded by institutional pressures and experiential conditions.[4]

What was clear to me from the beginning was the overriding sense of paradox that I faced every time I attempted to mother under the constraints of visitation. To explore this experience, I placed an advertisement in a local newspaper asking to speak to other women who were no longer living on a regular basis with their young children. Although I had decided it was time to research this issue, I knew publishing the announcement would erase the privacy of my own experience and status. I did not have much time to confront my uneasiness about this, however. Prompt responses were simultaneously comforting and disarming.

All the women with whom I spoke appeared eager to share their stories of noncustody. Our narratives provided us with a valuable tool with which to process and "make sense" of our unique circumstances. Our narratives revealed our personal accounts of noncustody as well as intricate, yet common, social and cultural systems of values, attitudes, and beliefs concerning the topic of mothering.[5] Every woman with whom I spoke voiced her heretofore repressed thoughts, fears, and anguish with me.[6] As they continued to speak to me over the course of several years, we coproduced rich descriptions of personal experiences. I found common threads of experience interwoven throughout these women's lives.[7] These reveal their struggle to "mobilize" motherhood by continuing to transform its meaning while simultaneously caring for their children.

Mothers' Essential Dispositions

As noncustodial mothers, we experience an overwhelming sense of remorse or depression as remembrances of regularly being with our children impinge upon a present existence that appears disjointed. Whether our status as noncustodial is voluntary or not, there is much pain and anguish as we try to adjust to daily life without our children. One mother I interviewed attempted suicide on two separate occasions. She was unsuccessful, in telephone conversations with her children, at reestablishing the depth of closeness she desired. During our initial interview, Elaine asked me, "Is this going to hurt forever? I just kind of wonder sometimes when things are going to be better because I don't feel like a mother anymore." She continued:

> The first four times that we visited, I was constantly in tears. I was real short with them [the children] generally because I didn't have any patience. They would cry when they had to leave, and I would be saying, "I'm sorry but you've got to leave. You've got to go home with dad. . . ." I should have been strong enough to not constantly be in tears.

Elaine's experience with her children is not atypical. Especially for mothers who have recently acquired the ambiguous status of noncustody, the ability to monitor emotional outbursts is quite difficult. The sight of the "familiar other" (in the case of either parent or child) in "unfamiliar" circumstances triggers unsettled emotions for all involved. As Jane (a noncustodial mother of two years) related, amidst tears of pain:

> It was awful. The kids would call on the phone, and I remember my son calling and saying, "Mommy, please come home . . . the house is so empty." They [would come to visit] and I can just remember the first few times seeing them sitting on the floor and crying and hugging each other and not wanting to leave and me telling them that it was best for them to go home.

The realization that family life is changing hits us like a ton of bricks and shatters our worlds. Our functions in our children's lives are suddenly called into question, and we find ourselves scrambling to reconstruct parameters that can assist us in developing a sense of relatedness with our children.

Elizabeth (a noncustodial mother of 2 years) feels emotional pain most intensely when preparing her children for bed. She describes some of their regular visits as "devastating." In her words: "It would get really hard to hold them, rock them, and sing to them, put them to sleep. Then I would walk out of the room . . . break down and sob. I didn't think my heart could break that many times." In such cases, it is the memory of past contentment that intrudes upon the ambiguous present.

Dealing with this emotional pain produces a "restless" state of mind for many women before, during, and after visitation. Impending visitation can create excitement, apprehension, and anxiety. A noncustodial mother for 4 years, Yvonne likens her emotional state of mind in preparing for her visits with her daughter, Dawn, to how she might feel if she had a date with Prince Charming. "I figure out what I am going to wear. My heart races. My palms sweat. I feel like I am going to cry and shake all over. Ya know, how you do when you are going to go out with somebody real fine! The exhilaration is incredible."

Whatever sense of excitement or apprehension we might have been feeling before the visit gives way to a sense of awkwardness at our initial point of contact with our children. Sometimes we feel the need to *act*—i.e., perform—in a particular way that may be contrary to what we are really feeling. Yvonne explains:

> Then, the second I see her, it's really weird. Because I would think that I would like smother her . . . want to kiss her . . . hold her. . . . But, I guess I act just like you would with Prince Charming. You try to act ordinary! If you smothered him with kisses and said you're so happy, you're so gorgeous, you're everything I ever dreamed of . . . he'd be running away before 5 seconds had gone by!

Obviously, the tenuous circumstances under which we are attempting to mother threaten us. We realize the precariousness of our new positions and we are often intimidated. In her 6 years of experience as noncustodial, Laura indicates that these initial greetings still exude an awkwardness that makes the point of contact uncomfortable for both her and her children. She attributes this awkwardness to the children's temporary confusion about parental loyalty. Because Laura's relationship with her ex-husband is strained, the children have, unfortunately, been privy to nasty confrontations between them:

> When I go to pick up the children, there is always a lack of freedom of expression because they are not used to the feeling that I really missed them. Their father had put in their minds that "your mother gave you up . . . she doesn't love you. . . ." But once we are away from the house . . . they also have the issue of loyalty. They try their best to keep peace between both places. . . . And once we are away from the house . . . they are no longer like strangers.

Visitation time itself is often chaotic, contributing to mothers' overall feelings of restlessness and anxiety. Because the boundaries and patterns of normal relating have been broken, the visits are often devoted to renegotiating interpersonal boundaries. Although mothers want to give to each child individually what the child needs, the brevity of the visit often produces only fragmented interactions. Children often argue over who gets to sleep in "mother's room" during visitation, highlighting their need to remain physically close. Or, upon reuniting, children will scramble to get their fair share of needed reassurance in the way of affection. Elaine has a

45-mile drive once she picks up her children from her ex-husband's house. She describes the car ride back to her house as usually chaotic because the children all talk at once, wanting to share school stories or stories of how their father has angered them recently. She tries to make them take turns communicating with her so she can hear each one and respond accordingly, but often, she indicates, that is easier said than done.

Diane told me that during many of her visits in her 10-year experience as a noncustodial mother, she felt anxious and tense. "There was joy in being with them," she said. "There was love, there was harmony, and yet there was discord because they needed discipline, but I didn't know how to go about it. I had not established a pattern of what to do when they misbehaved." Because the visits were often intense, Diane admitted that "sometimes . . . the visit was kind of a letdown. Oh my word, sometimes I almost couldn't wait to take them home because it was very intense." Diane's reactions to visitation are not uncommon. In Laura's case, witnessing her children exhibiting unacceptable social behaviors that typically are overlooked in their everyday lives creates much stress, tension, and disruption during visitation. As Laura explained, "I had doors knocked down . . . dishes broken . . . smart talk, and really disrespectable things." Sometimes her frustration

> would reach the point that I don't want to see them anymore!!! I would reach the point of thinking, "Oh my God, they are coming this weekend . . . 3 days . . . oh, no!!" I got rid of this life, this sick thinking . . . of this sick cycle . . . and now I have it every other weekend in my house with my kids.

Although Ann has only one 4-year-old daughter, her visits with Sara also exhibit similar signs of disorder. Ann's visits typically take the form of unstructured activities due to the inherent chaotic life-style she lives. A noncustodial mother for 3 years, Ann does not currently have her own home and thus carries her belongings in a suitcase wherever she goes. At the time of our interview, she was temporarily staying in town with friends. Visits with her daughter require flexibility, she explains, in how they are structured. "We use the time together to go swinging and sliding at the local park, or to go to the grocery store or mall. We bake cookies and play 'dress up.'" Because Ann does not have a place of her own, holiday celebrations, such as Christmas, pose special problems in this regard. She related:

> I don't have a place to go for Christmas . . . I am going to buy her [Sara] presents and take her someplace. Last year we went to the university stu-

dent center. They have a tree there . . . plenty of sofas . . . whenever they were open . . . there was no one around . . . we'd play on the sofas. I won't see her on Christmas. We'll invent our Christmas day. . . . We'll go somewhere and celebrate Christmas and take pictures.

Jane appears to have made some inroads in counteracting the often disordered nature of visitation. Her success is due in part to the regularity with which she has been able to negotiate both the time and the space she spends with her two children. As she indicated:

They came Friday nights and we went out for dinner and rented a movie. We maintained a sense of continuity. We would go to the market, get pastries on Saturdays, come back, and have breakfast. We would have a day planned. Because I didn't drive, I had to have a plan. We kind of did the same things. We'd have a rhythm. We'd go to the library, go to the Goodwill store, to the Christian bookstore, rent a movie, or visit friends.

Because of the uniqueness of the visitation experience, it becomes especially difficult for mothers to settle down emotionally afterward. It is difficult to make the immediate transition from the idea of "mother with children" to the reality of "mother without children." It is troublesome to resume our "child-free" everyday lives and the behaviors that are necessary to remain productive and contented. Often, the restlessness after visits is the result of experiencing a slight "glimmer of normalcy" or sense of settledness during the visits. As Elaine related:

It almost isn't fair to almost get it . . . that feeling of settledness . . . then it's gone and you have to start all over again. So, it's a battle. You try to get as much as possible out of it, but it leaves you wondering a lot. There are a lot of times that I feel that maybe I should wait until I can see them for a longer period of time. But the kids need consistency. Even if our visits aren't everything that my expectations say that they should be, I think my kids get something from them . . . even if it is pretty wild for them. . . . I can't believe how much it hurts.

Besides the feelings of pain, depression, and anxiety, noncustodial mothers also experience their share of loneliness. Many mothers told of instances such as socials where "typical" families are gathered, when it is especially difficult to interact. Mothers experience their unique status as "mother, yet not mother" poignantly during these occasions. Most often the result is a stark realization of their loss, and they are left feeling lonely. Ann feels this sense of loss most intensely when she is in church.

I feel least like a mother when family relationships are being talked about or when you are to bring your family. Who am I going to bring? Sara is 3 or 4 hours away. This situation feels like you are all alone . . . like someone has taken something from you and it's hidden. It's hiding from you. Mother's Day . . . that really kills me. I really miss her on Mother's Day because they [the congregation] ask all the mothers to stand, and I don't have a kid by me.

As we begin to see, the comments or responses we receive during our visits and in everyday circumstances affirm an ambiguity that lies at the heart of being a "mother, yet not mother." Our unique status separates us as social actors, and we struggle to improvise new parts. The standard of traditional motherhood that specifies stability in our relationships with our children looms large in our consciousness as we unsuccessfully struggle to reenact its mandate. We are continually "shrouded" by standards of motherhood that functioned in our past but that no longer match our current situations. At an experiential level, then, our status as noncustodial manifests in unsettling states of corporeality.

All the above threads of common experience (pain, anxiety, restlessness, and loneliness) are examples of what we typically identify as moods. Existential philosopher Martin Heidegger (1962) considers mood (disposition) as one of two important correlating dimensions that comprise an existential structure he identifies as "care." For Heidegger, care is not limited to a physical or emotional concern for self and/or others. Instead, he sees care as the essential way (experienced temporally) that we engage with the world as we strive to make sense of our experiences.[8] He thought that mood reflects a predisposition to the world that arises from our preexistent urges and/or drives as bodily subjects. Moods disclose these states of mind derived from circumstances experienced in the *past* that are continuing to impose upon or influence the present.

It is not surprising that these moods reveal how the past continues negatively to influence our current sense of self as mothers. Being noncustodial predisposes us to a negativity that appears in a number of forms. These negative evaluations of self by self and others "throw" us into an ambiguity that produces more anxiety about our situations. Our emotional struggle seems to be activated by our personal desire to somehow "preserve" a semblance of our past associations with our children, to not lose whatever bond we previously had established. This response of "preservation" reflects an aspect of what feminist theorist Sara Ruddick (1980) identifies as "maternal thinking." According to Ruddick, maternal practices are motivated by an overarching concept of "attending" or the virtue of "love."[9] Heidegger's concept of "care" and Ruddick's concept of "attending" bear resemblance. As we see, both care and attention inform our understanding of noncustodial mothers' experiences. The influence of the past and this interest in preservation appear to motivate our current maternal, yet noncustodial practices.

The theme of preservation also figures prominently as mothers become hard-pressed to maintain some semblance of mother-child bonding. Tokens and/or snapshots of one another take on special significance. Ann tells us about her experience with Sara:

> We take pictures . . . that's how we really have fun. I take pictures of her doing all these crazy things. That's what keeps her remembering things. It helps me remember, and it gives her a fun time. She likes looking at these pictures.

As Ann indicated to me later, these snapshots, along with small souvenirs of her visits with Sara, are safely stored in her suitcase and accompany her wherever she goes. Elizabeth has her son's photos on her key chain. Jane and her daughter have created "memory boxes" filled with exchanged notes, letters, photos, and mementos of times spent together. Mothers nurture these memories with their children because, for the most part, they are the only constant "image" they have of themselves as mothers.

Making Sense of an Ambiguous Situation

One of the strongest threads of experience that I saw woven into noncustodial motherhood was that these mothers lack what philosopher Alfred Schutz (1967) would identify as "recipe knowledge" in structuring their interactions as mothers. We apparently lack a sufficient understanding of how to be noncustodial mothers and to relate to our children under the constraints of these new conditions. Although we may "project" ourselves into the future when visualizing and anticipating upcoming visits, these projections often enhance a generalized state of anxiety that accompanies visitation. This state of anxiety is prompted by past role expectations and norms that we no longer can meet or correctly enact.

As Carol describes it, she learned early on in this experience that attempts to continue to enact the typical role of mother only result in failure, a negativity that only adds to a mother's already lowered self-assessment. Carol's 10-year status as noncustodial adds credence to her insight. To cope with the inherent deficiency, Carol attempts to remain focused on continuing a relationship with her son, Jeremy, in whatever form that might take, rather than on enacting a specified role or function. Alternately, she serves as a confidant, a teacher, a friend, or an entertainer for Jeremy. This helps Carol remain focused in the present when she is with Jeremy. Carol has managed to practice the often difficult task of visualizing and creating an alternative family structure.

Many mothers like Carol find themselves appealing to other primary interpersonal roles for guidance in dealing with their children. We realize that we must adapt to our changing circumstances because the survival of our relationships with our children depends on it. Diane is convinced that the word *mother* locks us into a mind set that no longer serves us. She sees some advantages to her children now knowing her more as a *person* than a mother. Her children, over the years, have come to interact with her based upon her caring personhood rather than on her affiliation with the institution of motherhood. As Diane says, "The facade of being the perfect parent is broken down" under these circumstances. Instead, children "see you working through a failure, and I think that is the best teaching tool you can give your children." Yvonne agrees with Diane on this point. Yvonne sees disadvantages in assuming such a rigid role as dictated by traditional motherhood because women end up "playing roles instead of being themselves." Yvonne finds the enactment of her personhood with her daughter, Dawn, "wonderfully liberating." Dawn finds out who her mother really is as a person and as a woman.

Although some mothers have embraced their ambiguous situations and are attempting to adapt, it appears that we tend to remain hypnotized by aspects of our past associations with our children and the typical role we enacted. In varying degrees, we *resist the future* because it persistently evades any attempt to mold or predict it. In Elizabeth's case, the familiar past and the unpredictable future appear to collapse into a "26-hour burst" of interaction every other weekend that remains unrewarding. She is also restricted to a 15-minute window of time during the week in which she can telephone her sons. She calls from pay telephones, at shopping malls, or at grocery stores, attempting to take advantage of this limited opportunity. However, the brief conversations are often unfulfilling. They serve to remind Elizabeth of the "abnormal" conditions under which she is attempting to mother. When I asked if she feels better after the conversations, she replied with some insightful comments:

Not usually, no . . . I feel aborted. Like . . . "this moment of motherhood has been brought to you by" . . . and it's over, just like that, it's over. Someone pulled the plug, and that's it. You can't have a meaningful conversation. It's very short, brief. It also makes me feel like I'm not being a mother because I am not there to talk to them. [I wonder] what kind of mother does that make me? There is the traditional [mother] role and the "oh-what-have-I-gotten-myself-into?" role.

The "abortion" of traditional motherhood creates an extremely difficult situation for noncustodial mothers because the "oh-what-have-I-gotten-myself-into?" role questions our future status as mothers.

Appealing again to Heidegger's (1962) concept of "care" brings us to the correlating moment that he identifies as "understanding." Heidegger's concept of understanding describes our process of interpreting the world around us or how we assign meaning to our experiences. He postulates that in trying to achieve understanding we are always future oriented because we attempt to realize what is yet to be "known." Lacking a sufficient knowledge base from which to draw, we find it difficult to visualize and understand what the future of noncustodial motherhood will bring.

What we *do* understand is that our present situations with our children lack the power and authority they once possessed, however transparent those powers might have been. And this becomes a primary obstacle in envisioning new ways of mothering our children. Strictly enforced visitation schedules emphasize feelings of powerlessness and loss of control over our children's lives. Legally, Ann has visitation for the summer, but according to Ann's description, her ex-husband typically sets the rules about when she can and cannot see her daughter. Fearful of losing any or all visitation rights, Ann goes along to "make him [her ex-husband] happy" so "he can't hurt me." Wanting to play a significant role in her daughter's development, she finds the strength to cope with the difficult schedule. Ann states, "My ex-husband constantly informs her [Sara] of his superiority, and this depresses me. At times, I feel as if I must act like a superior being to have a visit free of . . . 'it's nobody important . . . just mommy'. . . type of introduction at the door."

Elizabeth feels "very powerless over helping my kids through problems because I have been so shut out as far as communication with them." If she accidentally meets her sons on a public outing, they are not allowed to speak to her. "It's a miserable experience," she explains. It becomes readily apparent that these circumstances, continued over a period of time, will necessarily foster a lower sense of self-esteem for mothers.

The lost power and authority also manifest as problems with disciplining the children. Either the children ascribe a "vacation" status to the visits and thereby present discipline challenges, or we are reluctant to spend precious visitation time "policing" our children's behavior when we would rather be having fun with them. Ruddick (1980) maintains that the "growth" of a child is of vital interest to a mother and governs maternal practices during typical enactments of "attention" and "love." It follows that our future-directed attempts to understand reflect our concern for the continued "growth" of the mother-child relationship. Mothers are attending to their changing patterns of being and relating in order to develop healthy futures with their children.

A Renewed Sense of Caring

We can see how the discourse of noncustodial life is structured according to both Ruddick's (1980) concept of "attention" and Heidegger's (1962) concept of "care." These threads of experience highlight the reciprocal relationship between the dimensions of mood and understanding as they pertain to the structure of care. Maternal interests of preservation and growth are ways of interpreting the development of our relationships with our children. Both mood and preservation necessarily focus our attention on the past as it becomes an unwelcome intruder upon our present unstable position as mothers. On the other hand, understanding and growth focus our attention on the future as we continue to envision ourselves as active, influential mothers. However disruptive noncustodial experiences may be, continuing to provide attention and care appears to be a guiding principle in the lives of the women with whom I spoke.

Equally important to our comprehension of what it means to visit our children is our capacity to be transparent to ourselves—i.e., to be self-reflexive, to be able to examine our thoughts and actions and to evaluate them critically. Without self-reflexivity, we cannot make sense of our experiences in the world.[10] These narratives exhibit a high degree of self-reflexivity as we struggle to grasp and reconcile the differences between the conventionality of motherhood represented to us by past socializations and the unconventionality of motherhood presented to us by our status as noncustodial mothers. Because the future offers us little in the way of prescriptive advice concerning how we might cope with this struggle of reconciliation, our present situation causes us to call into question both our identities as mothers and our functions as mothers.[11] Many mothers experience daily the negativity the term *noncustodial* implies. Although publicly we have historically been marginalized by a male-dominated society (O'Barr, Pope, & Wyer, 1990), this particular classification of women is now experiencing another form of "marginalized" existence, albeit on a private level. Our morality is often suspect as we are questioned about our commitment to and/or love for our children. Such negative societal evaluations oppress us to the degree that we continue to define ourselves in terms of traditional gender roles.

Again, Ruddick's (1980) concept of attention sheds some light. "Maternal thinking," she says, is also governed by our concerns with producing children that society will "appreciate" and accept. Not that we necessarily agree with the criteria upon which acceptability is established. As Ruddick insightfully points out, generally the standards for acceptability are established by the dominant, male patriarchal system. Noncustodial mothers are concerned that society "accept" or adapt to *our new ways* of mothering. And, we are continually attempting to accept ourselves while redefining the morality of motherhood. On a positive note, according to feminist Sandra Bartky (1990), the questioning of morality signals the very existence of a budding feminist consciousness. As she suggests, feminist consciousness entails a moral ambiguity as women learn new ways of being and relating without compromising beneficial elements of what it means to be a woman. An increased awareness of oppression, then, often fosters various degrees of behavioral uncertainty. Privately, we should take some comfort in the fact that we are beginning to make evaluative judgments about ourselves and our morality as we sort out the conflicting messages we receive concerning our mothering practices.[12] What kind of mothers are we? Are we bad mothers because we no longer tuck our children into bed every night? Are we good mothers because we made difficult choices regarding the welfare of our children? Jane indicated to me that her typical retort to accusations of her apparent neglect is, "Crucify me that I left my children in a four-bedroom home in the suburbs rather than taking them to a one-bedroom apartment!"

Unfortunately, our uncertain existence cannot be erased simply by incorporating a few words of advice from a "veteran" noncustodial mother. Every noncustodial mother's situation brings with it peculiar circumstances. Nor is it an ambiguous situation that we should necessarily seek to clarify too quickly. The uncertainty may be a necessary requirement in our process of mobilizing what it means to be a mother and in nurturing our relationships with our children. Just as a child is prevented from healthy growth and development by a strict mother or father who adheres to rigid definitions of acceptability, so too are we prevented from realizing and actualizing our new conceptualizations of motherhood by adhering exclusively to either conventional themes or unconventional categories. The consequence of vacillating between such definitive categories is that we can become "immobilized" on a number of different levels: psychologically, socially, and culturally. Examples of this abound. Mothers like Ann sit staring at a wall for several hours in the local YWCA, where they are temporarily sleeping as a result of shattered family traditions. Mothers like Diane are in and out of mental health wards and find it difficult to maintain decent-paying jobs. Mothers like Elizabeth shut themselves in their rooms for days at a time, unable to face their apparent failure as traditional mothers. Mothers like Elaine try to commit suicide. Mothers like Yvonne struggle to go through each day when cultural stereotypes of motherhood serve as poignant reminders. This psychological, social, and cultural "immobilization" is generated by our perceptions that we are somehow locked into a paradoxical category that simultaneously defines us as "mothers yet not mothers." This way of thinking does not serve us in our attempts to mobilize our definitions of motherhood by choosing new contexts of discursivity. We do see examples of employing new contexts of meaning in Diane's commitment to be a *person* to her children instead of a typical mother and in Carol's commitment to allow her relationship with her son, Jeremy, to "take different angles."

I believe the struggles we are facing as mothers serve us as women living in a changing world. Our ambiguous situations require us to disclose our thoughts, fears, and aspirations on many different levels, which can lead us to greater levels of self-realization as mothers *and* women. In our attempts to preserve what it means to be feminine, to grow in character as women, and to establish new criteria for morally acceptable ways of mothering, we demonstrate an intentional "grasping" for a renewed sense of caring. This caring is the necessary condition for our future success as mothers. Caring for our children at the physical level of existence, although an important role, only meets sufficient standards for what it means to be a mother. Elizabeth voices this realization clearly:

> Maybe I am not the one who is doing their laundry, cooking their meals every day, or sending them off to school, but that's okay. That's a physical mom. Anyone can cook the meals and do the laundry. But it's a lot harder to listen to your kids and be fair to them. I gave them everything whether I had it or not, being nothing. I am every bit their mother now and maybe more so because now I listen to them. Now I talk to them. I didn't before. I was worried about feeding them, and wiping their noses, and keeping them out of their father's way.

Noncustodial mothers are venturing to enact maternal "care" in a presentness that foregrounds the relational aspects of their beings as mothers *and* women. This presentness motivates a mobilization of motherhood's symbolic meaning and evidences the continued desire to remain open and attentive to their children's welfare.

Discussion Questions

1. Do you agree or disagree with the author's assessment concerning the difference between the experiences of noncustodial mothers and noncustodial fathers?

2. The author incorporates the broadly defined concepts of "care" and "attention." How are these concepts also applicable to social and cultural practices other than parenting?

3. Noncustodial mothers' dispositions (their past) seem to overshadow their attempts to change relational patterns for the better (their future). As gendered beings, how difficult is it for us to remain "present" in a given relationship, successfully thwarting intrusions from the past and fantasies of the future?

4. How advantageous is it for our society to think about "mobilizing" motherhood's meaning? Should social institutions such as parenthood be flexible and responsive to changing circumstances, *or* do they present us with the social stability that we need during changing times?

5. The context of visitation necessarily makes motherhood problematic because it constrains interaction to a specified time and place. Drawing from your own experience, do you think that the contrived context of visitation prohibits genuine interaction?

6. Can you identify your standpoint on what mothering signifies by assessing your reactions and/or responses to this essay?

References

Bartky, S. (1990). *Femininity and domination: Studies in the phenomenology of oppression.* New York: Routledge.

Chodorow, N. (1978). *The reproduction of mothering: Psychoanalysis and the sociology of gender.* Berkeley: University of California Press.

Dally, A. (1982). *Inventing motherhood: The consequences of an ideal.* London: Burnett Books.

Greif, G. L., & Pabst, M. S. (1988). *Mothers without custody.* Lexington, MA: Heath.

Heidegger, M. (1962). *Being and time.* New York: Harper & Row.

Knowles, J., & Cole, E. (Eds.). (1990). *Motherhood: A feminist perspective*. New York: Haworth Press.

Lanigan, R. L. (1988). *Phenomenology of communication: Merleau-Ponty's thematics in communicology and semiology*. Pittsburgh, PA: Duquesne University Press.

Murdoch, I. (1971). *The sovereignty of good*. New York: Shocken Books.

O'Barr, J. F., Pope, D., & Wyer, M. (Eds.). (1990). *Ties that bind: Essays on mothering and patriarchy*. Chicago: University of Chicago Press.

Rich, A. (1976). *Of woman born: Motherhood as experience and institution*. New York: Norton.

Rothman, B. K. (1989). *Recreating motherhood: Ideology and technology in a patriarchal society*. New York: Norton.

Ruddick, S. (1980). Maternal thinking. *Feminist Studies, 6*, 341–367.

Schutz, A. (1967). *The phenomenology of the social world* (G. Walsh & F. Lehnert, Trans.). Evanston, IL: Northwestern University Press.

Van Manen, M. (1990). *Researching lived experience: Human science for an action sensitive pedagogy*. London: Althouse Press.

Von Eckartsberg, R. (1986). *Life-world experience: Existential-phenomenological research approaches in psychology*. Washington, D.C.: Center for Advanced Research in Phenomenology and University Press of America.

Weil, S. (1962). Human personality. In R. Rees (Ed.), *Collected essays* (pp. 313–339). London: Oxford University.

Endnotes

1. Greif and Pabst (1988) estimated that there were more than 700,000 noncustodial mothers in the United States in 1985.

2. See Dally (1982).

3. In part, this is because women historically were defined solely by their role as mothers. As Rothman (1989) states, "Mothering was not something women *did,* it was something women *were*" (p. 22).

4. Refer to Rich (1976).

5. Narratives are "life texts" that serve as especially fruitful sources for revealing what theorists describe as "intersubjectivity" (i.e., shared attitudes, values, and beliefs). Refer to Von Eckartsberg (1986).

6. The mothers included in this manuscript (whose names have been changed) range in age from early 20s to mid-40s and have from one to four children living with grandparents, relatives, or ex-husbands. For some women, noncustody was a recent experience. For others, separation had taken place years before. Most women cited financial instability as the primary reason for their noncustodial status, although some lost court battles. All mothers were bettering their economic situations by furthering their education or improving their job skills.

7. An existential phenomenological reflection was performed on these narratives. Phenomenology as a human science attempts to grasp the "internal meaning structures of lived experience" (Van Manen, 1990, p. 102). I used a three-step phenomenological method of description, reduction, and interpretation (see Lanigan, 1988).

8. According to Heidegger (1962), if we attend to or reflect upon a situation with the intention of grasping its meaning, we are demonstrating existential "care." Noncustodial mothers exhibit this "grasping" as they struggle with the symbolic power of traditional motherhood and attempt to mobilize it from the shackles that constrain its enactment.

9. Ruddick (1980) draws these concepts of "attending" and "love" from both the works of Weil (1962) and Murdoch (1971). For Ruddick, the act of attending orients the reality of the mother-child relationship according to three basic interests: preservation, growth, and acceptability. Attention seems to "invigorate preservation and enable growth" (p. 348). Along with social acceptability, all three factors help to shape the practice of attending to children.

10. Heidegger (1962) suggests that it is by means of our disclosure in the world that we come to realize who we are and actualize who we want to become. Disclosure to ourselves is an integral aspect of this demonstration of "care."

11. Chodorow (1978) suggests that our identity crisis is due, in part, to the fact that "women define and experience themselves relationally" (p. 207).

12. Of course, custodial mothers also question their effectiveness as mothers. For discussions, see Knowles and Cole (1990).

13

"Return to Life"

Communicating in Families of the Holocaust

Lynn H. Turner, Ph.D.

Department of Communication Studies
Marquette University

Visit

Down corridors of women too tired
to tie their hair back I make my way
to where you live since Poppa died,
since they cut off your leg
and you got too old to struggle.
A man strapped to a chair coughs
as I pass. A woman stares at walls
as though they were windows.

Your room. One sink, two beds
and against the north wall a television.
There a huge woman sits, swelled with dropsy.
"Cora," you call to her there in sunlight,
hair feathered by the breeze from the open window.
You watch her all day from your wheelchair—
your roommate, though you haven't shared
a room in thirty years.

The nurses tell me you are mean.
You hoard, you curse, you will not wash
and when you get the chance you pinch Cora,
smile when the doctor rushes in.
They open your bureau, find twenty oranges
rotting. You steal, they say, from greed
but I know different. Once I met a woman
who raised children from Dachau:
they took everything, could never get enough.
They'd search the house at night,
forever hungry. Children are one thing.

If Poppa could see us now, his squint
would narrow, his head would tilt to the side
and from his blinded eye a tear would tremble.
I tried to come before he died, but I could not
meet the stare of Poppa dying. Nor yours now.
I do not want to know you laid so bare.

    —Phyllis Kahaney

*ecently, I discovered that my mother and uncle suffered as children
from anti-Semitic taunts as they walked along beaches in Lakeside, Michigan, where they were not allowed to swim. Many emotions accompanied this
discovery, but I was also curious as to why my mother had kept silent about
this for so long. She did not have much in the way of an answer for me, but
the discussion we had sparked my interest in silence and taboo topics in
family communication. In the early 1990s I was privileged to work with a
project at Marquette University called Return to Life. This traveling photog-
raphy exhibit pictured the activities of Jewish refugees after Liberation. During this period I met members of Milwaukee's Jewish community and women
who belonged to Second Generation, an international support group for
children of Holocaust survivors. In talking with these women, I was struck
by the depth of silence that had pervaded their families' communication, and
thus, this essay was born. I had two main objectives in writing it. First, I
wanted to describe communication issues that exist within Holocaust survivor families, to further understand family communication under conditions
of stress. Second, I wanted to provide an opportunity for daughters of Holocaust survivors to voice their concerns and memories. The four women I
interviewed suffered in silence as children and young adults. They deserve a
voice now. In listening to their stories, I also saw a way to understand the
pain my mother experienced as a child, but kept silent from her children.*

Our handicap, that of the Second Generation, is that we were not given any
memories!   (Helen Epstein, quoted in Shoshan, 1989, p. 201)

Providing opportunities for women to gain voice is important. There are
times, however, when silence (which sometimes speaks louder than words)
has worked as a coping mechanism for them. That is the case with many
children growing up in Holocaust survivor families. Silence about the
Holocaust sheltered the children from knowing the atrocities their parents
suffered and seemingly helped the parents cope with their personal histories. Still, to grow up in a family with no spoken history and with few
intergenerational ties is painful. At some point, the silence needs to be broken so that the past is not forgotten and the future can be shaped. This
essay is a step in providing a voice to second generation daughters of
Holocaust survivor families. What was the context from which many of

these families sprang? How did that context shape the silence that evolved?

The context of Holocaust survivor families is a context larger than the individual demographics of those families. The contextual frame surrounding these and other survivor families consists of a veritable rush to reestablish family life after Liberation. Having a family, replacing, in a small way, what was lost, was seen as a "return to life" after the death of the Holocaust. Of the four daughters I interviewed in search of an answer to my questions, one said that the rush to reestablish family life resulted in marriages that were made between people who really may not have known each other very well. "My parents and many of their friends married in the resettlement camp. It's amazing they could have stayed together all these years after such a short and strained engagement." And most certainly marriages were made and children were born to people who were undoubtedly still suffering from "confusion and acute distress" (Shoshan, 1989, p. 195). In addition to the hurry to marry and have children, most survivor families are characterized by either silence or incessant talk concerning the Holocaust, which demonstrates the importance of communication in Holocaust survivor families. Although the "return to life" often prescribed either ignoring or testifying to the atrocities suffered during the war, all four of the daughters I interviewed shared the experience of being in families that used silence as a coping mechanism. This essay focuses on family silence about the Holocaust, including an overview of what family rules prevailed.

Much has been written about the Holocaust and its devastating effects on the lives of families and on Western culture. The Holocaust represents a special class of unpredictable stressors like those that McCubbin and his colleagues (1983) conceptualize as extreme environmental stress that creates a uniquely oppressive environment. Families that contain a member or members who experienced life in a concentration camp are subject to the repercussions of these extreme stressors. Some of these repercussions, such as guilt and pain, may be passed down to the children of survivors. Danieli (1985) calls this "the intergenerational transmission of victimization" (p. 295). In victimization, loss occurs. This sense of loss often includes a loss of confidence and self-esteem. The resulting emotion is often shame, which can extend beyond the individual level and may pervade the family system (Fossum & Mason, 1986). Shame can create stress, which represents a disturbance or a force for change within the family. The change in the family's system may be desired or undesired. Regardless of the outcome, stress is inevitable because families experience growth, change, and decay over time. In families of Holocaust survivors, this stress may be the outcome of a desire for things to stay the same, to not undergo drastic changes as they did during the Holocaust. Though we may want life to continue in a predictable pattern, we are often mistaken and, thus, get shaken by unpredictable stress (Galvin & Brommel, 1986).

In this essay, I focus on the extremely complex internal family context of Holocaust survivors. Boss (1988) suggests that extreme family complexity necessitates a qualitative approach in data gathering. "Family researchers and professionals must rely on each family member's story" (p. 35). Stories are powerful connections to our past and shapers of our present identity (Baldner, 1989). I was interested in retrieving narratives from daughters of Holocaust survivor families to reconstruct a picture of what family communication was like in their homes.[1] What I discovered were some of the family rules that had evolved in families whose roots were grounded in the extreme stress of the Holocaust.

To examine these families, I chose to focus on daughters' stories for several reasons.[2] First, women are often the narrators of family stories. In fact, the archetypal mother is seen as a storyteller (Tonn, 1992), telling stories to pass on family lore and teach children moral lessons. Second, family problems posed by a parent or parents who were Holocaust survivors seem clearly tied to Gilligan's (1982) portrayal of care. Gilligan suggests that a care orientation is expressed through a sense of connectedness to others, of being in-relationship with them. Thus, being in-relation to a Holocaust survivor might involve active care in dealing with stress, victimization, and shame—the residue of survival. In addition, Gilligan and others (i.e., Chodorow, 1978; Noddings, 1985; Wood, 1994) have asserted that this vision of care is associated with the feminine gender identity. As such, daughters should be particularly attuned to the family stress of Holocaust survival. In the interviews I conducted with four such daughters, six rules to live by seemed to repeat themselves.

Rules to Live By

Six family rules were repeated in each of the separate interviews. These rules echo issues expressed in other literature about survivor families (e.g., Fogelman, 1988a, 1988b; Shoshan, 1989). The six family rules indicate what can and cannot be discussed within this unique family context. They are: (1) We must not talk about the Holocaust; (2) We are unique; (3) We must celebrate life; (4) We must look to the future and success; (5) We must parent our parents; and (6) We must bear witness.

We Must Not Talk About the Holocaust

All the interviewed women commented, at some length, that their parents' experiences and information about the Holocaust were not explicitly discussed in their homes while they were growing up. Yet, somehow this heritage was known without a great deal of direct communication. The words of three of the daughters are indicative of the way these women described talk about the Holocaust in their families:

> "It was simply a fact of life."
>
> "You don't ask a lot of questions, it's just part of our life."
>
> "You realize, in bits and pieces, that something horrible happened— too horrible to talk about in any detail."

Although they all knew about the horror of the Holocaust, they also knew not to talk about it.

Not talking about it makes the Holocaust a taboo topic, at least intergenerationally. Some of the daughters said that they thought their parents did talk to one another about the topic. Fogelman (1988a) observes this same phenomenon in second generation therapy groups she conducted in Boston: "Intergenerational communication in these families [is] manifested as patterns in which the second generation tends to learn about the Holocaust through snatches of conversation and intense non-verbal messages" (p. 621). As one daughter commented, "My father would simply get that look—an intense, yet far away glazed over expression—and my brother, mother, and I would know immediately to stop talking. It was such a clear message, I never thought to question it."

Because all of the interviewed daughters were members of the group Second Generation, they all seemed to react to the family taboo by talking about the Holocaust with peers. In this way, the subject of the Holocaust seems different from other family secrets such as alcoholism. Although the family members did not talk about it during the daughters' childhoods, some members did speak of it outside the family. Of course, membership in Second Generation was an adult choice, activated after these daughters no longer lived with their parents.

We Are Unique

A second family rule discovered in the interviews was the sense that the survivor family is unique and all of its members individually are special. Part of this message was conveyed nonverbally as respondents recounted their discovery that they had no extended family. Unlike their friends at school, "We had no grandparents, aunts, uncles, and cousins." "We had to make our friends our family. And many of these friends were other survivors—other families that began with our parents' generation." This sense of being different from the majority and banding together with others like themselves permeated the interviews.

The sense of being special or unique was not all negative and not always conveyed nonverbally. The women mentioned how frequently their parents praised them by telling them that they were special, unlike any other child. Further, parents occasionally did refer to their surviving the Holocaust by invoking the notion of a special plan God must have had for them and their family. "My mother would say, 'I must have been saved for this reason, to have this wonderful family.'" Of course, this sense of being special carried burdens for these women in the sense of having to live up to parents' expectations. "Sometimes I wished we weren't carrying the weight of my parents' hopes and dreams so much. All parents probably think their kids are special, but I don't believe all kids feel so motivated not to disappoint their parents as we did."

We Must Celebrate Life

Most of the women mentioned that talk in the family often centered on being happy and "enjoying what we have." Children were often told by parents that the small irritations of growing up, which can feel so onerous, were not important. "My parents were consistently telling me not to mope around about such small issues as an argument with a friend at school. They often didn't seem to have a lot of patience to listen to what seemed like little problems." "Sometimes it was a burden to have to act happy." "My parents often stated that life was a joy and a gift; I agreed, but I didn't always really believe it." Celebrations were also tinged with sadness because there was no extended family to gather around the table. One of the women commented that her family always invited other families of Holocaust survivors to join them for Jewish holidays and other celebrations. "Our extended family was really my parents' friends and it was very important that we include them in all our birthdays and other parties."

We Must Look to the Future and Success

"My parents are extremely resilient people and they seemed to never look back. Their focus was always on our future, especially our future successes. My brother and I were held to some pretty high standards." The daughters all suggested that their families were future oriented. "In our house there was a lot of planning talk—where we will go for our vacation, what we will do for Hanukkah, you know, stuff like that." "Jewish families are always said to value education and this was really true with us. There were lots of conversations praising our teachers and planning college and future occupations. And, of course, there was absolutely no question that we would go to school and be successful." Another respondent commented that "I sometimes wondered, now as an adult, if we talked so much about our future because my parents felt they could never bear to talk about the past. Other families reminisce—we couldn't."

We Must Parent Our Parents

Two main aspects relating to this family rule were present in the interviews. First of all, the daughters were all concerned that they not cause their parents any more suffering. "You know, they have suffered so much already I really couldn't bear to say or do anything to make them unhappy." "It was kind of difficult growing up in the '60s—everyone was rebelling, but we just couldn't do that type of thing. It would be too awful to hurt my parents that way. I pretty much had to repress my rebellion. I wanted to agree with my parents more than I wanted to test them." "The worst thing I could ever do was to say something that would cause my father to feel that terrible hurt." "My parents were often demanding; they had to know where I was every minute of the day and night. I tried to get them to relax and let go of me, but it was hard, and I didn't want to say anything that might hurt them."

Second, these women mentioned a rationale they believed accounted for some of their family interaction. Several women mentioned that their parents had no role models for parenting teenaged children since they themselves lost their own parents at a young age. "My parents had no normal adolescence themselves and experienced no models of parenting during that time. It was like we were equal in some weird way." Another woman commented, "In some ways I felt as though I had to teach my parents how to be parents. I don't know why I felt so responsible for this, but I did."

We Must Bear Witness

Survivors' children often sounded the family rule of action, although this was probably a rule that came to them as adults rather than through the immediate, daily interaction in their families-of-origin. As Fogelman

(1988a) observes, when guilt, rage, and helplessness are worked through, this energy can profitably be transformed into deeds. Fogelman discusses the behavioral changes reported by members of her second generation therapy group. "Some began to learn Yiddish, others took courses in Jewish history, or went to Israel for the first time. Some joined Jewish organizations or attended religious services. Others have become Jewish community leaders" (p. 636).

This type of service work and connection to Jewish roots also were expressed by the women I interviewed. The daughters' adult sense of responsibility seemed to come from the overall experience of having been raised by Holocaust survivors. It seemed to be a culmination of the other rules expressed within the family. "It's an important thing, a responsibility to live a life where we never forget and we don't let the world forget what happened in the Holocaust." "It could happen again; it *will* happen again if we forget, if we let others forget, if we're not watchful and careful." "Something like this, all the suffering, has to be memorialized; it can't be forgotten and life just gotten on with."

Conclusion

Therapists have observed that Holocaust survivors exhibit an amazing resilience and fortitude (Fogelman, 1988b) despite their degrading experiences with extreme inhumanity. Their adaptability and spirit is clearly demonstrated by their willingness to renew family life. Most survivors married and began having children as soon as possible after the Liberation. One American official commented that the refugee camps were crowded with baby carriages; everywhere there were infants (S. Sorrin, personal communication, December 14, 1989).

However, survivors bring with them into family life a particular stressor, a legacy that is communicated to their children in a variety of ways. As these daughters of Holocaust survivors discussed, their parents did not talk openly with them about their feelings of loss and pain. Many survivors use denial as a coping strategy, and thus are silent on the topic of the Holocaust. As a result, the second generation suffers from an incomplete knowledge of their family's heritage. This causes the children of survivors to feel some guilt and pain themselves, which, in turn, they may suppress. This suppression occurs because it is a pattern learned through family interaction and because their pain seems too insignificant when compared to the enormity of their parents' suffering. Therefore, members of the second generation silence themselves within the family. This notion of repressed anger, mentioned by one of the daughters, who said, "It would be awful to hurt my parents; I pretty much had to repress my [adolescent] rebellion," was echoed in many ways by the other respondents. This may be an admirable desire on the part of the daughters, but it certainly may have resulted in problems for them, similar to the problems women, in general, have experienced due to silencing (Hayles, 1986).

Overall, these four women were extremely positive about their families-of-origin. They were careful to point out the strengths of their family's communication. This may have been a reflection of the emphasis on being happy and successful they had learned in their family's interactions. Even when criticizing what might be seen as lack of parenting skills, they were quick to find an excuse for their parents (i.e., "They never had role models" or "They suffered so much"). It seemed very important to all four of the women that I leave the interviews believing that their childhoods had been happy and their family communication had been positive. However, much of this positive experience came as a result of silence, or keeping the parents' histories a taboo topic. None of these four daughters reacted to this suppression with anger, as some children of survivors are reputed to have done (Fogelman, 1988a). The women reported that they understood why their parents would keep silent on this topic.

Possibly silence was reported as a relatively successful communication strategy in these four families for two reasons. First, although the families did not talk much about the Holocaust, they belonged to an active and cohesive Jewish community. As Klein (1973) points out, community is an important link to survival. The community provides social support and an outlet for communication. What cannot be discussed in the family may be discussed in the larger community. The women I spoke with found that kind of community by joining a support group for children of Holocaust survivors.

Second, the women I interviewed all managed to make positive use of many aspects of their family life (e.g., future orientation and emphasis on success). These women all became successful, active members of the community. They transformed their feelings into productive action by becoming involved in Jewish life. Possibly they were able to do this because communication in their family-of-origin contained many messages that built self-esteem. The family rules these women revealed in the interviews often contained messages geared to bolster self-confidence (e.g., "You are unique and special" and "You should celebrate life").

The lessons of the women's narratives are threefold. First, the value of listening to the stories told by those who experienced growing up in Holocaust survivor families seems confirmed. Second, silence may not be a completely maladaptive way of dealing with stress in a family. It seems important that there be some communicative outlet for people under stress, but perhaps a community of friends can substitute for the immediate family. However, this is a tentative conclusion, at best. Perhaps the women talking to me were so distanced from their experience of anger, and so silenced by their experiences, that they were unable to give or perhaps even acknowledge to themselves more negative accounts.

Finally, the voices in this study seem to speak of a contradiction in the context of family communication. The women did not express any problems in dealing with what may seem on the face of it to be conflicting messages. "We must not discuss the past" yet "we must never forget." This apparent contradiction may honor the two important responses to the stress of Holocaust victimization (be silent about it or talk incessantly about it). Future investigation of family communication and stress might profit from an examination of family narratives, an openness to the functions of silence, and careful consideration of the expression of contradictions in family discourse. These elements will further our understanding of the internal context that families bring to bear on the stressors they experience. For daughters of Holocaust survivors, these discoveries might aid their own understanding of how family silence may play a key role in their parents' ability to "return to life."

Discussion Questions

1. Does it make a difference that the second generation members in this essay are daughters? Do you think the rules and issues might differ if sons were questioned? How?

2. Although this book is concerned with giving women voice, this essay indicates that there may be times when silence says more than words. Do you think silence is a functional coping strategy for dealing with family stress and victimization? How so?

3. Is the Holocaust unique, or can you think of other stressors that might produce similar communication issues for families?

4. The women interviewed expressed strong devotion to their parents. How do you think these families managed to produce such strong ties among their members? Do you think the sons would have expressed the same level of personal caring?

5. All four of these families chose not to discuss the Holocaust with their children. We know, however, that other families do talk about their experiences. What do you think would be a good way for families to talk about such trauma?

6. Do you agree that talking about something that has been labeled shameful is an empowering act? Why or why not? How might this relate to other types of stressors women face today, such as rape?

References

Baldner, C. A. (1989, April). *Creating connections through family narrations*. Paper presented at the annual conference of the Central States Communication Association, Kansas City, MO.

Boss, P. (1988). *Family stress management*. Knobbier Park, CA: Sage.

Chodorow, N. (1978). *The reproduction of mothering: Psychoanalysis and the sociology of gender*. Berkeley: University of California Press.

Danieli, Y. (1985). The treatment and prevention of long-term effects and intergenerational transmission of victimization: A lesson from Holocaust survivors and their children. In C. Figley (Ed.), *Trauma and its wake* (pp. 295–313). New York: Brunner/Mazel.

Fogelman, E. (1988a). Intergenerational group therapy: Child survivors of the Holocaust and offspring of survivors. *Psychoanalytic Review, 75,* 619–640.

Fogelman, E. (1988b). Therapeutic alternatives for Holocaust survivors and second generation. In R. L. Baum (Ed.), *The psychological perspectives of the Holocaust and its aftermath* (pp. 79–108). New York: Columbia Press.

Fossum, M. A., & Mason, M. J. (1986). *Facing shame*. New York: Norton.

Galvin, K. M., & Brommel, B. J. (1986). *Family communication: Cohesion and change*. Glenview, IL: Scott, Foresman.

Gilligan, C. (1982). *In a different voice*. Cambridge: Harvard University Press.

Hayles, N. K. (1986). Anger in different voices: Carol Gilligan and *The Mill on the Floss*. *Signs, 12,* 23–39.

Klein, H. (1973). Children of the Holocaust: Mourning and bereavement. In E. J. Anthony & C. Kovpernik (Eds.), *The child and his family: Vol. 2. The impact of disease and death* (pp. 293–401). New York: Wiley.

McCubbin, H. I., McCubbin, M. A., Patterson, J. M., Cauble, A. E., Wilson, L. R., & Warwick, W. (1983). CHIP—Coping health inventory for parents: An assessment of parental coping patterns in the care of the chronically ill child. *Journal of Marriage and the Family, 45,* 359–370.

Noddings, N. (1985). *Caring.* Berkeley: University of California Press.

Shoshan, T. (1989). Mourning and longing from generation to generation. *American Journal of Psychotherapy, 18,* 193–207.

Tonn, M. B. (1992). Effecting labor reform through stories: The narrative rhetorical style of Mary Harris "Mother" Jones. In L. A. M. Perry, L. H. Turner, & H. M. Sterk (Eds.), *Constructing and reconstructing gender* (pp. 283–293). Albany: State University of New York Press.

Wood, J. (1994). *Who cares? Women, care, and culture.* Carbondale, IL: Southern Illinois University Press.

Endnotes

1. To gather these stories, I tapped several sources. First, I attended a group discussion of members of the organization Second Generation, a group of children of Holocaust survivors. Second, I attended a speech delivered by Lucy Steinitz, editor of the book *Living After the Holocaust: Reflections by Children of Holocaust Survivors in America* and herself a child of survivors. I also viewed a film, *Dark Lullabies,* made by the child of a survivor, based on her feelings about her experiences with her parents and her quest to discover more about her heritage.

   Based on the issues raised by these sources, I interviewed four adult daughters of Holocaust survivors. These women were all members of the support group Second Generation. The women ranged in age from 38 to 47, and all were members of two-biological-parent families-of-origin. In two cases, both mother and father were survivors; in one case, the father only was a survivor; in the remaining case, the mother only was a survivor. The four women all had at least one other sibling. The families were all middle-class. I interviewed each woman separately in a semistructured interview process. We met in a neutral setting, a local Jewish Community Center. The interviews lasted from 1 to 1½ hours each. From these interviews, I induced several rules descriptive of life, and especially communication, within survivor families. Because these women had many demographic characteristics in common, perhaps it is not surprising that their accounts were strikingly similar, making a thematic analysis relatively easy to accomplish.

2. The composition of the Milwaukee Second Generation group is primarily female. The speaker I heard and the filmmaker are also daughters of Holocaust survivors.

14

African American Women

Voices of Literacy and Literate Voices

Cheryl Forbes, Ph.D.

Writing and Rhetoric Program
Hobart and William Smith Colleges

African-American women's voices sing out but are not always heard.

That White Thing

Sometimes I wish I could just
quit.
Quit talking to white people.
Just zaps your energy
When they do that
White thing

    What do you mean?

See?!
It's that
White thing—
Like for some reason
Everything we say
Is supposed to
Make sense to *them.*
Never can just talk
Always have to explain.
Always have to have a reason.
Can't just talk.

    Will you show me how?

Man, you just don't get it!
You just don't get it, do you?
I'm sure glad I'm not white.
Sure would be tiring
Always having to have things
Explained to me
Never just listening

Never seems you guys *know* anything.

    —*María Cristina González*

*R*ecently I taught a course called "Power and Persuasion," a history of rhetoric from the Renaissance to the late 20th century. The latter half of the course provided students an opportunity to make speeches. One of the students, an African American woman, gave a forensic speech defending herself against charges of ignorance, illiteracy, and frivolity because she occasionally writes in Black English vernacular. Her speech reminded me of the following essay, which I had begun writing before I met her. But Brandon's struggle with voice, identity, and role rang just as true as had Alicia's, Kenyett's, and Nikki's. I realized as I listened to Brandon that not much had changed for women of color. This is why I wrote this essay. Call it forensic rhetoric, if you will. Because I learned so much from these women, I wanted to share that with others . . . to allow others to hear them as clearly as possible, given my mediating role. These women helped me better understand racism, feminism, and literacy. These women challenged me to change.

*T*hese are the stories of four women of color with different experiences of literacy, yet whose experiences merge to become one story, the story of women of color who refuse the silence our society offers them. I know these women. I have talked with them, eaten with them, written and worked with them. Their stories are worth listening to. I was Alicia's, Kenyett's, and Nikki's colleague and teacher. I know Alicia's mother, the fourth woman, through her daughter, through phone conversations, and through her writing. Although the women come from different geographic places, from different social places, and from different generational places, they share a desire for an authentic literacy that does not violate their identity or their ethnicity. They know that literacy is the way people become heard in our society. People with the wrong literacy remain voiceless, as the story of these women shows. Alicia and her mother (and through her mother we hear the voices of two more generations) have struggled against the obliteration of their voices, as have Nikki and Kenyett. These women reveal the tension, the ambivalence, and the celebration of their literate voices, even though they must live with and through more than one kind of literacy, even though their literacy is frequently attacked.

I repeat. Their stories are worth listening to. But before we listen, I want to make one point clear. Literacy is not, simplistically, learning to read. For me, as for these women, literacy is a matter of relationships among the four language processes of writing, reading, speaking, and listening; literacy is also a matter of relationships among people. Relationships naturally lead to storytelling. Full literacy, therefore, is thoroughly and intimately feminist; it cannot be anything else. Now, let's listen to the stories of these women.

Alicia comes from a middle- to lower-middle-class two-parent, traditional family, outside of Chicago, Illinois. She attended private, Christian schools and chose a private, Christian, liberal arts college with a nearly open-door admissions policy. Both her secondary schooling and her undergraduate schooling have been, then, in predominantly white, middle- to upper-middle-class institutions. Alicia attends a racially mixed church which, according to her mother, has much racial conflict between the Black and White members. There also is racial and ethnic conflict at her daughter's college.

Alicia has been schooled in a particular kind of literacy—traditional White, American, male, academic, objective, impersonal literacy. When Alicia wrote "Black English" as a first-year student, she was just beginning to confront the complexities of ethnicity, identity, and literacy. In it, she repeatedly turns to the question of relationships. Her familial relationships, church relationships, school relationships, and the final, most sensitive relationship, the relationship of herself with herself, are all connected to the kinds of literacies she chooses.

Now a senior and still concerned with this question, Alicia describes herself this way: "When I talk with my family and Black friends, it's important to me that they know I have White friends. But it's just as important that my White friends understand that I am not White, that I am an African American and don't want to be White." She wants her White friends to realize that her ability to use only White standard English and write a "White" way does not make her White. If anything, her literacies should tell others that she is African American.

Although Alicia uses a different vocabulary today to describe her position, her concerns have not changed. She does not want to be mistaken as a black-skinned White person. Literacy, then, is not an objective achievement, but is a matter of relationships, an integration of subject and object. Because of varying relationships, Alicia uses different literacies with different people and social contexts.

Compare Alicia's attitude to that of high school student Maya Angelou (1969).

Shame made me want to hide my face. Mrs. Flowers deserved better than to be called Sister. Then, Momma [her grandmother] left out the verb. Why not ask, "How *are* you, Mrs. Flowers?" With the unbalanced passion of the young, I hated her for showing her ignorance to Mrs. Flowers. It didn't occur to me for many years that they were as alike as sisters, separated only by formal education. (p. 78)

Mrs. Flowers, who profoundly affected Angelou's literacy, emphasized the spoken word as a path to literacy. "Your grandmother says you read a lot," Angelou reports Mrs. Flowers as saying, "Every chance you get. That's good, but not good enough. Words mean more than what is set down on paper. It takes the human voice to infuse them with the shades of deeper meaning" (p. 82). Mrs. Flowers insisted "that I must be intolerant of ignorance but understanding of illiteracy" (p. 83), almost as if she had understood Angelou's shame at her grandmother's illiteracy about verbs. Alicia, as a first-year college student, was trying to move beyond the shame and to identify what in Black English was acceptable for her and what was unacceptable.

Her essay begins with these words: "Slaves didn' be having no heirlooms tah pass on tah they childrun; unless maybe you is countin' Black English." Alicia announces herself and her position on Black English in her version of Black English vernacular—and in metaphor. The literacy she immediately proclaims is not that of academic argumentation, but African American style, using the word *style* as Smitherman (1977) does: style is the *way* you use your words. Alicia wants to argue metaphorically, narratively. She wants to tell a story about Black English as an heirloom, something to cherish, to pass on, to give to others. Her sentence, though, reveals her ambivalence and confusion, despite its declarative posture, for an heirloom is *not* something to be used. It is an object that has moved beyond the functional to become merely decorative, no matter how costly. Here Black English has turned into a museum piece, only to be studied and stared at—to rest on velvet, no doubt, but never to be put to the stresses and challenges of daily living, to the trials of finding and maintaining relationships. In the next paragraph she declares that Black English is a legitimate language of a legitimate culture, her own. Recognizing this, however, leads her to ask, "Should I as a Black American choose Black English (BE) over standard English (SE)? Or is it a matter of 'taking sides'? How conscious should I be of it?"

Despite her written and spoken statements to the contrary, Alicia has long been conscious of the differences between her two competing ways of asserting her literacy. Her Black high school friends who did not attend a

White high school ridiculed her for talking "proper"—an African American euphemism for talking White. Her friends didn't leave room for more than one kind of literacy. If she wanted to be their friend, she had to leave school literacy, as she puts it, "in my locker." She learned early "to keep a careful watch on my tongue." Even so, school literacy would seep out, just as her African American literacy did at school. When it did, White kids laughed: "That only pointed out one more falling short of the standard." The standard, of course, was that of White literacy. Alicia intended to make sure that no one could say she "could not speak their language. . . . I was determined to speak just like them, to speak their language better than them." In other words, she would become more literate than the White students around her.

What does a woman like Alicia do? The question isn't merely one of what does an African American do, but what does an African American *woman* do? She is trying to please everyone in her life, as well as satisfy the culture-in-power, that White culture where "green power," not "Black power," rules. Because green power is "where it's at," her mother says, "If that means talking the White man's language, then so be it. 'Money talks, so honey hush.'" Notice the moral and psychological bind in which Alicia finds herself. She is to strive for green power, the power the predominantly White culture has to offer. To get it she must talk the White *man's* language—or must she? Is *she* to talk at all? Or is she to "hush"? How can she talk without talking? How can she please all the warring and contradictory relationships and cultures in her life? She is a woman as well as an African American, and a woman's role is to make everyone happy (or conversely, not to displease anyone). But can she? If she plays one role successfully, by doing so she may play another unsuccessfully. Her roles cancel each other out, and so may cancel herself. To please her mother, she must not only talk like a man but like a White man; yet as a woman and a Black woman she shouldn't be heard. To please her Black friends, she must reject her mother, and she must risk success. To achieve success, and to be acceptable to her White friends, she must leave her African American literacy outside the school door.

These two literacies, White and African American, force Alicia into a state of near paralysis. She simply cannot make herself acceptable, no matter what she does. She can't talk and remain silent, which is, ultimately, what both sides want her to do. "When it comes down to it, the judgments are made: this person's intelligent, this one's not, this one is to be feared, he tryin' to be White by talkin' so propah. It's more than just talk." Is it possible for Alicia to be considered "educated"—or "literate"—without sacrificing her ethnicity and her identity? How can she learn to speak "propah" when for an African American woman the only really "propah" language may be silence?

Marge Piercy's poem "Unlearning to Not Speak" is apt for Alicia's struggle. Piercy (1973) begins her poem with a direct reference to what we commonly think of when we think of literacy—school and paper. "Blizzards of paper / in slow motion / sift through her," she writes. The woman of the poem is a sieve through which the White storm of literacy causes nothing but anguish: "Why don't you speak up? / Why are you shouting? / You have the wrong answer, / the wrong line, wrong face" (p. 38). Alicia would add, "the wrong voice, the wrong language, the wrong literacy." It seems that she has no "right" voice, Black or White, loud or quiet. She complains, "White students have stereotyped Blacks (including speech patterns) in my presence only to explain that I'm different. I'd been given a kind of honorary citizenship"—a citizenship she rejects. At the same time, it's the citizenship she is supposed to want.

Alicia makes the conflict clear. "I had to respond," she writes about the accusations of her Black girlfriend. "My response was an awkward shrug of silence. And now when my speech is brought to my attention, I put on that same awkward, silent shrug. And I keep a careful watch on my tongue." Is silence a response? A literacy? Has she come to the place where she juggles three literacies and not just two?

Throughout Alicia's essay, the words and voice of her mother hover. Listening to Mrs. Wilson, we recognize the echoes of her voice in that of her daughter. She writes and speaks about language, about listening and speaking, writing and reading. She wonders what words will overcome the barriers between people schooled in separate literacies. "I find it hard to know you, hard to talk to you," she quotes a White acquaintance, who defends herself with, "I live in a mixed neighborhood. I'm different, I live in the city not the suburbs. It's hard to converse with you." Mrs. Wilson refuses to accept the excuses, yet realizes, as does her daughter, that she and the White woman have traveled different paths. She responds:

> How can that be? Isn't this the first time you've ever really tried to hold conversation with me? Isn't conversation two way? Willing? Honest? Learning? How can you converse with the hypocrites and not converse with me. I notice that every Sunday. I can play the game much better than they can. I know a [woman] that can converse with anyone. She is quite guileful and a straight A student in White man. You can't converse with the real [me].

In Alicia's mother's voice, "a straight A student in White man" means the way White men talk, the way they approach literacy, the way they decide what is acceptable as literacy and what isn't. Compare this statement to her daughter's: "I was determined to speak *just* like them, to speak their language better than them." Alicia doesn't want to be just "a straight A student in White man" but a straight A–plus student. Both mother and daughter proclaim that they can—and will—converse with anyone. Mrs. Wilson sounds more confrontational, perhaps because she has lived through more confrontations or because she hears in her own voice the echo of her grandmother, Alicia's great-grandmother, saying, "Don't worry, I'm not going to let you get that black. You can know of it, you can feel it, you can relate to it, but you can't be it." Here I think of Alicia's question to herself, "Why does not using BE mean sometimes feeling 'not black'?" Her first literacy teacher—as with most of us—was her mother, by her own admission a "straight A student in White man."

Again, we hear the deep moral and psychological dilemma, this time of Alicia's mother, and her mother and her mother before her, and so on. To succeed, to become educated, to become literate, to be able to talk to those outside of her immediate context and family means becoming straight A in another language. Or silence. Alicia reflects the fear of division—and not between races, languages, and literacies—but between African Americans *because* of literacy. It echoes the old story of the house slaves and the field slaves, divided by dialect, by talking proper, by a desire for literacy to lead them into American culture. Or as Mrs. Wilson puts it, "I recall once saying, 'Big Mama, the teacher says it's pronounced pink not pank.' 'You tell that teacher it's pank in my devilish house.'" "Most people," she writes, "would have me be quiet and shut up." Better to say nothing than to say pank. Better silence.

And so mother and daughter come to the same conflicts in the end: voice or voicelessness, talking proper or not talking at all, learning to be literate the White man way or being judged unlearned, illiterate. Whose voice should they adopt as the appropriate path to acceptable literacy? Can they take the path of Black English vernacular? Or do they need to travel multiple paths to multiple literacies? Is this a burden or a journey to fulfillment and understanding? If Alicia and African American women like her choose the path of a "straight A student in White man," will they lose something precious that they cannot regain? As Alicia asks herself, "In my learning the standard, did I lose something?" This is the fear of the last two women to whom we will listen, Kenyett and Nikki. Their stories and their essays are inextricably intertwined. They are friends and colleagues. We cannot hear the story of one without also hearing the story of the other; and because both women had read Alicia's essay, Alicia's story is also part of their story.

Kenyett comes from a lower- to lower-middle-class nontraditional family in Detroit, Michigan. "Mama" appears frequently in her discourse, as it does with Alicia. The male figure who plays a major role in Kenyett's life is her multilingual uncle, who taught her to hold a newspaper on her own when she was 3. But "Who told this man that I could read?" she wanted to know. In Alicia's text, too, her uncle is the male figure she mentions. Kenyett claims that she "never really had a childhood." At the age of 6, after her sister was born, she began doing all the household chores, cooking included. She attended predominantly Black public schools and chose a state university that offered a scholarship, which she needed to attend college. Her family had no money to give her. For Kenyett, to change her speech would be to reject her history and her relationships. That is too great a price to pay for school literacy, as we learn from her essay "This Letter You Will Learn From."

Kenyett's friend Nikki, too, writes about Black English. But her essay tells us a great deal about her background, so different from either Kenyett's or Alicia's. It is significant that her first personal comments compare her social class with that of inner city African Americans: "When middle and upper class African Americans *like myself* are raised and educated in predominantly White neighborhoods they have an advantage over inner city African-Americans who only speak Black English." Here she combines the objective and the subjective: "they" with herself as an example. Could she have Kenyett in mind when she writes of disadvantaged inner city Blacks? Throughout her text she distinguishes between the dialect of a lower socioeconomic class and her own socioeconomic class.

At the time, her emphasis on social class failed to impress me as significant. Now, when rereading her essay, I hear the tensions between Nikki and Kenyett revealed in an acceptable, objectified form. Now I recall her visit to my office, ostensibly to discuss her research, but actually to talk about her anger at her friend. Why, she asked me, had Kenyett called her and all African Americans "illiterate"? Nikki's essay "Bilingual African-Americans" becomes a defense of herself against Kenyett's charge of illiteracy. "Maybe you and all those from the inner city. But not me," she seems to be saying. She is also trying to understand who she is, what voice she should adopt. In her own way, she is trying to answer Alicia's question, "By adopting the standard, did I—or *will* I—lose something?"

Reading Nikki's and Alicia's texts with and through each other, I find remarkable similarities. Remember that though the two women do not come from the same socioeconomic class, both women attended predominantly White schools, and Black English was not encouraged in their homes. Listen to Nikki.

I have learned from experience that young middle and upper class African-Americans find it difficult to be accepted by African-American kids from the inner city and ghetto. I have had the opportunity to be around both White and African-Americans from my same background all of my life, but I have also been around African-Americans from the inner city, who spoke strong Black dialect, I would find myself trying to talk the same way they were talking, and they would say I sound "country," and if I spoke the way I normally would speak they would say "Why do you talk so White?" I would find myself explaining that I talk the way I talk because I grew up in a White neighborhood and went to integrated predominately White schools all of my life. Now that I am more aware of my language if someone makes a comment about the way I speak, I respond by saying, "I don't talk White I use appropriate English." I found it difficult to be accepted by inner city African-Americans when I was growing up, because they thought I was either stuck-up or trying to be White. What my peers did not realize was that they were actually complimenting me when they would talk about my so-called "White" language.

Nikki and Alicia have similar experiences: accusations by friends—and by relatives—that they are trying to be White. Unlike Alicia, however, Nikki has refused to lapse into silence. Instead, she chose the response "appropriate English" and sees the jeers as compliments. At least as far as her spoken language is concerned, she has become comfortably assimilated into the dominant culture—and, in fact, seen it as positive. Alicia is still troubled by that assimilation, and Kenyett steadfastly rejects the necessity.

Kenyett's rejection and Nikki's acceptance are the root of their disagreement about literacy. Nikki can't accept the label "illiterate" because she does not speak an "illiterate" dialect. In effect, she has accepted that "illiterate" is the appropriate label for Black English, at the same time that she defends Black English against the charge. She reveals her ambivalence in such statements as:

This Black English is not all negative. It gives a certain comfort and inner strength that middle and upper class African-Americans frequently cherish or seek as shelter from the fast pace that is set by White Americans. For instance when I return to Gary, Indiana to visit my grandparents, aunts, and uncles it [Black English] gives me a sense of comfort, relaxation, and pride. It makes me appreciate the hard long struggle that African-Americans have endured. It is a great feeling that touches the very soul of our existence.

Notice that Nikki connects the spoken language of her extended family, Black English, with her identity and ethnicity. She and her family have moved ahead, quickly, have endured "the hard long struggle" from illiterate to literate, from lower class to upper class. She is proud of their movement *away from* Black English, yet glad that someone she knows still speaks it for the sense of history and movement that it gives her: "the very soul of our existence." Black English becomes a geography, a place to visit, like the battlefield at Gettysburg. Most of us don't want the responsibility of maintaining such places, but, like Nikki, we're glad someone does. Notice, too, that Black English is, like a vacation home, a place to slow down, to escape from the "fast pace that is set by White Americans." But slowness is often equated with stupidity in our culture, a stereotype that Nikki unwittingly attaches to Black English, a stereotype that is close to the image of "lazy" that many White Americans hold about the way some African Americans talk.

Yet, her metaphor shares characteristics with Alicia's "heirloom." Black English is something to cherish, to museum, even if it is not something to be used in the day-to-day requirements for literacy in this country. Rather, it is ethnically special, like folk costumes, dances, or food (Alicia connects it, disparagingly, with chitt'lings). Nikki connects language (and implicitly literacy) to identity and ethnicity, by comparing her culture to that of Italian- and Polish-Americans.

Although she is proud of what her family has accomplished, moving from Black English to the standard, she cannot bring herself to reject outright the use of Black English, as if such a rejection would be tantamount to feeling—or being—"not black." Nikki reveals her deep ambivalence by the structure of her argument. From sentence to sentence she moves between saying yes to Black English and saying yes to the White man's standard. She wants both, while avoiding the label "illiterate"; yet by her own experience she knows the difficulty in trying to speak both Black English and the standard. She has been condemned by both groups of people. Finally, though, as she attempts to define the emotional and psychological impact of Black English for understanding African American identity and ethnicity, she declares that "Black English is just as important as Standard English. Standard English is important when it involves the work-place. Black English is important because it involves the language of the African American culture. . . . Black English is our foundation; it is our roots." Only through Black English, then, is it possible for an African American to understand herself, her ethnicity, her relationship to the dominant culture. To forget or ignore Black English, for Nikki and for Alicia, even in the cause of literacy, means to forget or ignore the past.

Kenyett begins her essay by referring to Alice Walker's (1982) *The Color Purple,* in which Celie is another rebel against the idea of one-way literacy. Like Alicia's Big Mama, it's pank, not pink, in her devilish house. Darlene, her sewing companion, thinks otherwise, as Celie explains in one of the most important letters in the story, written to her sister Nettie: "Darlene trying to teach me how to talk. She say US not so hot. . . . Every time I say something the way I say it, she correct me until I say it some other way. Pretty soon it feel like I can't think. My mind run up on a thought, git confused, run back and sort of lay down" (p. 222). Darlene worries that Celie isn't educated, though clearly she can read and write. Celie's Black dialect is, as Darlene puts it, "a dead country giveaway." White folks *and* Black folks "think you dumb." Or, as Alicia puts it, "Some Blacks looked down upon BE, regarding it as backwards."

Adopting the letter format of Walker, Kenyett thrusts her readers into an epistolary essay, involving three people: Nikki, whom she calls Nigeria; Victoria, a White friend; and herself, whom she calls LaTeece, the authorial persona. (When I refer to the fictional characters I will use LaTeece/Kenyett and Nigeria/Nikki; when I refer to the actual women, I will use just their first names.)

LaTeece/Kenyett has sent a copy of Celie's letter to Nigeria/Nikki and Victoria, who have read and discussed it, without seeing any "significance" in it. They write LaTeece/Kenyett, asking her "to express [her]self a little bit more." She gladly complies.

"Dearest Loves," she writes, "I fail to see why you both can't see what is so easy to see. Had been a snake, sure bite 'cha nose off." Using Black English vernacular and metaphor, similar to the beginning of Alicia's essay, LaTeece/Kenyett tells them to read Celie's letter again, an appeal to use the literacy skills she assumes they have. If they still "don't git it, then I's try to explain," she concludes. Nigeria/Nikki tries, and she still is confused: "What you be saying child, 'cause you's really wasting my time." In other words, speaking Black English vernacular is a waste. LaTeece/Kenyett understands her friend's love-hate relationship with the talk.

The next letter switches to another approach, out of frustration, it appears. Nigeria/Nikki has inadvertently accepted a definition of literacy that excludes her own speech and so, her own ethnicity. The essay reflects a reality in which Nikki refers implicitly to Kenyett's socioeconomic class and native fluency with Black English, and Kenyett refers to Nikki's apparent rejection of Black English for "the standard." Recall that Nikki has chosen to interpret accusations that she was "stuck-up or trying to be White" as a compliment.

The conflicts between the two underlie the letter LaTeece/Kenyett writes in Nigeria/Nikki's voice. The words from Celie just sit on the page, because Nigeria/Nikki cannot see or hear them, as if Black English by definition is a language of silence. Black English is not a language that fosters literacy; it is not a language through which Nigeria in the essay or Nikki in reality can be literate. For Nikki, the standard is the language of thought and of professional relationships; Black English is the language of feeling and of family relationships. Kenyett in her essay rejects that position. For her, success, education, work, literacy, need not—and will not—come at the expense of her language. But understanding her friend as she does, LaTeece/Kenyett writes the following letter:

> My dear Nigeria,
>   I apologize that you did not comprehend the letter that I sent to you. I thought you of all people would understand the letter and exactly what Celie was saying in the letter. You do speak the language which is known to be Black Dialect, am I correct? I thought I was. So why don't you understand all of my propositions in the letter? So many times people have tried to change the way you speak and you get very perplexed in your own words. So many times you have been called illiterate and uneducated because of the way you speak and many times you have gotten offended. Take one more look at the letter and tell me if you still don't understand. I think that you will see this time.
>
>   LaTeece

What is startling, disturbing, and clever about this letter is that LaTeece/Kenyett switches to standard English to get Nigeria/Nikki's attention. She accommodates Nigeria/Nikki's position regarding standard English by using it effectively, almost as a weapon against her. Nikki in her essay makes a point that African Americans need to learn when standard English is appropriate or correct, and when they can risk Black English, for she does view Black English as a risk, socioeconomically, though she also views it as a comfort. She appears to advocate a linguistic segregation, analogous to the geographic segregation advocated today by many middle- and upper-class African Americans. Speaking the standard and associating with White Americans is reserved for the workplace, as is wearing a suit; at home African Americans slip into something "comfortable," Black English.

Kenyett senses this dualistic position and hints that her friend has fallen for the lie that she has been told many times: that Black dialect, intimately connected to their ethnicity as Alicia has shown, is illiterate and uneducated. In Nikki's words, Black English is inappropriate professionally. Kenyett rejects the position that Black English is professionally inappropriate. If it were, then how could anyone write meaningfully with it, as Alice Walker has done, whether the genre is a novel or a research paper? By using standard English in this particular letter, Kenyett momentarily accepts her friend's position to show her the irony of it. It is also ironic that despite Nikki's insistence in her essay that she is fluent with Black English, in Kenyett's essay Nigeria/Nikki fails to understand LaTeece/Kenyett, who must switch into standard English to communicate with her. And, thus the relationship breaks down.

When her friends don't write back, LaTeece/Kenyett assumes "you both were still lost. Must be. Folks like you just don't stop writin' little ole me for nothing. Since you can't figure the letter out then I'll tell you what my point was for sending it to you. How do you feel when I say that BLACK DIALECT IS A POWER DRIVEN JAGUAR?" From here to the end of the essay, this metaphor dominates LaTeece/Kenyett's voice. Like Alicia, she "argues" metaphorically, rather than propositionally. She calls out a refrain, "Black dialect is a power driven Jaguar," and waits for a response.

Kenyett's Black dialect functions and functions well, unlike Alicia's heirloom or even Nikki's soul or roots, where the language has been put under glass. But Kenyett's language and ethnicity do not simply function; they exhibit power, real rhetorical power. They have strength, speed, and beauty. Alicia and Kenyett use an economic metaphor. Nikki, despite her concern with economic matters, chooses what we might call spiritual or metaphysical metaphors, though she claims no religious beliefs or affiliation. To own an heirloom, or a Jaguar, a person (usually) must be wealthy. Yet to maintain Black English as a major vehicle for ethnic identity, to insist that it is a path to literacy, risks failing to achieve wealth. Alicia's mother and great-grandmother weren't willing to take the risk: "I won't let you get too Black." Nikki is not entirely willing to take the risk, either. Kenyett, on the other hand, shouts "I'll be as Black as I want. For I've got a power driven Jaguar at my control. Just hear me talk." She also uses a symbol of male dominance, a symbol of the elite. Like Alicia, she takes something that has been considered of absolutely no value and reverses and redefines it, but only by connecting it with what the dominant culture calls valuable.

Control is the key, for Kenyett insists that the control she reveals over Black English—and over White English—indicates that she is indeed literate and educated. But more than that. It isn't just that she has control of her languages, but that Black English in and of itself is a sign of control, of power, and of strength. On the other hand, for Nikki as for Alicia, Black English has always meant a *lack* of control over future success.

LaTeece/Kenyett ends her essay in silence, which returns us again to the confrontation of voice and voicelessness:

Dear Loves,

Now that you's know what I's trying to say with that letter from The Color Purple, if you didn't figure that out, I hope you feel the power of the language. Our "Black dialect" has a big effect on folks of all races. Some be wanting us to talk different from it and other says do what is comfortable to you.

And for the first time, she fails to sign her name.

Must African American women, as Gloria Naylor, Toni Morrison, and Alice Walker have shown, be left with the polarity of voice or voicelessness? Must they live with the tension between speaking or being silent, between having words that they and their cultures accept as legitimate, worthwhile, educated, and so literate, or being "lost for words"? If they must choose, they may be lost for other things as well: for a history, a heritage, an authentic and respected ethnicity, an identity.

These women are struggling for survival in a culture that fails to hear their literacy. In fact, they show that they are literate in two distinct dialects and in two modes, spoken and written discourse. By doing so, they demonstrate that it is possible to be powerfully literate in Black English, just as powerfully as in White English, perhaps even more powerfully. Yet it does no good to speak and write with such strength and purpose if the audience is both deaf and blind. This is the dilemma each woman faces, as it has been the dilemma of Alicia's great-grandmother, grandmother, and mother.

Alicia, Mrs. Wilson, Nikki, and Kenyett care about reading, writing, speaking, and listening. They have thought a great deal about the demands and definitions of literacy. They care about relationships. Despite her reiteration that Nigeria/Nikki is not illiterate just because she speaks Black English, LaTeece/Kenyett falls into silence, as if the struggle to attain literacy without rejecting what makes her an African American woman overwhelms her in the end. Even the relationships she promotes in her letters fail her. As she writes, "Does you think I's be dumb when I's say US instead of WE? I know you says no, but other Whitefolks and some Blackfolks, too think I's be dumb." Are there too many "others" to overcome, even with a power driven Jaguar? Even with an heirloom? A soul?

Although these interpretations are possible, finally I do not read this silence as the equivalent of Alicia's resigned shrug of the shoulders or of Nikki's defense of her speech. Rather, I read Kenyett as asking for a response: "I've had my say; now let me hear you." It is a move to further the conversation, using her silence to prompt the others into speech. As I said, she is adept at reading silence. And here, at the end of her essay, she shows her skill at using silence so that the voices of others might be heard. This seems to me the kind of literacy all of us ought to want: to hear the written and spoken voices of others, to speak and write with a voice of our own, and so to value the voices of all.

Discussion Questions

1. Think about a time when your own language proved to be a barrier, a handicap, or a stigma. Then think about the stories of these women. How did you respond to the tensions your language created? Why did you respond in that way? How would you respond today? Why?

2. What do you hear in these women's voices? Do you hear anger? What leads you to this conclusion? Should these women be angry? If you do not hear anger, then what emotions do their voices convey? How appropriate do you judge their responses to be?

3. When scholars and teachers talk about literacy education, "correctness" always becomes a focus. These women do not always or necessarily write "correctly." Are women expected to use correct grammar more so than men? Why?

4. Women of color share with White women some of the same issues about appropriate and acceptable language use. For women of color, it often is adopting a particular dialect. What are the implications of these language expectations on the roles women are "allowed" in our society? How might a change in what we value in language-use change social norms and expectations for women?

5. Interview several women of color about their language experiences. How do they compare with the experiences of Alicia, Kenyett, and Nikki? What conclusions can you draw about the values we place on language?

6. What does it mean to have a public voice? A private voice? How many voices is a woman expected to have? What happens when a woman's

two main voices conflict? How might a woman reconcile her voices, if she could?

References

Angelou, M. (1969). *I know why the caged bird sings.* New York: Bantam.

Piercy, M. (1973). *To be of use.* New York: Doubleday.

Smitherman, G. (1977). *Talkin' and testifyin': The language of Black America.* Boston: Houghton Mifflin.

Walker, A. (1982). *The color purple.* New York: Pocket Books.

15

False Eyelashes and the Word of God

Speaking as an Evangelical Woman

Lynne Lundberg, Ph.D.[1]

Department of Speech
Augustana College, IL
and
Department of Rhetoric
Coe College, IA

I am the eldest of four daughters of an evangelical man of God. My father made every decision after praying and consulting Scripture. One of the lessons he and my mother taught their daughters was that God specifically ordained certain roles for men and for women. Women, in the evangelical church, are not allowed to speak or act with authority in public. My sisters and I have struggled to overcome the barriers of our childhood faith in the effort to live meaningful lives. The most important element of that struggle, for me, was to research and write about other women's struggles against religious authority. This essay discusses the special difficulties posed by religious authority for evangelical women and gives examples of what women do to live within, circumvent, or escape these boundaries.

Back on television after a scandal-ridden absence, Tammy Faye Messner exemplifies a common stereotype of the evangelical woman. She is well-known not only for her piousness and religious devotion, but also for her excessive makeup and frequent bouts of tears on the air. Jan Crouch, her successor on the Trinity Broadcasting Network's *PTL*, fits Messner's image down to the false eyelashes and deference to her husband.[2] Of course, God doesn't require evangelical women to wear false eyelashes or display emotional excesses in public, but many evangelicals believe that God does require women to defer to men.

I grew up in an evangelical family. My experience as a young woman in the evangelical tradition has included the conflict that many women in this tradition experience. I have often wondered how intelligent, articulate women allow themselves to be silenced, or alternately, how they justify speaking in the church context. Paul's prohibition of women's speech in 1 Corinthians begins a tradition carried through much of Christianity, delimiting the authority of women to speak.[3] Women are viewed as ineligible to speak because they lack authority. The authority to speak in a spiritual context is especially important because this authority is moral authority (Meredith, 1970, p. 43). The rigid gender roles of the evangelical Christian church in America allow women no spiritual authority to speak in religious contexts, thus limiting their potential. These restrictive rules for evangelical women have detrimental effects not only for them but for the evangelical church as well.

The Evangelical Church Mandates Rigid Gender Roles

The term *evangelical* is interpreted in many ways, but for polling purposes, George Gallup, Jr. and Jim Castelli define evangelicals as "those who describe themselves as 'Born-Again' Christians" who believe that much of the Bible is literally true (1989, p. xix). Some evangelicals are also fundamentalists; others are also Pentecostal or charismatic. Gallup and Castelli estimate that nearly one third of Americans are evangelicals, 58% of them women (1989, p. 93).

The traditional gender roles of the evangelical church are especially powerful because they have the weight of eternal life or damnation behind them. In their earthly lives, evangelical Christians are to live as biblically as possible, following a patriarchal family and church structure. The correctness of this tradition is argued on the basis of the authority of God. For example, the ninth amendment of the Moral Majority's "Christian Bill of Right" states, "We believe in the right to receive moral support from all local, state, and federal agencies concerning the traditional family unit, a concept that enjoys both scriptural and historical precedence" (Wald, 1987, p. 191).[4] Within that traditional family structure, evangelicals advocate traditional gender roles for women. With a "social agenda deeply opposed to liberation from the patriarchal family" (Hadden & Swann, 1981, p. 98; Wills, 1990, p. 332), evangelicals say that women "should return to their traditional role in society," in the home raising children (Gallup & Castelli, 1989, p. 195). To be clear, the hierarchical structure of authority in evangelical Christianity places Jesus in authority over men, who are in authority over women and children. Thus, women's only proper exercise of authority is over their children. Although the weight of a woman's authority increases when she acts for her children (Janeway, 1971), all of her actions and demands must be according to the dictates of her husband and church. During my evangelical childhood, every family decision (where to live, where to attend church, etc.) was made by my father. My mother took part in discussions about education and discipline of children, but my father's authority was ultimate—"a benevolent dictatorship," he called it.

Women have no authority in the church but still are expected to work for the church. Gallup and Castelli report that "religious leaders across virtually all denominations point to women as the backbone of the local congregation" (1989, p. 51). In the evangelical church, women use their voices primarily to sing. They also are allowed to teach, but only as long as their students are not adult males and they do not hold positions of power. Even the appearance of authority must be avoided by women in their spiritual lives. During a prayer on the March 30, 1990, episode of *PTL,* for example, Paul Crouch and the male guests on the program sat in a semicircle of chairs to pray, while Jan Crouch knelt next to her husband. The more-assertive Sheila Walsh on the *700 Club* discusses theology, but always cites a male source for her insight. She usually cites Pat Robertson, but on one occasion seemed to feel so strong a need to cite a male authority that her source was "a man on the staff."

If evangelical women question their lack of authority, they face a great risk, the risk of eternal damnation. Social anthropologists Susan C. Bourque and Donna Robinson Divine, in *Women Living Change,* note, "Some women may accept subordination because the prospects for change are both too limited and too costly" (1985, p. 7).

Rigid Gender Roles Limit Evangelical Women

The gender roles advocated by the evangelical Christian church have a variety of consequences for women and girls. Some of these consequences are experienced as a double bind. All evangelical Christians are expected to devote their lives to serving God, especially by making the most of the skills and talents God gave them. More than half of those people, the women of the church, however, are prohibited from any activity involving authority or speech, which may, as it turns out, be their God-given talent. To know and believe oneself to be a talented speaker or preacher yet to simultaneously know oneself to be disqualified for the activity solely by one's sex is frustrating. When I was a child, my career goals involved public speaking, but I was discouraged from these "inappropriate" choices. I was told to get a college education so that I could support myself if need be. I was encouraged to become a teacher rather than a lawyer (because nice girls shouldn't want to argue for a living) or a minister (because women shouldn't preach). I was told that learning to cook and keep house were my most important lessons. I was trained to be a wife and mother and discouraged from developing myself as a person.

Evangelical women develop many strategies for reconciling themselves to their ordained gender roles, negotiating those roles within the evangelical tradition, or rejecting the roles along with the tradition. Some women manage to convince themselves and those around them that the mandated gender roles are worthy ideals. Jan Crouch, for example, often assumes a childlike, giggling demeanor in contrast to her husband's authoritative manner, perhaps to prove the wisdom of his "headship."

Women may negotiate a place of limited authority for themselves within the evangelical tradition. Women on evangelical television programs often sing, a ministry traditionally approved for women, and read from the Bible. They are allowed to read from the Bible because they are not speaking their own words. Women who want to remain true to their tradition and at the same time speak, do so deferentially. For example, on one show Jan and Paul Crouch conversed with Joseph Good, a Hebrew scholar, about the role of cosmetics in Jewish wedding tradition. On a later broadcast, Paul noted to another guest that Jan had proven that makeup is allowable for Christian women. She responded: "Brother Good did that. I just agreed with him."

When evangelical women carve out small spaces in which to speak and act with authority, they are bound to feel cramped. Evangelical women's gender roles force them to apologize for and minimize their accomplishments, leaving them little space for self-esteem. The discomfort that accompanies the realization that women are considered inferior to men can be seen in a dialogue about feminism between Pat Robertson and Sheila Walsh on November 28, 1989. After Robertson commented that he would believe women were intellectually equal to men once a woman became the world chess champion, Walsh initially responded hotly, "I like chess—and I'm pretty good." She continued by explaining that women in the church should be encouraged to use their gifts (implying that a list of those gifts would include intellectual ones) for the good of the church.[5] Walsh was careful that day, however, to proclaim: "I am not a feminist; I'm a Christian woman."[6]

Because of their prescribed place, women within the evangelical church are discouraged from asking questions or voicing opinions that contradict male-defined church doctrine. This doctrine is derived, of course, from a *literal* interpretation of the Bible that is assumed to be in line with God's intent; it is not up for contemporary interpretation at all (Hadden and Swann, 1981, p. 100). Carol Virginia Pohli argues:

> Moral Majority women are locked into a space which is psychologically and emotionally confining, and . . . the high walls around them are not easily climbed from either side. They are walls built by acceptance of a belief system which values spiritual "truth" and spiritual "progress" more than it values honest inquiry. (1983, pp. 543–544)

Because this belief system does not value inquiry, women who manage to speak tend to do so in carefully prescribed ways, echoing the views of evangelical men rather than articulating a woman's experience (Pohli, 1983, p. 544). Because women's inquiry is limited to what is already assumed to be true, these women must see themselves as lesser beings, people without ideas worth considering. They are a step further removed from God's inspiration than are men; otherwise, their ideas would be equally considered. Although some evangelical parents try to develop the self-esteem of their daughters, the church's devaluation of women's ideas undermines this goal. Because a woman's legitimate power in the evangelical tradition comes through motherhood, which is respected only in marriage, women must become subordinate to men to have any authority at all. A woman raised in the evangelical tradition has little hope of valuing her own ideas or those of other women. She has a difficult time viewing herself or other women as appropriate authority figures.

The values of an evangelical home may sound more fitting for the 19th century than for today. Indeed, there are significant similarities. Pohli argues that evangelical women of today are put on pedestals, as were their Victorian counterparts (1983, p. 544). Although Pohli explains that evangelical women stay on their pedestals and out of political life because they are closeted in a hegemonic belief system, Andrea Dworkin (1983) credits these women with an awareness of the outside world. Evangelical women, aware of the dangers the world holds for women, seek the protection of men. Dworkin explains:

> Right-wing women have surveyed the world: they find it a dangerous place. They see that work subjects them to more danger from more men; it increases the risk of sexual exploitation. They see that creativity and originality in their kind are ridiculed; they see women thrown out of the circle of male civilization for having ideas, plans, visions, ambitions. They see that traditional marriage means selling to one man, not hundreds: the better deal. . . . They see no way to make their bodies authentically their own and to survive in the world of men. (1983, p. 68)

Whether we accept Pohli's or Dworkin's interpretation of the reason for evangelical women's response to the Bible and religious tradition, the response remains one of unquestioning acceptance of the tradition as interpreted by evangelical men. This interpretation results in an extremely limited sphere of influence and a role of subservience for women, who are viewed as ineligible to speak because they lack moral authority. Thus, a woman's development of her potential, even when it would benefit the church, is a task at odds with the unquestioning acceptance of tradition demanded of one who wishes to remain in the church.

Rigid Gender Roles Limit the Evangelical Church

There are clearly negative implications for the women who are part of the evangelical tradition, but it is also important to note the negative implications for the tradition itself. As Charles Conrad (1983) points out, the evangelical church sees the world in a dichotomized way, viewing the secular world as outsiders not to be trusted. Because church leaders are suspicious of any influence from outside the church tradition, new ideas stand little chance of a fair hearing. Secular ideas are held up to scrutiny and rejected, but theological ideas receive even more scrutiny. Erling Jorstad points out the suspicion evangelicals have for biblical criticism: "The [*700 Club*] preachers also deplored the influence of liberal theology and sophisticated analyses of biblical texts" (1981, p. 34). Secular ideas are given unusual attention by the evangelical church. Many social trends that are thought by many to be positive, such as the increasingly positive treatment of women in the work force, are seen as moral threats by the evangelical community. For example, on September 27, 1992, Pat Robertson, appearing on *Meet the Press,* argued that day care was responsible for nearly all of America's social ills. Robertson's view that the women's movement is to blame for "the breakdown of the American family" (Jorstad, 1981, p. 90) keeps many evangelical women from exploring an enhanced role for themselves, one that might enable the evangelical church to better make use of all of the talents given by God.[7]

The church also loses membership as many women raised in the evangelical tradition find that they must leave the tradition to become fulfilled adults. I could not find a way to develop my talents such that they fit within the tradition's tightly bound gender roles. Like many other women, I left the church. One of my former students was raised in a different religious tradition with similar gender roles. She felt a great deal of tension and contrast between her life at college, where she was a political leader, and at church, where she was not allowed to vote. Her supportive parents wanted her to remain a member of their church but could not help her resolve her frustration with the church's view of her as a woman. The church will not receive the benefits of her God-given talents whether she stays with the church or leaves it. If she stays, she and her talents will be stifled and limited. If she leaves, she will feel that she is damned.

It has not been my intent in writing this essay to ridicule evangelicals but to closely examine one of the group's beliefs and the ramifications of that belief. According to the evangelical church, women are inherently unqualified to speak with spiritual authority. This has profound moral consequences for those without the power to change the religious institution, so it is important that it be evaluated from outside the institutional framework. I harbor no illusions that my writing will overturn centuries of tradition. However, I do nurture the hope that parts of my message will make sense to a few people, who might begin to view their own religion with critical attention and thereby give voice to women of all religions.

Discussion Questions

1. How does the concept of authority differ when God enters the definition? Does religious authority affect women differently than it affects men?

2. What does your religious tradition say about women's roles? How were your childhood and adolescent questions treated (welcomed, discouraged, silenced)? What female role models exist in your church, synagogue, or religious community?

3. Are there differences between male and female religious speakers? If so, what impact might these differences have on their audiences' religious experiences?

4. What are the sources of theological prohibitions on women's speech? How are theological prohibitions similar to or different from secular prohibitions?

5. What are the implications of silencing women on the subject of religion (for the women of the church, for the men of the church, for children, for people outside the religion)?

6. What does it take to break childhood role-model lessons? How does what we're taught about the way men and women ought to behave affect our lives as adults?

References

Bourque, S., & Divine, D. (1985). Introduction: Women and social change. *Women living change* (pp. 1–21). Philadelphia: Temple University Press.

Conrad, C. (1983). The rhetoric of the moral majority: An analysis of romantic form. *Quarterly Journal of Speech, 69,* 59–170.

Dayton, D., & Dayton, L. (1975, May 23). Women as preachers: Evangelical precedents. *Christianity Today, 19,* 4–7.

Dayton, L., & Dayton, D. (1976, January). "Your daughters shall prophesy": Feminism in the Holiness movement. *Methodist History, 14,* 67–92.

Dworkin, A. (1983). *Right-wing women.* New York: Perigee.

Gallup, G., & Castelli, J. (1989). *The people's religion: American faith in the 90's.* New York: Macmillan.

Hadden, J., & Swann, C. (1981). *Prime time preachers: The rising power of televangelism.* Reading, MA: Addison-Wesley.

Janeway, E. (1971). *Man's world, woman's place: A study in social mythology.* New York: Morrow.

Jorstad, E. (1981). *The politics of moralism: The new Christian right in American life.* Minneapolis: Augsburg.

Meredith, A. (1970). *The theology of tradition.* Notre Dame, IN: Fides.

Pohli, C. (1983, Fall). Church closets and back doors: A feminist view of moral majority women. *Feminist Studies, 9,* 529–558.

Wald, K. (1987). *Religion and politics in the United States.* New York: St. Martin's Press.

Wills, G. (1990). *Under God: Religion and American politics.* New York: Simon and Schuster.

Endnotes

1. The author wishes to express appreciation to Professor Kenneth Kuntz, Department of Religion, the University of Iowa; her mother, Gail Lundberg; and her sisters.

2. The women who appear on evangelical television programs are virtually the only women seen by the average American in a leadership role in evangelical religious contexts. Jan Crouch is a rarity because most evangelical television programs do not feature women in prominent roles. Of the five most prominent evangelical television shows, only two programs—Jim Bakker's *PTL Club* and Pat Robertson's *700 Club* —have included women. These evangelical television programs have a large impact on evangelical women because, as Gallup and Castelli

report, "For a significant portion of Americans—older, female, lower income, poorly educated, Evangelical—religious television has become a part of their religious routine" (1989, p. 164).

3. The role women play in the evangelical church is an effort to follow the teachings of the Bible, specifically those of Paul. In his first letter to the Corinthians, Paul advised the fledgling Christian church: "As in all the congregations of the saints, the women should remain silent in the churches. They are not allowed to speak, but must be in submission, as the Law says. If they want to inquire about something, they should ask their own husbands at home; for it is disgraceful for a woman to speak in the church" (1 Cor. 14: 33b–35, New International Version).

4. Ironically, evangelical churches, particularly the Holiness sects, were among the first in America to give women the authority to speak in church. Dayton and Dayton (1975) go so far as to call 19th century Holiness churches feminist. However, they note that the same churches are no longer bastions of feminism. They explain that a number of factors have diverted the Holiness churches away from their early feminism: The "increasing 'professionalism' of the ministry" (p. 7), that is, the authority of experience gave way to the authority of the professionally trained minister (1976, p. 92); "the rising impact of fundamentalism on the Holiness movement and the consequent tendency to drop back into biblical literalism on the issue of women" (1976, pp. 91–92); and the influence of the larger patriarchal society, which led to the elimination of "strange practices" such as women preaching (1976, p. 92).

5. It may be coincidental that Pat Robertson's program included a relatively strong woman soon after his unsuccessful presidential bid in 1988, during which he tried to appear concerned about women's issues. In what Garry Wills took to be an appeal to women, Robertson boasted that adviser Connie Snapp was his highest paid staffer (1990, p. 178).

6. Since Sheila Walsh's departure from the *700 Club* in January 1993, evangelical women have no role models who challenge, even in a limited way, the traditional conception of women's role in the church or the home. I wondered whether her deviance from evangelically correct behavior had resulted in her being fired. A representative of the *700 Club* told me on March 9, 1993, that Walsh left the program because she and her husband were having marital difficulties and were in counseling. The representative stressed that Walsh had "an open invitation"

to return to the program. A news co-anchor on a secular network probably would not feel that marriage counseling was a reason to leave his or her job. Perhaps the role-model status inherent in Walsh's position made her departure unavoidable. After all, an outspoken woman with marital difficulties looks more like a "feminist" than like a "Christian woman." Walsh's departure leaves evangelical women with only the simpering Jan Crouch on whom to model their lives.

7. See the parable of the talents in Matthew 25: 14–30.

16

Courageous Talk

Empowering the Voices of Recovering Female Alcoholics

Kelley R. Chrouser, Ph.D.

Manager of Research
American Dental Hygienists Association

Jack Kay, Ph.D.

Department of Communication
Wayne State University

Sympathetic Ailments

My mother was an alcoholic
And my father never came home.

I find a sort of solace
With a people oppressed
I find a sort of healing
From shared suffering

Can we heal together?

—*María Cristina González*

*W*omen recovering from alcoholism are somehow "displaced" in a rather voluminous quantity of scholarly work. Although much is known about responses to alcoholism, physiological changes, and environmental conditions, little is known about how women "talk" in recovery. Our interest was stimulated as scholars through personal relationships and experiences with women in recovery. All in all, these are incredible women with inordinate courage. Although it might be interesting to speculate on how women literally talk themselves into new identities and acquire different life skills, mostly we just stand in awe.

There tend to be two kinds of alcoholics, grandiose and depressives. The men tend to be grandiose; the women, depressives. I remember I used to pull my fingernails down my face, and I would smash my hand through windows. It drove my boyfriend, soon to be husband, nuts. He can't deal with that depressive, self-loathing person. He thinks I shouldn't feel that way. So I just don't show him that side of me anymore. I just can't. Maybe I just don't know very much and should just shut up, listen, and learn something. But I know that in order to understand, to not drink, I need to share, and I know that it's important to hear that depressive message. I hate not finding—I keep hoping to find a message—a story—that's me.[1]

We live in a culture that mystifies, conceptualizes, and ignores the truths of people's lives. Our culture, according to Miller, "encourages us not to take our own suffering seriously, but rather to make light of it or even to laugh about it. What is more, this attitude is regarded as virtue" (1990, p. 7). Miller goes on to say that many readers of her book, *The Drama of the Gifted Child,* felt that she had described their own lives. They say, "It was *my* life you were describing in your book; how could you have known?" (1990, p. xi). Miller responds that "surprisingly, it was the child in me, condemned to silence long ago—abused, exploited, and turned to stone—who finally found her feelings and along with them her speech, and then told me, in pain, her story" (p. xii). Indeed, the excerpt leading into Miller's indicates a similar need and similar pain, "Will someone *please* read me my story?" (Miller, 1990, p. 8).

Both Miller (1990) and the collective voices of recovering female alcoholics address the issue of "muted voices" living and breathing, speaking (without voice) within(out) our culture.[2] The consequences of voicelessness are disastrous. We end up "preferring . . . to plan self-destruction on a gigantic atomic scale" and inflicting our own abuse histories upon the next generation (with the rationale of doing it for their own good) without even "a trace of a bad consciousness" (Miller, 1990, p. xiv). In fact, it is the process of removing the pain into abstraction that blinds us to the lived realities of oppression. It becomes a closed system that gives the dis-empowered no movement, no voice, no chance for change, and no story.

The voices of addicted women have been muted, with disastrous consequences. In fact, women in Alcoholics Anonymous self-identify "40 percent" of their membership as incest survivors and "another 40 percent" as sexual assault survivors. Addicted women cover sexual violation by "planning self-destruction" on a microscopic scale and inflicting their abuse histories on a world that does not listen—but still pays the price.

The need, then, to empower and "hear" the voices of female recovery extends beyond our concerns as scholars. As friends of recovering female alcoholics, we stand in recognition of their need to hear the voices of other women in recovery. Our work focuses on a collection of voices that need to be heard, privileged, and enfranchised. We hope our efforts help create order out of chaos and self-esteem out of self-abasement for recovering female alcoholics.[3]

"Her" stories are read from a frame that takes seriously the concept of "difference," "otherness," and "mutedness." The reading of the androgyne (Flowers, 1982) gives us a way to read the dominant and the muted. "Androgyne" refers to "a u-topic desire, not by means of separatism or the destruction of men but in terms of integration . . . a way to coexist" both as subjects with constructed (fe)male sides and as subjects interacting with other gendered subjects (Meese, 1990, p. 162). In other words, (re)covery for female alcoholics begins with women hiding behind masculine voices, eventually incorporating more feminine voices, and finally constructing a combined voice, or the "androgynous." Androgyne as a perspective, then, enables us to examine the split/unity of fe/male discourse—a split that women themselves perceive within their conversation.[4]

We present three major "stories" within female discourse: (1) the story of bondage, (2) the story of tug-of-war, and (3) the story of emergence. Each story is followed by a meta-story that serves as an analysis. Finally, we provide tentative conclusions concerning recovering discursive arrangements.

The Story of Bondage, or Houdini's Conundrum: How Do You Bind That Which You Cannot See?

I used to celebrate my birthday. It was special to me, you know? I made such a big deal out of it. Anyway, it [my birthday] stopped being important—somewhere I got lost. I think I must be pretty visual or something, because sometimes I still see her, this child of 3 running naked through the forest, and she's all beat up, raped, molested, and screaming. My father said that people get their just desserts. So, I just drowned her. I wanted her to quit this ugly world, you know? To drink was to die, and she felt no pain in drunkenness.

Once, I was with a man, and he dumped me cold. I downed two quarts of scotch and some tranquilizers. For some crazy reason a woman from AA was worried about me, and she drove all around the city until she found me. I was pronounced dead on arrival, but they revived me. So, anyway, when she didn't die, I acted like I just didn't give a shit. I wore black leather and spit and fought and drank a lot. It was all part of the game. To lock her in an ivory tower.

People were scared of me too. Oh God, I remember once these six bitches beat up on one of my friends—but they didn't want to fuck with me. I acted and talked like I didn't give a shit. They were scared of my mouth— they just weren't free to fuck with me anymore, just the other 40%.

So now, today, I celebrate my AA birthday. One of the coolest things that you told me was that AA didn't promise me heaven, but it opened up the gates of hell long enough to let me out. It's what's become important, but there are things that still I can't tell you. You see—women alcoholics don't want jackshit to know how they feel about that 3-year-old girl. Christ, it's cold in here, isn't it? I'm always so cold.

Meta-story

The story women in Alcoholics Anonymous tell is essentially the story of desired loss. The women who construct the stories have felt a hostile world. That hostility forces the female into hiding. As a result, whoever subjectively uses the word *I* in the story is never revealed. She is hiding somewhere deep inside herself. What the world sees is a shell, a facade, a mask. The shell is cleverly and patiently wrought to protect the wounded female inside from the hostility of the outside. She is purposely lost from view.

Reading a synopsis of loss automatically creates a series of questions. Is she really lost, and how do we know that? If she is lost, what happened to her? Why would a woman do that to herself? How does she quit? Can she? Remarkably, women in recovery confront, perhaps for the first time, the very same questions.

Women tell us about loss, they tell us they are tied up inside a place where others are not supposed to enter. T(he) imprisonment of the female is constructed through her use of male language, male clothing, her rejection of feminine posturings and language, and t(he) use of the word *I*, which is really just an "eye" (you get what you see, only anything else— me—is concealed). First, women disappear within t(he) language. They construct a discourse that reflects masculine language, which is cold, without feeling, rational, and hard. In their eyes, men do not get hurt. Women do. To conceal the woman, to protect her from hurt, women speak "his" story, "his" language. For example, women appear with men who "dump them cold," women lock themselves in "ivory towers," "bitches are frightened of the [encased female's] mouth," and it becomes important not to let "jack(shit) know" how they feel. If we look at the examples separately, a pattern of linguistic protection begins to emerge.

When women are with men who dumped them "cold," they paint a picture of a masculine, feelingless discourse. In fact, within their stories all references to either cold or cool are preceded/succeeded by a male pro/noun. Inversely, all references to warm or hot take on a female pro/noun. Not surprisingly, then, when the *I* that appears in the story announces, "I'm always so cold," we see him—not her. The female is inside somewhere protecting herself with the armor of a feelingless discourse. In fact, the preceding locution indicated her loss, "There are things that still I can't tell you."

The speaker even describes for us the armor of such a discourse. She locks herself in an "ivory tower." The metaphor of the academy posits a male language that is rational and again without feeling. She gets hidden in the language of knowing. The female is somehow "locked inside" the fortress of rationality and appears "like stone," "strong," and importantly, impossible to reach without a fight.

The appearance of fortification serves a vital function. Females (bitches) are frightened by the power of a feelingless discourse. So the adoption of linguistic numbness, of a language premised in absence of feeling, is the equivalency of power and steel. Women construct a painless world by locking themselves inside a language that no longer reflects vulnerable selves. We have instead nothing (importantly nothing) more than fortified exteriors.

Within the story, women talk about building the facade, brick by brick, through the adoption of male clothing and male posturings: "I wore black leather and chains"; "I fought and spit and drank." For all appearances, "she" is meant to be "he."

Posturing, in and of itself, is only one brick helping to form the exterior barricade. A female who postures as male cannot stop herself from entering the exterior anymore than she can stop others from encroaching upon the interior. The power of the woman in masculine attire is no match for the power of the woman who has "mastered" the feelingless discourse of the male world. In fact, "bitches" (who have just the attire) are not a match for the woman who acts like she just doesn't "give a shit." They (the bitches) are frightened of t(he) "mouth." The loss of the woman is merely the entrapment of the woman, constructed by the woman to ward off encroachment and to ward off her own betrayal of herself by letting "her" engage the world.

The reasons women opt for hiding themselves within a male exterior are disquieting. One reason is to end the violence and violations with which they have lived. When the image of the little girl is drawn into the story, our automatic response is to want desperately to envision a pretty child smiling, carefree, and happy. Instead we are reminded—when it would be easier to hide—that the image is no more than a mirage. An image is slashed, beaten, raped, and abandoned. The lure of a fortress is not to be taken lightly. When women *are* encroached upon, their natural reaction is to fortify themselves. These women have a real need to adopt both a language and an appearance that defy further encroachment. By posturing as a male, there is no woman left to violate, to rape, or to burn. People no longer want to either figuratively or literally "fuck with them."

Furthermore, women in Alcoholics Anonymous have a real need to numb themselves. Posturing as male does not create a male. When language cannot sufficiently numb the females' feelings, alcohol, the great anesthetizer, does. Women in recovery frame their abuse of alcohol as a tool for oblivion—of being without a soul; if a body has no soul, violation cannot hurt. In their words, "There was no pain in drunkenness." Thus, drinking is not the problem; waking up sober is. "Sobriety hurt, and I never wanted to feel anything."

Interestingly, women never seem to talk about their drinking as an attempt to kill the body, only as an attempt to kill the female inside the body. Alcohol is now the double-edged sword, "To drink was to die (kill the female which is now killing the male) and to not drink made me feel (female) like dying." The behavior of alcoholism becomes a vicious cycle, and the language of alcoholism reflects the same cyclical and vicious process. "I made me numb, which hurts; I tried to kill her and they revived her, so I made me numb, which hurts." What is comforting and at the same time heartbreaking about the cycle of language and behavior is that it is the beginning of the tug-of-war that signals either recovery or, conversely, death.

The Story of Tug-of-War, or the Unbalanced Scales

Today, I don't try to figure out my mother anymore. Once, when I was drinking and my life was fucked up, it was important to see her so I could avoid me. Well, my mom isn't an alkie or anything—she drank when my dad died, but everyone else [in my family] is just sick. My mom, she just didn't want the neighbors to see. So she snuck cigarettes into the house. Even when I drank, I never drank in public. Only my sons saw their drunken mother. I didn't have a role model, but I know I have to learn to love me first.

That's important [loving me first] because when I was a little girl I thought no one loved me. I was a bastard and "bastard" meant something bad. My mother loved me and I couldn't feel it, but I felt my stepfather when he molested me. He was nice. I found out later it was wrong [the touching] so I didn't let anyone love me no more. I cried, last year, at my [real] father's grave site. Shit, I didn't even know him, and so I cried for me —for me, damn it—and I was worth it.

I know survivors. I can spot them. Around 18 months sober—up it comes, all that abuse women hid from themselves for so long. Take the fucking chemicals out and there it is. Oh God, I remember that pain too, I remember that fear. When I was 18 months sober, I felt so crazy and I just started screaming. All I could get out was my stepfather's name. I remembered, I saw pictures first, a hand, an arm, and then his face and cigarette burns, and the rape. I don't want anything to do with him. I'm changing my name. He should just be stopped. His name.

So now, I listen to female speakers. I *need* to hear *her* depressive story, not *his* grandiose one. His story doesn't understand my self-loathing, depressed one. I see the eyes of the woman alcoholic and they're full of life, eyes that once felt nothing. Women, we don't have to have those eyes anymore. We don't have to drown ourselves cold.

When I remember how painful my hell was, I have a lot to be grateful for. Once I was at a meeting and a guy brought in his 5-year-old daughter.

It was like looking in a mirror. A woman told me that maybe God wanted me to see something. She [the little girl] was so pretty. Maybe I need to get rid of that father thing now—release me. Maybe the little girl finally died and maybe not. Maybe I just need to grieve for the parts of her that are gone. One sick man killed her. It took a long time to realize that—he was just one sick man.

Sometimes I still want to curl up in a fetal position and I can't talk. I won't talk. I get so sick and so lost—sort of untreated alcoholism. When I'm there now, though, I know that my God cried for me. Just for me.

Meta-story

Growing up in Alcoholics Anonymous looks and feels very much like adolescence, with one major exception. The women in Alcoholics Anonymous image themselves as inside, and the desire to stay there can be overpowering. Adolescents may image themselves inside as well, but there is more desire to be outside. The concept of unbalanced scales is played out in women's discursive formations as a process of "growing up." When we first encountered the phrase "to grow up," we thought it was ridiculous and demeaning. These were, after all, grown women. When we stayed around long enough to figure out what growing up entailed, we recognized the courage it took to do so.

For women in Alcoholics Anonymous, the outside is frightening. The world they encounter is initially painful enough to have sent them scurrying inside themselves. Coming out and encountering the world without the benefit of alcohol or other mood-altering chemicals is an incredibly courageous journey. Recovering women shape that journey in three ways: (1) engaging in a tug-of-war between the self and the image of the mother; (2) beginning separations of the self from the father; and (3) facing the occasional emergence and disappearance of the self. All three create an image of scales, with the self on one end and mother/father on the other end. Growing up in Alcoholics Anonymous sways back and forth between dependency and autonomy of self in ways similar to the emerging adult in adolescent youth.

Growing up in Alcoholics Anonymous is always contingent upon abstinence. In other words, women do not begin adolescence until they begin sobriety. There is an often-iterated belief in recovery that alcohol stunts emotional growth. The logic appears in this format: If a woman began drinking at 13 and entered Alcoholics Anonymous at 28, she would be a 13-year-old feeling child in a 28-year-old body. If she remains sober, the process of emotional development begins as a struggle against the image of the mother.

The mother, for women in recovery, is most often imaged as the one who created behavioral rules for the alcoholic. Nearly all of the women in Alcoholics Anonymous talk about their mothers as literal or figurative missing entities. She "left me at 5" or "I couldn't feel her love" or "She wasn't like us." Thus, the mother's behavior becomes a model for absence; "Being a mother today is difficult with no role model." The mother is portrayed as an emotionally unavailable woman. Growing up in Alcoholics Anonymous is cast as a separation of the self from the image of the emotionally unavailable mother.

The rejection of the mother as image (not as person) places the self directly before what is entrapping the female. The inaccessibility of mother is rejected. The mother is the image of entrapment, and entrapment of the recovering woman is what was killing her. A woman in recovery first has to reject the image of bondage in order to confront the jailer. The rejection of entrapment places the woman before the image of the father. When drinking, women see themselves as donning the mask of the male. That mask needs to be removed in recovery. She needs to literally (re)cover herself by confronting the tale of the father.

The story women tell of the father shifts ground as women grow up. When the father is first encountered, he is bigger than the voice of the female. She speaks as a little girl to this godlike male. To the little girl the father is that giant. In recovery, women (re)cover the father's face as well as their own. He loses his stature, and she gains whatever she takes away from him. She (re)covers the father sexually and linguistically.

The father is (re)covered sexually. In fact, to talk as a recovering woman is to first talk as the little girl to the father and later to talk as the woman to a faulty man. When the little girl speaks in recovery, she is thought of by others in the program as regressing. Little girls in Alcoholics Anonymous discourse are in "fetal positions," are "bruised and beaten" and "burned by his cigarettes." His (the father's) power is literally sexual. The abuse of the little girl aids in the construction of fathered discourse in recovery.

Women in recovery do not initially talk about sexual abuse issues. Most women are silenced. The power of that silence is frightening, and women in recovery acknowledge the force of breaking silence. They "scream his name." They "shake." They "go crazy and scream that horrible scream that comes from their gut somewhere deep inside." Alcohol has dimmed the memory for so long, and "when the chemicals are out of the system—up it comes." Recovery is partially the refusal to hide the abuse from the self. Women are encouraged to "remember." The images of re-membering are at first visual in that she "sees the father" and "remembers the rape." To age in Alcoholics Anonymous is to move beyond the visual memory and into the feeling memory "to remember the pain and remem-ber the fear." To recover becomes a matter of feeling what that girl-child felt and of breaking the silence of the father's tyranny. Women begin to recover when they acknowledge their own pain and refuse to remain silent.

Breaking the silence is to break with the little girl who "does not talk." An old adage tells us children (in this case, little girls) should be seen and not heard. To "not speak" in Alcoholics Anonymous is portrayed as a move backward in time, a move back toward the power of the father over the little girl. The "little girl" is the voice that refused to speak and the voice that sought chemicals to subvert her own femininity. Only when a woman begins to polarize the little girl with the voice of a grown woman is she truly in recovery. The little girl is in "untreated alcoholism." The woman is in "recovery."

Recovery is a story about reaching adulthood and "grieving over the lost little girl." When women in recovery speak as women, they also speak differently about the father. They "get rid of that father thing" and "cry at the father's grave." Women grow up. They let the "little girl" heighten and mature. The father loses his ability to dominate because he is no longer speaking from a space bigger than the woman's.

When women in recovery begin to reject the model of the mother and the dominance of the father, the question still remains: Why is this story called the unbalanced scales? The scales remain unbalanced in terms of the self.

The scales are unbalanced because there remains little room for the fe-male to speak: Her (his)story is laden with the entrapment of the mother, the dominance of the father, and the entrapment of the self. The self begins to emerge in Alcoholics Anonymous with the rejection of the image of the mother and the father. The woman gains priority on the daughter-mother continuum ("I need to love me first"), and she reduces the size of the father ("I need to get rid of that father thing") because to do so "releases the self."

There is little in this world that serves as a role model (not mother) for the woman's emergence as both a rational and a feeling person (nor father). There is certainly little in the alcoholic woman's life to suggest that being on the outside of herself will be rewarding and worthwhile. She is beaten and abused and silenced. Speaking is easier when there is consensus for your opinions or authority behind you. It would be easier to talk about feminist theory than feelings of femininity. One seems so rational; the other, so personal.

Women alcoholics tell a surprisingly similar story. The self who is emerging is so tentative she occasionally falls back on herself. Sometimes she speaks with the authority of the man she portrayed when drinking. She "knows" and she "shuts up and listens" and she "sees," but she does not "feel."

In different ways, some women refuse the journey. One woman simply could not image a life that made her feel what she had hidden from herself for so long. She chose a masculine suicide attempt (gunshot) aimed at the feminine (the chest/the heart). Other women refused to "feel" the pain of the little girl. "I hid her from myself for so long. I figure she must be pretty bad." Other women are talked about as simply "unwilling." (Re)covery is the story of growing up. Women are asked to let their little girl age herself and to let the woman finally meet the world.

The Story of Emergence, or the (Re)casting of a Life

Today I stay sober by suiting up and showing up. My children are scarred. My friends tell me to suit and show because I might be the only Big Book[5] my children read. Yesterday, I got a call from my son's wife. My son just went to treatment. So I'll continue to suit up and show up to be the Big Book that someone else's children read because you showed up long enough to let my children read yours.

I remember once I didn't want to show and suit up. I wanted to quit, and I didn't want to feel the pain of memory. I hated what one sick man did to me. My sponsor,[6] God bless her, told me to go through the tunnel because the other side was worth it. I wouldn't have to fight anyone or anything. My hardness has been softened.

When I was drinking, I thought I could talk with the best of them. When I started coming to Alcoholics Anonymous, I couldn't even say I was an alcoholic for a year. Today, I have opinions and I can say them out loud. That's kind of nice. Today, I know that my God cried for me. I can now look in the mirror daily and love myself through the fellowship of Alcoholics Anonymous. I was at the beach once and on the horizon was a ship. Off in the distance was another ship, a "fellow" ship. That ship was there to help the other through rocky waters. They were close enough. I thank you, Alcoholics Anonymous, for being close enough and for show-ing me the other side. It was worth it.

Meta-story

In the "She Story" a new voice emerges. The voice belongs to a female who has (re)covered the image of the female and the image of the male: the androgyne.

When the little girl grows up, the father goes down. In the eyes of a recovering woman, the father becomes faulty. The image of the male is (re)cast in accordance with the changing image of the woman. She has a voice of her own. She does not appear in man's image any longer. She can now listen "to *her* depressive story, not *his* grandiose story." Her story is as important as his. He can no longer "shut her up."

The male is (re)cast, however, in ways similar to the (re)casting of the woman. By rejecting images of the mother and the father that dominated her, the woman grows up in her own discourse. Growing up gives her a new perspective. For example, most of us perceive our parents very differ-ently today than we did when we were teenagers. We probably changed a whole lot more than our parents did. Women in Alcoholics Anonymous change the image of the father in similar ways. After all, they know the language of the man, but the "he" within their worlds is now feminine as well. They can now comfortably "suit up and show up" in masculine metaphors to be the "Big Book that their children read." The "she" of her own discourse is both masculine and feminine—androgynous.

Conclusion

The ability to leave a trace that can be "read" is never taken lightly in the world of Alcoholics Anonymous. When women are in regression (when they speak/do not speak) as little girls, they do not leave a text for other women to read. They are silent. When women in Alcoholics Anonymous begin to speak as a "woman," they begin to be "heard" and they leave "her story to be heard." That story is important to other women in recov-ery. Other women now hear "her" depressive story, and in the words of a recovering woman, "Her depressive story was important for me to hear."

The story of (re)covery is (re)cast as a willingness to go "through the tunnel" because "the other side is worth it." It is worthwhile to find the female inside and "stop fighting [a masculine reference] anyone or any-thing." Women in recovery begin to quit fighting the male because and only because they stop fighting the female. Her "hardness has been softened," and she can now "talk about it and it is nice." The male and the female become enjoined in recovery discourse. To talk like a recovering woman is to talk in both feminine and masculine ways that allow neither component to dominate the other. Alcoholics Anonymous is (re)cast as a "fellow"ship where males and females are on the same plane—"same horizon"—and they are "close enough."

Unfortunately, women still know the language of the man, and the combination of a female voice with a male voice is tentative. The weight of tradition and history is on the side of rationality and subverted feminism. The combined voice speaks the language of seeing (little girl seen) and feeling (woman heard) simultaneously, but with a tendency to weigh down the masculine. In other words, women in recovery are constructing an "androgynous" voice through the emergence of a feminine voice that is incorporated into the masculine voice. Although the combined voice may be just "tentative," recovery is a process of making the androgynous voice more prominent. Fortunately, women in Alcoholics Anonymous appear to be (re)constructing a story of their own, a (her)story to be seen and, most importantly, read.[7]

Discussion Questions

1. If the three stories were read from differing cultural perspectives, what would these stories sound like? Feel like? Why?

2. What significant polarities or contradictions seem to recur in each woman's story? Why do you think this happens?

3. What assumptions did you make about women and alcoholism from this reading?

4. What implications does this essay raise concerning women, their bodies, and constructions of health?

5. Do you see yourself or someone you care about in these stories? What emotional responses do you have to the similarities?

References

Alcoholics Anonymous. (1976). *Alcoholics Anonymous: The story of how many thousands of men and women have recovered from alcoholism* (3rd ed.). New York: Author.

Barthes, R. (1986). *The rustle of language* (R. Howards, Trans.). New York: Hill & Wang.

Beckman, L. J., & Amaro, H. (1986). Personal and social difficulties faced by women and men entering alcoholism treatment. *Journal of Studies on Alcohol, 47,* 135–145.

Bissel, L. (1985). Introduction. In Rachel V., *A woman like you: Life stories of women recovering from alcoholism and addiction* (pp. xvii–xxvi). San Francisco: Harper & Row.

Chrouser, K. R. (1990). *A critical analysis of the discourse and reconstructed stories shared by recovering female alcoholics in Alcoholics Anonymous.* Unpublished dissertation. Lincoln, NE: University of Nebraska–Lincoln.

Derrida, J. (1972). *Positions.* Paris: Minuit.

Fillmore, K. M. (1984). "When angels fall": Women's drinking as cultural preoccupation and as reality. In S. C. Wilsnack & L. J. Beckman (Eds.), *Alcohol problems in women: Antecedents, consequences, and intervention* (pp. 7–36). New York: Guilford Press.

Flowers, B. S. (1982). The "I" in Adrienne Rich: Individuation and the androgyne archetype. In G. Mora & K. S. Van Hooft (Eds.), *Theory and practice of feminist literary criticism* (pp. 14–35). Ypsilanti, MI: Bilingual Press.

Foucault, M. (1982). The subject and power. In H. L. Dreyfus and P. Rabinow (Eds.), *Michel Foucault: Beyond structuralism and hermeneutics* (p. 208). Brighton, MA: Harvester Press.

Geohegan, V. (1987). *Utopianism and Marxism.* London: Metheun.

Hegel, G. W. F. (1975). *Lectures on the philosophy of world history* (H. B. Nisbet, Trans.; D. Forbes, Introduction). Cambridge: University Press. (Original work published 1930)

Hermann, A. (1989). *The dialogic and difference.* New York: Columbia University Press.

Lacan, J. (1988). Freud's papers on technique 1953–1954. In J. A. Miller (Ed.) and J. Forrester (Trans.), *The seminar of Jacques Lacan: Book I* (pp. 7–18). New York: Norton. (Original work published 1975)

Meese, E. A. (1990). (Ex)tensions: Refiguring feminist criticism. Urbana: University of Illinois Press.

Miller, A. (1990). *The drama of the gifted child* (R. Ward, Trans.). New York: Basic Books. (Original work published 1979)

Sarup, M. (1989). *An introductory guide to post-structuralism and post-modernism.* Athens: University of Georgia Press.

Showalter, E. (Ed.). (1985). *The new feminist criticism: Essays on women, literature, and theory.* New York: Pantheon.

Stevens, S., Arbiter, N., & Glider, P. (1989). Women residents: Expanding their role to increase treatment effectiveness in substance abuse programs. *International Journal of the Addictions, 24,* 425–434.

Weedon, C. (1987). *Feminist practice and poststructuralist theory.* Oxford: Basil Blackwell.

Endnotes

1. All texts of conversations presented in this essay are reconstructed from field notes of ethnographic observations that occurred at open meetings of Alcoholics Anonymous or during private interviews outside formal meetings.

2. The process of silencing is a cultural and social production that is implicated and practiced in discourse. Western rhetorical philosophy, for example, has a long (his)story of wrestling with polarity. See, for example, readings of German dialecticism (Geohegan, 1987; Hegel, 1930); French poststructuralism (Barthes, 1986; Derrida, 1972; Foucault, 1982; Lacan, 1988; Sarup, 1989). Unfortunately, whenever there is a difference, or two poles, one pole takes on a positive evaluation, whereas the other takes on a negative evaluation. The legacy of patriarchy is to present us with a dominant cultural view while others remain inconspicuously absent (see Flowers, 1982; Hermann, 1989; Showalter, 1985; Weedon, 1987). Furthermore, research on alcoholism serves as exemplar of "her" exclusion (see Beckman & Amaro, 1986; Bissel, 1985; Fillmore, 1984; Stevens, Arbiter, & Glider, 1989).

3. The voices of recovering women (re)presented in this text were gathered utilizing ethnographic research practices. Stories and conversations were listened to, participated in, and written up as both verbatim accounts and thick descriptions. Field notes were taken over a 10-month period. Notes were restricted to open meetings and private interviews in deference to the requirements of Alcoholics Anonymous.

More than 90 voices appear in the text (see Chrouser, 1990). For complete field notes see Chrouser, 1990, Appendix.

4. See also Flowers (1982). For a more thorough discussion of how "androgyne" is utilized in this text, see Chrouser (1990, pp. 166–171).

5. Big Book is an Alcoholics Anonymous slang term for *Alcoholics Anonymous: The story of how many thousands of men and women have recovered from alcoholism* (1976). This text details the principles of recovery for Alcoholics Anonymous members and may be referred to in their conversations as either the Big Book or the Alcoholic's Bible.

6. The term *sponsor* refers to a specific relationship in Alcoholics Anonymous. Long-standing members serve as sponsors for new members. *Sponsoree* refers to the person being sponsored.

7. Our language is one in which women are absent. When discourse tells women to be silent, that they do not exist (even while they live and breathe), then discourse figuratively anticipates/welcomes their death. Furthermore, men are implicated in women's stories as well. If men and women are in some essence the Jungian anima and animus, then men are incomplete within their own discourse as well. Our language tells men that it is not appropriate for them to find ways of expressing their grief or their pain. In other words, the omission of the female is tantamount to the castration of the male/fe.

Finally, we wish to clarify that our analysis of the discourse is limited to one particular forum of female recovery from addiction, Alcoholics Anonymous, and to a small segment of even that group. Other voices within Alcoholics Anonymous itself (i.e., class, race, sexualities, nonabused counterparts, etc.) need the empowerment of critical understanding as well. We believe that the locations of "women" are plural and multifaceted. In fact, in the larger work from which this is drawn (see Chrouser, 1990), two additional readings exist of the same texts. We would applaud efforts to imbricate other treatment modalities and approaches. This analysis is not intended to exist as "the" reading, just as "a" reading, "a" way to let others read "herstory."

17

"I'm Alive, Thank You"

Women's Accounts of HIV/AIDS

Judith Liu, Ph.D.
Kathleen Grove, Ph.D.

Department of Sociology
University of San Diego

Donald P. Kelly, Ph.D.

Department of Sociology
University of California, San Diego

Inscribing Your Name
in the Book of Life

for N. Z.

I have grown to hate the sun
that floods your consulting room.
Once I left my colored scarf there
while outside the bluejays
built a nest, while outside the wind
wailed as if it were my own sorrow,
when you appeared before me like a dream
and said "That's all for now" and I
believed you. I believed the anguish
of my own heart would stop, the pain
would stop and I'd be free again,
in a white room I would leave you,
lay you to rest, the healing done,
the deed done, and you would resurrect,
you would rise up, your own miracle—
me, the healed one, your mirror.

In the deep, soft silence of the afternoon
we are touched and cast around us
dappled light. When the empty wall
is only a shadow, when the moonswept wall
is only a ladder you climb up to me,
peer down as circles form themselves
into mirrors absent of our reflections.
You say "We are absent of ourselves"
then disappear just as the hologram expands—
smoke, silver, lightning white.

    —Phyllis Kahaney

Our initial involvement with this disease was the result of a caregiver's retreat during which Judith became involved with Dale, a young man with AIDS. They were friends for almost 4 years before he died on May 31, 1995. This association, in turn, affected Donald who, through Judith, also came to know Dale. Kathleen went to school with one of the women in the study and has known her for more than 20 years. These personal relationships with sufferers of AIDS, along with the relationships developed with the women in this study, have made us hope that our research will help people to empathize with anyone who has become HIV positive by giving a human face to a social problem that is affecting our society. In this essay we have attempted to give voice to HIV positive women who might not otherwise be heard, and who may be nothing more than mere statistics to most people.

"If you find out early, there's a lot of life you've got to live."

Wearing a black jumpsuit, a white frilly blouse, and a black fedora, she is striking as she enters the room. A strawberry blond, at 5 ft 7 in. slender and statuesque, Nicole, with her large eyes and dazzling smile, immediately captures your attention. Eyes turn to her; a small group gravitates toward her and the questions begin. "You can see the surprise in their eyes. They don't mean to look so shocked to see me walking around, but they are. 'How *are* you?' is what they want to ask." Because Nicole is all too familiar with doctors and hospitals, the question is inevitable. But Nicole's lilting laughter fills the room as she replies, "Yes, I'm alive, thank you. I'm still here." With a wave of her hands, she goes on talking about her children, and her husband.

Despite her appearance of health and vitality, Nicole begins to cough. At first the episodes are short and sporadic, but as the evening wears on, there are a series of long, hacking episodes. They are of such severity that it becomes clear that something is very wrong. And what is wrong is that Nicole has acquired immunodeficiency syndrome (AIDS).

As early as 1982, Nicole had extreme fatigue, chronic yeast infections, pelvic inflammatory disease, and viral pneumonia, yet she was not diagnosed with AIDS until 1989.

> I had pneumonia, viral pneumonia in 1987. Couldn't figure that one out either. It was bizarre. The doctor gave me [a medicine], and he says, "If you're not better overnight, if you feel like you can't breathe, and you're not going to make it, I'm going to hospitalize you."

And although she was hospitalized, the doctors were hesitant to test for the presence of the human immunodeficiency virus (HIV), and did not do it.

> Oh, hell no. Do I fit the risk group? I must look right. . . . The doctors kept saying when I went into the hospital, "No, not her, she's—look, she's white, she's been married for almost 7 years, she's been with her husband for 7 years, she has a child, the child is well. Her husband is well. They come from a good family," and, uh, "No, it couldn't possibly be [AIDS]." What's funny is I'm dying. I'm on 100% oxygen and I'm saying, "Hey guys, in September of 1982, I had this flu." And I'm trying to tell them I was really sick initially. . . . And I was not sick for 2 or 3 days; I was sick for weeks. I lost 30 pounds; I was so sick. . . . Every gland in my body was swollen. There was a period of a week when I couldn't even walk. . . . It was horrible. And I went into emergency three different times and they told me I had the 24-hour flu. And I'm going for 3 weeks!

Nicole's problems with diagnosis are not uncommon because physicians tend to overlook gynecological manifestations of the disease, such as recurrent vaginal infections and/or pelvic inflammatory disease. All too often, these symptoms are not given serious consideration as indicators of a more serious disease. Nicole recalls:

> I had pelvic inflammatory disease, and I've had chronic yeast infections since my first daughter was born. And I just called the doctor up, I didn't even have to go in anymore. He says, "Instead of three, let's make it six [prescription] refills" because I was having them so frequently. It was not unusual to have a yeast infection, a severe discharge, for 3 weeks out of the month for a year straight.

In desperation, Nicole finally wanted to "find out what was wrong," so she had herself tested. Not only was she HIV seropositive, but she was finally diagnosed as having AIDS.

Nicole believes she was infected by the man she was living with in 1982.

> In 1982, I met a man, and I moved in with him; we were supposed to get married. I ended up leaving him because I found out that he was an IV [intravenous] drug abuser. He was using while I was living with him. I

knew that he had been clean for 10 months prior to meeting me. And he had gone back into it.

Although she admits to "using drugs," but never intravenously, and being sexually active, when she was diagnosed, she began thinking about her past partners. Nicole zeroed in on this relationship because "this one, it just fit."

> I could prove the intravenous drug use [by my partner]. But I couldn't prove the [bi]sexual thing, so I don't even bring it up. Because I know he would do anything to get a fix, and I knew what area he was in; I met him here in [town], and I knew the kind of people he hung with. And his family warned me that he was involved in very extremely high risk behavior. They warned me.

"J didn't go out and ask for AJDS."

Cuddling Tony, her 13-month-old baby, in her lap, Lynette coos, "Who is this little boy? Who is this boy?" The telephone rings, and Lynette stiffens. "We had to spend what little money we have to buy one of those damn answering machines because it is getting to the point that the creditors are out to get us, and I can't handle the stress." Lynette—an articulate, attractive brunette with expressive brown eyes—dejectedly drops her head while she listens to yet another message demanding her to "call the following number immediately or your bill will be sent to a collection agency."

> We had to get an answering machine because we need to know who is on the other end. Because we have only one car, Jim has to call me to pick him up. It got so bad, you know, that I was afraid to answer the phone 'cause [the creditors] were calling all the time and I, you know, just can't handle it anymore. Now I can just listen and pick up when it's a call I need to take.

When Lynette was 24 and Jim—a tall, slender, blond—was 26, they "met each other and it was just incredible; we were best friends for almost a year and it was just like [we were] soul mates."

> It was like soul mates, and we finally realized that there was more to this, and if we got married, we had always talked since we very first met about wanting to find someone that wanted a big family and how hard that was these days because everyone is so career-oriented.

So they married, and they moved to California. "We were married about 6 months when we started trying to get pregnant. It took us almost a year-and-a-half. We got pregnant at the end of 1989, November of '89, um, we went home for Christmas and told everybody. We were all excited." Lynette and Jim decided to have the baby naturally and found a birth center.

> We were all excited; we were going to have our baby at a birth center; we were very naturally-oriented people. Went into the birth center and the first day we were there, they said, "You know we do all these preliminary tests, and you know we're going to do this, and we're going to do this, and we're going to do an HIV test, and we're going to do this." "Sure, fine," you know, "where do I sign?"

Two weeks later, Lynette was called at work and was summoned to "come in immediately." Only after Lynette was reassured that "nothing is wrong with the baby, but you have to come in right now," did she decide to wait until the following morning so that Jim could accompany her. When they arrived, Lynette and Jim were summarily told, "Your test came back positive; you're HIV [sero]positive and you can't have your baby here." Lynette and Jim were politely—but firmly—shown the door with a list of doctors who could help them.

"Terrified, shocked, and in a panic," Lynette and Jim "desperately" sought out the doctors, who assured them that they would not only help them but also help their unborn child.

> Um, the woman at the birth center, when she told me that I was HIV [sero]positive, the second thing she said to me was, "It's not too late to terminate." "Yeah," and I said, "you don't understand. You don't understand. You know, since I was a little girl, I wanted to be a mom. That's what I've always wanted, you know. You don't understand. And that was the great thing about Dr. Smith. We walked in his office, and he said, "You know, you're going to be fine. You—we don't even need to think about terminating. If the baby is positive, we're going to be there for you, and if he is negative, we are going to be there for you."

Jim was tested as well and he, too, was HIV seropositive. Six months later, Tony was born and "he tested negative and we were all absolutely thrilled. And it was just wonderful. Just wonderful. He grew incredibly well, he did great, no problems." Seven months later, however, Tony was retested and the results were: HIV seropositive.

> [Tony] did really well, and then when he was about six months old, right before Christmas, I started feeling really weird about it. And um, I said,

"Jim, it's not okay. Things are not okay," and he said, "No, you're just being paranoid, you're just being a mom." And we went in for a checkup, and they said, um, "The tests have come back positive, but we're sure it was a mistake." Well, I knew it wasn't and I said, "Okay." They said, "We know it's a lab mistake; I mean, look at him, he's just healthy and beautiful. It's a mistake; we just need to do [the test] again. So we did it again, and we found out in January that he was [sero]positive. But I, I think I probably knew it in December. I feel really, really guilty that I gave this to him.

Lynette feels tremendous guilt because she believes she was infected by her first husband and is the source of HIV infection in her family.

I was married when I was 18, to a very, um, ill man, a mentally ill person who was apparently schizophrenic, had drugs in his earlier days, in and out of mental hospitals the whole 2 years we were married. I don't know, I don't know if I got it from George and I gave it to Jim or if Jim got it from somebody and gave it to me. Um, neither one of us have been wild, promiscuous people, but we have both slept with people that we didn't know incredibly well. You know, not often, but it only takes one. We don't really think about that; we don't really focus on that. I, you know in all honesty, when, whenever I sit down and think about it hard, if Jim and I had known ahead of time, we would have still gotten married. . . . I felt a lot of guilt that it was me, you know, I know it was me, it was me, it was me, it was me, but [Jim has] never acted that way, you know. You know, if I got it from him, if Jim had HIV before we got married and we had had AIDS testing before we got married, which we didn't do, I would have married him anyway because he is absolutely the most supportive person I have ever met in my life. He is my soul mate, like I said.

"J mean, J wouldn't know to this day
if J were watching for symptoms."

Nestled comfortably on her couch and surrounded by homemade pillows and needlepoint pictures in her neat, cozy apartment, Shelley tells her story. Smoking one cigarette after another, this 5 ft. 5 in., sandy-blond, blue-eyed dynamo with a bubbly personality concluded, "It finally got to me. We were together 8 years." After a tumultuous relationship, at age 30, Shelley decided that it was time to move on because her boyfriend was sleeping around. "I, he and I had split. I was going to New York to start a new life, the whole thing. And it [HIV testing] just seemed like the responsible thing to do. I thought it would be a good thing to know," especially since "it wasn't the first sexually transmitted disease [I had gotten from him]."

But in July of 1988, Shelley was not expecting the news the doctor called to deliver:

> He said, "We got your results back, and you tested [HIV sero]positive, and I need you to come in to get a T4 cell test to see the level." And it was like, "Okay." I don't really remember the rest of the day. I think it was probably 4:00 in the afternoon, and I had, maybe, an hour at work to go. When I got home, I told my parents. And that was pretty much it. It was one of those numb days.

Although she was aware that her boyfriend was sexually active, it did not dawn on her until after the results that she could possibly be HIV seropositive, because "my 'ex' is not a drug user; he is not bisexual. He is just heterosexually active."

When she learned of her HIV status, Shelley immediately called her ex-boyfriend.

> The major dilemma was, it wasn't a dilemma, but, how do I tell him? We had split, we were really negative, I mean, anti-relationship at that point anyway. And I had to tell him. But it wasn't okay. . . . He didn't know. I told him. And he turned around and tested [sero]positive. "Why? Why did you get tested? Why did you get tested?" You know, he freaked out at that. I think he would have been happier to not [know]. Now at this point, we do still talk, after he got over the shock, he got tested. And then after he got over that shock, it was like, he was real pleased to know at an early stage that this was the case [that he was HIV seropositive].

Later, Shelley and her ex-boyfriend talked about how he had been infected.

> We've talked about it, and I'm inclined to think, he does a lot of Third World travel. And when he went down to Brazil, and when he came back from Brazil, he had hepatitis. I'm inclined to think he probably picked it up down there. Just because that made sense.

For Shelley, the hardest thing about being HIV seropositive is

> Well, it wasn't until—well, actually, it hit me up front, and then it hit me again. And that was that I won't have any children. And that hit me the hardest, of anything else. I also went through the "I feel like a leper" period.

Despite the obvious differences in the routes that were taken in arriving at an HIV diagnosis, these three stories have several details in common. First, although it is generally conceded that anyone can become infected, the social constructions that ultimately define AIDS through risk groups make it such that even the medical establishment is "locked" into that way of perceiving the disease. Risk group identification produces a mindset and constructs a reality that obscures the possibility of recognizing HIV infection in people not associated with these groups. Further, many women are not diagnosed until their health has been compromised to such an extent that testing for HIV infection remains the *only* viable option to explain their condition.

Second, the fact that AIDS risk groups are associated with already stigmatized groups results in the immediate marginalization of women who are diagnosed as HIV seropositive—they have managed to "catch" a disease that only "bad" people get. Consequently, the women we interviewed are very careful in constructing their stories about how they were infected to maintain as much as possible the aura that they were and are moral individuals. Their stories are highly context-specific so that they can try to explain how ordinary their situations are. That is, there is nothing in their stories about how they or their partners were infected that would necessarily lead anyone to conclude that their behavior was in any way deviant. In the three cases illustrated here, all the women sought a causal link to their infection that made them the unlucky recipient of a deadly disease. Nicole's lover was an IV drug "abuser"; Lynette's first husband was a "mentally ill" drug user; and Shelley's ex-boyfriend managed somehow to become infected as the result of traveling in the Third World.

Despite their attempts to normalize their lives so as to mitigate the marginalizing and stigmatizing effects of an HIV diagnosis, HIV-seropositive women feel a sense of detachment that is exceedingly problematic for them. Women need to feel that they are attached to networks of caring individuals, yet an HIV diagnosis has the potential to shatter the existing networks to which HIV-seropositive women belong. Consequently, merely constructing their stories is not enough. Further complications arise as they consider the questions: "Who do I tell and why?"

"It's like I have taken one step out of the closet."

One of the problems of HIV infection is the stigmatization that accompanies its diagnosis. As a consequence, the women we interviewed initially made a conscious decision to delineate between the public and private spheres of their lives. What you tell is as important as whom you tell. Kristen, a 25-year-old, single restaurant manager, details the difficulties that accompany being infected with a disease associated with "bad" people:

> It's like any assumption they make about me is wrong, pretty much, unless they know the story. And it's a pretty personal story, and I can't tell you how many times I've had to tell it in the last year. Because every time I tell somebody that I have it, I tell them the story that goes with it because I want them to understand. Even though they know me and they really care about me and they have a lot of sympathy and they don't care how I got it, it's their concern that it is just bad luck that I have it. But I still feel more comfortable if people know how I got it.

Family, friends, and sympathetic employers are normally the first people who are told. But revealing one's HIV-seropositive status necessarily includes an emotional component that factors into the equation of whom one tells.

> At work, my boss, the chairman of the board, [and] upper management pretty much know because I work directly for upper management. And a few girlfriends. Like I said before, I've been there for 7 years so I've established relationships with people who've been there as long as I have that are really good friendships. And those people who I knew would be a really good support for me are the people I told.
>
> Not very many people really [know]. My mom and my dad and my brother. My grandparents don't even know. We think it would probably scare them too much. And one of my best friends knows. I have two. I can't tell the other one [because] I don't know how she would react. . . . A lot of the reason I don't tell certain people is that I'm afraid that they are going to tell other people.
>
> It was a little easier to tell my mom. . . . And my mom, when this started happening, heard I was having serious health problems and was going in and out of the hospital, and it was really stressful for her. And after a few weeks, she came down to visit me. And when I told my mom, I wrote her a note. [I wrote that] the doctors say one of the kinds of pneumonia I have is pneumocystis pneumonia, and uh, she said, "Yeah, I know." And I said, "Well, you know, pneumocystis pneumonia is a kind of a sign of AIDS." You know, she started crying and I started crying.

Initially, this division between whom to tell—and whom not to— seems to be a logical response for mitigating the stigmatization that results from an HIV-seropositive diagnosis; however, an HIV infection exacts an enormous physical toll. Trips to doctors and clinics become more and more frequent as the disease progresses, and consequently, more and more work days must be missed. To explain these increasing absences from work to individuals whom they had not told, the women we interviewed resorted to assigning their illnesses to a less stigmatizing disease, such as cancer.

Mickie, a 23-year-old sales clerk, explains her technique for disguising her HIV-seropositive status:

> The pharmacy knows because I was getting my drugs through them. My two assistants know. The receiver knows because we golf a lot together. The camera lady knows. When you work at a drugstore, you get so many new people in all the time, but then when you've been around—because I've been working there for 5 years or so, I've known these people a long time. So the girl that's in photo or [the] receiver are my friends, even outside the store. And my boss, I told my boss because I was having to call in sick a lot. But other than on a store level, they think I have cancer. . . . That's what the story is, that Mickie has cancer, terminal cancer.

Overall, these explanations are used by HIV-seropositive women to minimize the possibility of an interactional nightmare occurring, but this strategy is not without its own inherent problems. Some friends and family know, others do not; yet, they are all told that something is wrong. In addition, being infected forces one to interact with more and more people who would otherwise remain strangers—doctors, nurses, and other HIV-infected individuals. This increases the number of people involved in the lives of HIV-seropositive women. It also results in a constant need to remember who does or does not know their HIV-seropositive status—which begins to become a nightmare of its own. Roberta, a 39-year-old mother of three, describes the difficulty involved in sustaining this separation:

> I don't tell anyone who doesn't have a reason to know. And you have to be careful about who you tell. You have a choice, but you have to be careful. Then you have to keep your stories straight. "What did I tell you?" "How much did I tell you?" And the worst part of it is, sometimes I can't remember, so when they ask me how I feel, I have to think about whether or not they know. And when I can't remember, I start to panic and think, "Oh no, am I getting dementia?" I can't remember. I just can't remember.

It is clear that maintaining secrecy to preserve one's confidentiality is not all that easy, and this is further exacerbated by the need to connect with existing AIDS-related organizations. This means going public to a certain extent to find necessary support services; however, women often do not receive the kinds of assistance they need. This is partly due to the fact that they do not know what services are available to them. Before they are diagnosed, they encounter few people in their social world of "straight, married, monogamous, women" who are HIV seropositive. Because information about services is frequently disseminated only by word-of-mouth and because they are not usually members of the appropriate informational network, HIV-seropositive women tend to suffer in isolation. This is particularly evident among women who have no contacts within the gay community. Shelley describes the importance of having connections within the existing AIDS community:

> I have a gay male friend and he's full-blown AIDS; he is really quite sick, but he was wonderful. He sat down and he was telling me about how he gets a portion of his electric bill reduced because of his diagnosis. There is Maggie's Pantry [which delivers meals]; he was telling me about all these services available that he is currently receiving. And it's funny because women don't know these things. With women, it's a very private thing; you're not aware, and it's hard to get out there and make the calls and say, "Hey, what can you do for me?" We're used to being the caregivers, not the receivers.

"J just didn't have anybody to talk to, and J was going nuts."

Although knowing gay men may help women become aware of what services are available for HIV-infected individuals, women face the irony that these services were created by and for gay men, who have different concerns regarding the impact of HIV infection on their lives than do women. Doris, a 38-year-old divorced mother, relates her experience in trying to find a support group to help her deal with the social consequences of her infection:

> But the way they talked about safe sex was [crazy]. [One man] was saying, "Well, suppose you meet someone at a club that you want to go home with. You just practice safe sex—you don't need to tell them at the beginning. And then if you really form a relationship with this person, you know, then after a while you'll say: 'You know, the reason I really want to practice safe sex was because I'm infected.'" And it just kind of left me out in the cold. Like, I'm worried about kissing: can I kiss somebody? Can I share my coffee with them? What do you mean, you take people home and have sex with them and don't even tell them! It just astounded me. . . .

And one thing I really started to realize after a while, that, well, the first time, I was really shocked by the way the men talked about sex. But after a while it made sense. . . . If you're a gay man and you are picking up other gay men at the bars and taking them home, the odds are really high those people are infected. I mean, it comes down to the point that a lot of those people, even if they don't know or haven't been tested, you should just assume they're infected. It doesn't seem like a gigantic ethical reach to me necessarily that these people don't talk about it—that these people just practice safe sex, but it just didn't fit my world.

This lack of fit for women seeking support is evidence of the specific focus to which AIDS service organizations have tended to develop:

No, that [support group] was all men. About 15 men and me. It wasn't [very comfortable]. And so, I went to another support group. . . . It was 50 gay men and me. And sometimes they were saying, "Well, there was a woman here a few weeks ago that came a few times." I kept hearing about these women. And the receptionist at the doctor's office was infected as well, and she told me about a women's support group that I went to once, and there were three of us there. She and I and another woman who was very sick. . . .

This view is supported by Nicole, who sought out medical and support services for heterosexual women and found that "there were none." After numerous calls and limited success, she finally created her own women's support group because she saw a need and was frustrated:

I wanted a support group in the East County because I felt that support groups were the main thing that gave me the information I so desperately needed. I was able to network and to find services and things available to me that otherwise, I was getting misinformation. I was getting misled quite a bit. I wanted to be in the actual HIV community, talk to other persons, find out if there were other persons with the same diagnosis who were still living a normal life, and didn't give a bull cronky whether they were HIV infected or not. And I was able to find people, and people like that exist. It's just amazing.

Lynette was equally frustrated. She and Jim initially found a support group for parents, but Lynette felt out of place because the parents were not infected. Instead, these parents were dealing only with a child who had been infected through a blood transfusion. Consequently, she found that these parents had "different feelings towards the parents of the children who do have HIV, because that is how the kids got it" and felt ill-at-ease.

Fortunately, Lynette met Nicole at one of these meetings and learned of the support group Nicole was starting "and it made all the difference in the world for us. We dropped the other group and I have been going to [Nicole's] group."

The result of this constant search for "people you can relate to in a lot of different ways" is that the women involved in our study came to know each other personally. However, nothing existed institutionally to help them get together into their own support groups, nor did their gender socialization as traditional caregivers make it easy for them to actively develop large-scale, viable support networks. Their specific needs and concerns as women were not being addressed in the ways that existing AIDS service organizations functioned for gay men. Even though groups similar to Nicole's exist, they tend to be isolated anomalies that lack the resources of established AIDS service organizations. They are, consequently, the exception rather than the rule for women who wish to find assistance in dealing with their problems.

"HIV isn't the worst thing in the world to have."

Using risk groups as opposed to risk behaviors to define susceptibility to HIV infection limits the number of ways in which AIDS, as an illness, can be perceived. AIDS becomes cloaked in a moral fabric that obscures any consideration of the illness separate from the already stigmatized groups— gay men, IV drug users, and increasingly, underclass minorities. Unless they are IV drug users or the sexual partners of IV drug users (both of which take precedence over their gender identification), women are left out of the AIDS equation. Thus, the test for HIV infection is frequently given only as a last resort. Once a woman is diagnosed as HIV-seropositive, the present medical parameters make progression to AIDS status equally as difficult because those parameters were based on the progression of the disease in males. In other words, the medical construction of AIDS tends to render women invisible, which limits their access to whatever services are available to other HIV-infected individuals.

Given these seemingly intractable problems, why do women persevere? All the women we interviewed initially felt, "So what are we saying here? Am I going to die?" when they were originally diagnosed. With more information about HIV infection, though, they came to realize that an HIV infection manifests itself physiologically as a chronic illness punctuated by sporadic acute episodes of numerous diseases. Consequently, they decided "to get on with" their lives. How they go about doing this tends to take one of three directions. For Nicole, dealing with the endless medical examinations and the problems that accompany them are tolerable because, as she says,

> I'm doing this to keep myself alive, so that I can watch my children grow and be with my husband, and that's what's important to me right now. My kids and my husband come first, and [my involvement in furthering HIV awareness] is just icing on the cake.

All the women who were both wives and mothers tended to share this gender-related perspective.

The second path used by HIV-infected women to deal with their lives involves how their condition has changed their outlook on life for the better. As Kristen describes it,

> I think I look at things a lot more differently now. Things aren't as big a deal as they used to be. Things at work that used to be stressful aren't stressful anymore. . . . Since something so major has happened in my life, I can look at other things and say that's no big deal. . . . It's . . . such a big thing that I can look at other things in a better perspective, and go—well, things can be a lot worse—and it's not as bad. It's easier to have positive feelings, I guess.

Further, many feel that this view is applicable to others as well. As Nicole states it:

> Go on with your lives. If you've got a problem to work out, and you think it's dominating your life, [it was] probably there before you were HIV-[infected], and you better take care of it. Do it for yourself. And as far as being HIV, don't take yourselves too seriously. It's not the end of the world. I could think of worse things to have at this point. And what other disease do I know of, where I could be in such good company? It's been a good experience for me, and uh, I've been having a good time with it. I never expected it. If someone had told me 5 years ago that this would all happen, I would have said, "You're nuts," especially the speaking area. Because I never, ever, ever would have wanted a career where I stand up and talk to rooms of people. I do this now. All of the things that I thought would least likely occur in my lifetime, I've done. And I do them on a regular basis. No, HIV isn't the worst thing in the world to have. Prejudice is a real bad thing, and thank God I've got HIV.

Besides the view that softening one's outlook on life is important, it is also evident in Nicole's quote that her HIV infection has given her life a purpose. This perception was voiced by several other informants as well and represents the third route that the women we interviewed followed for adapting to their new life circumstances. According to Shelley:

> If there is anything I can do that will help somebody down the road, you know, cope with it, or whatever, then I'm doing some good. You know, you get to the point where you think, now I really have to make something of my life. . . . Now I have to really do something good and make a difference.

Although Shelley is planning on making a difference in the future, Mickie has found her role:

> And I can't even tell you how many thousands of people I have contacted through [Alcoholics Anonymous] and [Narcotics Anonymous] who have gone and gotten tested now. So, I feel like maybe it was meant to be. Maybe this is my mission in life, and my purpose. I always knew I had a grand-scale purpose, I just didn't know this was it. Never ever have I felt I've helped so many people. And people that find out after listening to me at a meeting, and go and get tested and find out they are [sero]positive, they are calling me, and they are saying that if it wasn't for you, I would have slit my wrists after finding this out.

Even from this brief look at women who are HIV infected, certain points are salient. Despite the identification of HIV with risk groups, women can become infected and, in so doing, become stigmatized. This stigmatization places women in such an awkward position that they must take great care initially in selecting to whom they should tell their story and deciding what their story is. This balancing act becomes more and more difficult as the disease increasingly exacts a greater and greater toll on their health. As a consequence, many women come to realize that in maintaining their secret they are, in fact, contributing to the perpetuation of the myths that make HIV infection so problematic for women. In telling their stories publicly, they are providing a service to society. For this act of courage, we are indebted to them. For giving others voice, as we have tried to do for them, we thank them.

"I'm always thinking about the future."

- On April 8, 1993, at the age of 34, Nicole died of complications of AIDS. This essay is dedicated in loving memory of her.

- Lynette, Jim, and Tony have moved to Texas to live with Lynette's brother because they are too ill to care for themselves. Lynette's

brother will have custody of Tony should anything happen to them
first.

- Shelley now has AIDS, has quit work, and receives disability.

- Kristen is still working as a restaurant manager and is involved in a
  relationship with an HIV-seronegative man.

- Mickie is on full disability and is too ill even to continue her speaking
  engagements.

- Roberta's husband died of brain cancer and she is raising their three
  children.

- Doris has recently relocated because of a new job. She continues to live
  an independent life, which includes public speaking engagements. Her
  health, however, continues to deteriorate.

Discussion Questions

1. What impact did this essay have on your understanding of AIDS?
   How do you think of the disease differently after hearing the women's
   stories?

2. If "good" people can get a disease that only "bad" people are "supposed" to get, then is there something wrong with the way American
   society constructs the AIDS problem?

3. In what ways does HIV/AIDS differ from other chronic terminal illnesses, such as cancer? In what ways do these differences affect
   patients and their caregivers?

4. This essay reveals how often HIV-seropositive women remain undiag-
   nosed, even when they are clearly symptomatic of the disease. What
   can individuals do to protect their health when risk-group identification often blinds medical professionals from diagnosing the disease in
   "non-risk" groups?

5. After reading this essay, what would you define as behavior that puts
   you at risk for becoming HIV seropositive? And in another light, what
   do you believe any one of us could do to support a friend or family
   member if he or she were diagnosed with this disease?

6. What are the benefits of the government's spending money on the prevention of AIDS rather than spending money primarily on treatment?

18

Thelma and Louise

Breaking the Silence

Linda A. M. Perry, Ph.D.

Department of Communication Studies
University of San Diego

Like the Badlands, violence against women is part of our national landscape.

Interior

The light and the light
within me are like a tree
unfolding, branch by branch
like tentacles caressing
dark but feeling in the light
the end of shadow. The tree
of the soul unfolds,
rises like a canopy.

The spirit moves as the spirit
moves me. And who am I?
And what in this heart
is light as flame, gently
as the touch of a god
that knows itself and knows
it is more than it sees?

—*Phyllis Kahaney*

I don't attend violent films. I believe there is enough violence in real life that we don't need to pay to see it. I would not have gone to see Thelma and Louise *if I had known there were attempted rape and murder scenes in it. When these scenes occurred, my instinct was to leave the theater. Much to my dismay, however, as the film progressed, I enjoyed it more and more. As I reflected back on it after seeing it several times, I realized that the reason for my enjoyment was that I had received some vicarious vindication for the violence I had experienced in my lifetime. There on the big screen were scenes that gave me a moment's revenge for my lost innocence as a 15-year-old rape victim, my disgust at truck drivers with women's undergarments hanging like trophies from their mirrors as they speed by me on the freeway, the countless disappointments with men in whom I had placed faith and who had ultimately robbed me of that faith—in other words, for the lifelong degradations, humiliations, abuses, and fears I have experienced as a female. Also there on the screen were the retaliations females are taught not to seek: to escape from abusive and ego-centered husbands, to take revenge for verbal and physical violence wielded against us, to degrade law officers whose power has degraded us when we needed protection the most, to humiliate men who destroy our freedom to move about freely without whistles and stares, and to choose to end the opportunity for more violence against ourselves and, ultimately, all women. Yes, I loved the film and I loved the way it made me feel. As a tribute to the millions of women who are caught with no visible or viable way to escape their daily subjection to violence, I dedicate this essay. It is far more about that violence and its continuation than about the fleeting few moments during which two women named Thelma and Louise help to give women a voice and to ease their pain.* [1]

Thelma and Louise is a movie in which two female friends leave town for an innocent weekend getaway. At a rest stop, Thelma meets and flirts with Harlan, whose later attempt to rape her is prevented by Louise. In retaliation for his physical violence, continued verbal assaults, and lack of remorse, Louise shoots him with a handgun that Thelma had brought along to protect them (which tells us a lot about what women expect when they go out in public). Thus, the film begins with two female buddies whose vacation consists of run-ins with men and a run from the law.

Louise states several times in the film that "you get what you settle for." Symbolically, the film offers women opportunities to no longer settle for male insults, sexism, and aggression even if they have to die (as Thelma and Louise do in the end) to escape it.

Thelma and Louise received many and varied critical reviews. Some critics defined the movie as a statement about changing gender roles; some identified it as a feminist film; others indicated that it gives feminism a bad name. Some said it was a male-bashing film, others said it was about time males were bashed. Other critics saw it simply as a "buddy" film, much like its male counterparts such as *Butch Cassidy and the Sundance Kid.* But whatever the critics said, they said it with passion. The film was loved or hated, admired or scorned, but not ignored.

Why did this film receive such strong responses? For those who disliked the film, especially men, *Thelma and Louise* may threaten the status quo of women's oppression, which is sustained through the physical and/or psychological violence against them. Violence, more than any other single factor, maintains patriarchy and the superiority of males. *Thelma and Louise* replaces that superiority by situating men in the background, a position women have traditionally held in films.

For those who liked the film, especially women, *Thelma and Louise* may work as consciousness-raising about, and vicarious vindication for, the violence against and oppression of women. That argument as advanced in this essay is based on relevancy. That is, the meaning each person derives from a film is determined primarily by how relevant the behaviors exhibited in it are to her or his life situation (Cohen, 1991). Sadly, the omnipresence of violence against women in American culture makes *Thelma and Louise very* relevant to women. Domestic abuse, rape, and sexual harassment levied against women have reached epidemic proportions. In fact, the United States is "among the most rape-prone" societies (Scully, 1990, p. 48).

Thelma and Louise has taken on a "cult" following because of its strong and timeless representation of women's daily burdens of addressing, avoiding, or ignoring the constant acts and symbols of masculine control through aggression. The first section of this essay explores the magnitude of violence against women. In the second section, some arguments for why and how this violence is maintained throughout our culture are provided. Finally, it will be shown that films like *Thelma and Louise* provide awareness of the magnitude of violence against women and momentary vindication for the physical and psychological violence wielded against women.

Thelma and Louise Demonstrates the Magnitude of Violence Against Women in Our Culture

Statistics on violence against women are devastating. Seventy-one percent of rapes are premeditated; 58% of rapes are planned; 53.7% of female college students report some form of sexual victimization since age 14; 34–37% of college men report they might rape if they knew they wouldn't get caught (Scully, 1990). Approximately one out of every three or four women is likely to be sexually assaulted at least once in her lifetime (Malamuth & Briere, 1986; McBride, 1990). Most surprising, studies show that a minimum of 30% of all reported rapes are committed by pairs or groups of men (Brownmiller, 1975; Johnson, 1991).

Specialists say that most abusive and/or violent physical and psychological crimes are left unreported and unrequited. It is estimated that only 20% of all rapes are reported; that means that more than 250,000 rapes are estimated to occur in the United States each year (Brownmiller, 1975). Blair (1986) points out that "these statistics may represent only the tip of the iceberg" (p. 38). In fact, a more recent report says these figures are underestimated and as many as 750,000 females are victims of sexual abuse each year in the United States. Statistics indicate that "sexual violence against women, rather than being the product of only a few deviant individuals, is committed by large numbers of men" (Malamuth & Briere, 1986, p. 75). In *Thelma and Louise* the lead characters travel though their daily lives remembering, experiencing, and fearing male superiority and aggression. This is demonstrated in scenes such as when Thelma is verbally degraded by her run-around husband, victimized by an attempted rapist, demoralized by a lover who steals their money, and taunted by the sexual crudeness of a truck driver, to name a few. The sadness comes in recognizing that I and a majority of American women have had these or similar experiences and *know* that these portrayals are relevant to our daily lives.

The result of the omnipresence of violence against women causes "the vast majority of women [to] have a constant nagging fear of violence, rejection or humiliation from men both strange or well known to them" (Price, 1988, p. 44). For example, in *Thelma and Louise,* Thelma brings along the handgun to protect herself and Louise against "psycho-killers" (as she puts it) during their weekend vacation. As Page (1991) notes, "*Thelma and Louise* is not everywoman's life; it is a worst case scenario, just close enough to the lives of many real women to give it a resonance that transcends its cartoonist script" (p. 9).

Most men who rape seem to go unnoticed as "normal," average males; that is, they outwardly do not appear to be deranged, sadistic, or scary. This means that women must always be on guard because there is no telling whom the aggressor might be. Another movie reviewer explains:

> I don't know a woman over the age of 16 who hasn't been hooted at by some trucker or hard-hat or gas jockey who just can't let a woman walk by without flicking his tongue like a water moccasin or jerking his fist in orgastic imitation. It's not about sex, it's about control. They simply can't let you by without trying to make you react. . . . Any woman who lives in a middle size city is a warrior of sorts. . . . You think kicking Iraqi butt was a strain? Try urban America, where a woman walks point every time she walks down a street, anticipating the worst and planning for it, ratcheting up her vigilance to combat readiness. Are my keys handy? Can I cross the street to avoid this guy? Is there an open store I can duck into? How fast can I run in these shoes? . . . If you gentlemen are squirming at the matinee, it's because a movie made you feel for two hours the way this culture has made women to feel for years. (Morrison, 1991, p. A7)

Throughout the film, Thelma asks Louise about her reasons for moving away from Texas. Through Louise's resistance to answering these questions directly and other hints throughout the film [such as her shooting of Harlan, her anger at Thelma for even bringing up her experiences in Texas, and Hal's (the "good" cop's) acknowledgment that he knows what happened to her in Texas], we know that she had, in fact, been the victim of some form of sexual violence. However, the lack of information explaining the details of Louise's experiences in Texas underscores the omnipresence of violence. This omission allows the viewers to envision all the types of possible violence Louise might have experienced rather than focus on one type. Schickel (1991) explains:

> Such an explanation would have quelled much of the "male bashing" criticism leveled at *Thelma and Louise* but it also would have cheapened the movie in some measure, suggesting that some kinds of sexual violence grant their victims murderous entitlement while others do not. By leaving Louise's mystery intact, the film implies that all forms of sexual exploitation, great or small, are consequential and damaging. (p. 54)

By the end of the film, Thelma and Louise have moved from being the objects of men's control to the subjects of their own choices. Their final choice is the ultimate one of suicide—a violent choice that ironically prevents further violence against them. Although this violence is at their own hands, it is an extension of and response to the violence they have experienced in this culture. Many viewers believed the suicidal ending of this movie was inappropriate. Some wanted the women to be captured and to pay for their crimes; some wanted them to escape to Mexico; others wanted them to fight it out with the law. Does Thelma and Louise's choice of suicide reflect what is known about victims of violence? Does it provide more relevance for viewers?

Blair (1986) found that suicide attempts are common on the part of abused women. She cites one study in which it was found that "50 percent of the women who had experienced abuse were diagnosed as depressed and 29 percent attempted suicide at least once" (pp. 41–42). Another study found that "victims of completed rape (44%), attempted molestation (32.4%), attempted rape (29.5%), completed molestation (21.8%), and aggravated assault (14.9%) reported up to six times higher [suicidal ideation] than that reported by nonvictims (6.8%)" (Kilpatrick, Best, Vernen, Amick, Ville-ponteaux, & Ruff, 1985, p. 869). It is no wonder, then, that many viewers and critics believed the suicidal ending to *Thelma and Louise* was realistic. Susan Sarandon, who played Louise, noted that this was the least compro-mising ending because the entire film centered around Thelma and Louise's development into women who were not going to "settle" (Schickel, 1991). Morrison (1991) provides the best rationale for the film's ending:

> *Thelma and Louise* finished up not as Joan of Arc martyrs, but as tank-top samurai whose code left the option of dying on their own terms, which is the way you win when your adversary insists that you play by his rules. It was triumphant and sad and liberating. (p. A7)

Unfortunately, whether we liked the film's ending or not, the fact is we can identify with the choices the lead characters made.

As individual women we know the fear of violence we experience in our day-to-day and night-to-night lives. As a group, women know there is something wrong with a culture that allows that violence against them to continue. But, what are the factors that maintain violence against women in our culture?

Thelma and Louise Demonstrates the Maintenance of Violence Against Women in Our Culture

Violence against women is maintained through social myths and realities that are two sides of the same coin. They both reflect and create each other, they both provide models for future behavior, and they both are the currency of social living. In this section, I explore some of the myths and realities that help to maintain violence against women and show how they are demonstrated in *Thelma and Louise*.

Social Myths Help Maintain Violence Against Women

Aside from the myth that abuse is not widespread, which is negated by the statistics above, other myths include (a) women want to be raped and (b) men are culturally superior and have the right to control women.

Social myth 1: Women want to be raped. Frye (1992) notes that "both heterosexual activity and heterosexual nonactivity are likely to be taken as proof that you wanted to be raped, and hence, of course, weren't *really* raped at all" (pp. 52–53). Further complicating this is the problem that if the victim knows the rapist or freely engaged in interaction with her assailant (inviting a person she is dating into her home or kissing him), it will lead to her story being discredited (Mynatt & Allgeier, 1990; Wilson, 1988). Baber's (1991) review of *Thelma and Louise*, published in *Playboy*, provides an example of how women become the accused when he writes, "Now, you might ask what signals Thelma is sending Harlan (her attacker) with her behavior, since she has been dancing and drinking and flirting openly with him for some time, but let that pass" (p. 45).

Baber (1991) classifies Harlan's sexually aggressive behavior as a "normal" response to Thelma's flirtations. Baber represents males who hold the belief that when a woman flirts, she is asking for sex and when she says "no," she is really covering her desire to be raped. Does the following excerpt from the attempted rape scene sound to you as if Thelma is requesting sex from Harlan?

[In this scene, Harlan and Thelma have gone into the parking lot because Thelma has gotten sick from drinking.]

H: How you feelin', little darlin'?

T: I think I'm startin' to feel better. [Harlan begins to pull her close to him.]

T: I think I need to keep walking.

H: Wait a minute, wait a minute, now where do you think you're goin'? [He grabs Thelma and sits her on a car hood.]

T: Oh no, no, quit it, stop it, stop it! [Harlan gets more physically aggressive.]

H: I'm not goin' to hurt ya'. I just want to kiss you.

T: No! No!

H: Come on, come on. [He kisses her.]
[Harlan laughs and rubs his hands up her dress.]

H: You are gorgeous! [Thelma struggles to free herself from his grip.]

T: Okay, let me go. I'm married.

H: That's OK, I'm married too. [Laughing and continuing to grab at her.]

T: I don't feel good, I've been sick.

H: Oh. [He slaps her across the face.] Listen to me, I said I'm not going to hurt you, alright?! Relax. [He pulls at the bustline of her dress.]

T: Harlan, stop it, please, I mean it. [He grabs at her breast.]

T: Wait, don't, I mean it. Louise is going to wonder where I am.

H: Fuck Louise. Fuck Louise. [Thelma slaps him.]

H: Don't you never fuckin' hit me, you fuckin' bitch, you hear me? [He punches her in the face.]

T: Don't hurt me, don't hurt me, Harlan, please . . .

H: Shut up, shut up, you fuckin' bitch. [He swings her around, pulls up the back of her dress and begins to struggle with her underwear and his zipper.]

T: Please, please, don't hurt me, Harlan.

We all agree that Thelma's cries for mercy cannot be easily mistaken as requests for sexual favors from Harlan. After Louise discovers Harlan attempting to rape Louise and prevents it by holding a gun to his head, he tells her, "We're just havin' a little fun, that's all." Louise's response says it all: "In the future, when a woman is crying like that, she isn't having any fun." Women wanting to be raped is, after all, a myth; unfortunately, it is a powerful myth that often provides aggressors with an alibi for their sexually violent behavior toward women.

Social myth 2: Men are superior and have the right to control women. The representations of men in *Thelma and Louise* offer caricatures of real-life male figures who seek control of women in our culture. Each lead male character represents an oppressor, an aggressor, or a manipulator. Darryl, Thelma's husband, is an ego-centered man who controls Thelma by treating her like a child and shows his superiority through his behaviors and attire. For example, he wears a necklace that reads "#1" and his vanity license plate says "The One." Jimmy, Louise's boyfriend, is emotionally bankrupt and cannot commit to Louise until he believes she is leaving him for another man; then he uses his offer of commitment to control the situation. Harlan, Thelma's assailant, is an aggressive and violent man who disguises himself with smooth flirtations until he no longer gets his way and then uses violence to control women. Even Hal, the law enforcement officer who tries to protect and save Thelma and Louise, enacts the role of a father figure with assumptions of self-importance who seems to believe that he can control the system and save his "girls" from other men. J.D., the young con man, uses boyish charm to distract women while he slips his hands into their pants and their pocketbooks and, thus, controls their emotional and financial fates. Finally, Earl, the truck driver, demonstrates his felt superiority over women by displaying silver silhouettes of apparently naked women on his cap and his truck's mud flaps. The growing sense of doom that surrounds Thelma and Louise's fates is based on the unfolding realization that all men are capable of violence of one sort or another, regardless of what their intentions may appear to be. Brownmiller (1992) contends that women's fear of rape, in fact, may have been one of the primary reasons women became subservient to men.

Although it is men women fear, it is men whose protection they must seek—sleeping with the enemy, as it were. Brownmiller (1975) states that "the ideology of rape is fueled by cultural values that are perpetuated at every level of our society and nothing less than a frontal attack is needed to repel this cultural assault" (p. 389). Indeed, that is what Thelma and Louise do. For every act of physical, emotional, and psychological violence pitted against them, their rebuttal is a "frontal attack." They leave their inadequate males for a weekend escape; Louise retaliates against verbal and physical violence wielded against her and Thelma; Thelma robs a male clerk after being robbed by a male lover; they (literally and figuratively) shoot down male oppression with female aggression. Would violence against women continue in our culture if men believed women might react as Thelma and Louise do?

When offering a critique of *Thelma and Louise*, Baber (1991) sarcastically states his belief that men were inappropriately portrayed as less superior and more demasculinized in the movie than they should have been. He describes actions in the movie thus: "[Thelma] and Louise get the drop on a state trooper who is suspicious of them and they lock him in the trunk of his car—but not before they steal his pistol and he cracks up and weeps and moans and groans (you know how those state troopers are under pressure)" (p. 45). And further, "At last, Thelma and Louise reach their finale. They are at the end of their road, trapped by insensitive lawmen and a police investigator named Hal (Harvey Keitel), who suddenly becomes meek and ineffective as the showdown develops (you know how those male police investigators are under pressure)" (p. 45). Thus, whether in the film, in some of the reviews, or in daily reality, an attitude of male supremacy is evident. Although it may seem that if women took on more of these masculine roles, the amount of violence against them would decrease, this does not seem to be the case. The following social realities point to that fact.

Social Realities Help Maintain Violence against Women

All men do not commit violence against women, but *all* men—the abusers and the protectors alike—ultimately benefit from it because it preserves male dominance (Scully, 1990, p. 49). Brownmiller (1975) takes the argument one step further when noting that "from prehistoric times to the present, I believe, rape has played a critical function. It is nothing more or less than a conscious process of intimidation by which *all* men keep *all* women in a state of fear" (p.15). The advantages males gain through violence against women are maintained through two social realities: socialization and silencing.

Social reality 1: Women and men are socialized to enact different and specific sex roles. The socialization of women as nurturers and relationship-builders in some ways prevents them from speaking out about the violence against them. When women gain self-worth through knowing how to maintain relationships, it becomes very difficult for them to admit failure in selecting a friend or a mate who may have come to behave violently toward them. Goldner, Penn, Sheinberg, and Walker (1990) say that

> staying put [in a violent relationship] is not about weak character, or morbid dependency, or masochism, but is better understood as an affirmation of the feminine ideal: to hold connections together, to heal and care for another, no matter what the personal cost. (p. 357)

Thus, the more feminine the female, the better the chances she has been socialized to see her self-worth as directly related to her ability to maintain relationships. Women may remain in a violent relationship rather than admit they have failed in their assigned sex role. However, they are caught in another double-bind because if they choose to alter that role, they may be subjected to additional violence.

Some have argued that changing sex roles create male aggression. Goldner and colleagues (1990) explain that as women take on more roles and responsibilities previously considered to be part of the male arena, a fear arises in men who want to maintain the status quo of male superiority. They note:

> This taboo against similarity, and the dread of the collapse of gender difference, operates silently and powerfully in all relationships between men and women. . . . *Indeed we have come to think about battering as a man's attempt to reassert gender differences and gender dominance, when his terror of not being different enough from "his" woman threatens to overtake him.* [Italics theirs.] (p. 348)

Both Thelma and Louise are subjected to increased violence as they move further away from stereotypically feminine roles (waitress and housewife) toward more stereotypically masculine roles (gunslingers and avengers).

Scully (1990) and Baron and Straus (1987) point out that violence is a learned behavior, more often existing in societies or cultural groups that support the subordination of women to men physically, socially, and economically. Taubman (1986) explains, "Much of domestic violence and exploitative behavior is culturally shaped. This society values violence as a means of solving problems and esteems those who are skilled at its use" (p. 16). These skills are evident in Mynatt and Allgeier's (1990) finding "that 43% of 201 college men surveyed reported that they had sex with a woman against her will at least once or twice" (p. 131). Unfortunately, the maintenance of socialized sex roles is rewarded, and altering them is resisted—even negative roles such as male aggression against women. One way these roles are maintained is by silencing women who, in their submission to men, have internalized fear of the verbal, psychological, and/or physical violence they will encounter should they speak out.

Social reality 2: The silencing of women's voices maintains violence against them. Males' sense of superiority is maintained through the control they demand over women. This being the case, then women speaking out about their fears as real and possible victims of violence should help to counter that control. So, why do women not speak out? Why did Louise not speak out about the violence she seemed to have suffered in her past?

Although "both the victimization and the anger experienced by women are real, and have real sources, everywhere in the environment, built into society, language, the structure of thought" (Rich, 1979, p. 49), women may not speak out against violence because speaking out sometimes is met with more violence. Whether women experience random violence by strangers or by male friends and family members, Frye (1992) explains:

It is often a requirement upon oppressed people that we smile and be cheerful. If we comply, we signal docility and our acquiescence in our situation. We need not, then, be taken note of. We acquiesce in being made invisible, in our occupying no space. We participate in our own erasure. (p. 52)

Thus, women fear violence because it is omnipresent, and they fear speaking out against it because they may inadvertently inspire the behavior they wish to extinguish.

It is especially difficult for women to speak out and report violent crimes because their aggressors often are family and friendship acquaintances (Scully, 1990). Mynatt and Allgeier (1990) suggest that the reporting of acquaintance assaults is typically only 2% of enacted incidents. The low report rate stems from several factors: reporting violence in a close relationship will bring shame to families, there are social taboos about being labeled a victim, the person reported may retaliate, and previous close contact might indicate the victim willingly participated. As Koss (1990) notes, studies suggest that there is

a scourge, if not an epidemic, of violence against women in the United States. Many people, citizens and officials alike, are unable to accept that this amount of violence could exist without coming to public attention. Cover-up may be facilitated by the forced secrecy that is almost uniformly demanded by perpetrators of abuse. (p. 375)

Of course, that would be the case because "the fact is, we do not believe women who seem to have no apparent motive for lying and not much to gain either. But we do believe powerful men even though they have a lot to gain from not telling the truth" (Rivers, 1991). And, why would a woman want to report a violent crime against her when she knows the odds are she will not be believed, especially by the legal and political systems that have been created and controlled by men.

Brownmiller (1975) notes that more reported rapes are determined to be unfounded when male law enforcement officers attend to the cases than when female law enforcement officers attend to them. For example, in New York City, 15% of reported rapes were determined to be unfounded by male law enforcement officers heading the investigations. Only 2% of rape cases were determined to be unfounded (the average for all crimes reported) when female law enforcement officers headed the investigations. In other words, "Women believe the word of other women. Men do not"

(Brownmiller, 1975, p. 387). This problem is acerbated when one recognizes that only 10.2% of police and detectives in public service are females (U.S. Bureau of the Census, 1991).

In *Thelma and Louise* it is made clear that Louise was subjected to violence in Texas. Although this appears to be the motivating factor in her shooting of Harlan, the audience does not learn what happened to her because she remains silent. She does not want to discuss it with the police or even with Thelma, her best friend. Yet, Louise's silence speaks loudly to the audience because through her silence "[her] individuality disappears and Louise's past, symbolizing the past of all women who have been assaulted, abused, or harmed in other ways by men, emerges as the dominant voice" (Griffin, 1995).

It is interesting that one of the criticisms of the film is based on the assumption that female friends would confide the stories of their past victimizations to each other. For example, Carlson (1991) argues that "the characters in the film don't confide in each other as real-life women would. When Thelma asks what happened in Texas that makes her murderous, Louise refuses to talk with her about it" (p. 57). Carlson, like many others, ignores the extent to which female victims are silenced through fear, intimidation, a sense of failure, and/or loyalty to the family whom she and the victimizer may share.

When women speak out (enact independent behaviors), the accounts of their behaviors are magnified and negatively labeled. Although the amount of violence against men in *Thelma and Louise* is much less than the violence against women depicted in most male-centered films, Thelma and Louise are trivialized in reviews as being man-haters and/or male-bashers. Rich (1979) emphasizes this when noting, "It is ironic, to say the least, that the first verbal attack slung at the woman who demonstrates a primary loyalty to herself and other women is *man-hater*" (p. 264). More reviews critique *Thelma and Louise* as exhibiting man-hating and male-bashing than any other description. For example, Baber (1991) states:

> I was attracted to them [Thelma and Louise] at first, and I did like them—until I realized that if I met them on the street, they would probably blow me away if I violated their standards of protocol and etiquette. And therein lies the meanest and deepest message of this slick cinematic exercise. . . . The most primitive message behind *Thelma and Louise* is that a lot of men need killing these days. (p. 45)

As Geena Davis (who played Thelma) noted, "Even if this film did convey some horrible man-bashing message—'Let's us gals all get guns and kill all the men'—it couldn't even begin to make up for all the anti-woman movies people don't even talk about" (Jerome, 1991, p. 90).

Even actresses who take roles of women who avenge the violence against them become negatively labeled. Reviewer Duncan Shepherd (1991), for example, states, "The whole business, including the entire pig-pen's worth of male chauvinists, arouses no feminist sentiment as strong as the one of pity and regret that actresses as engaging as Geena Davis and Susan Sarandon have to count themselves fortunate in today's marketplace to be allotted the title roles" (p. 37).

Unfortunately, until women join forces and speak out in large numbers about the violence they experience and fear, the vicious cycle of violence will likely repeat itself. Individual women are silenced because they believe they stand alone, because they lack the firsthand knowledge of other women's experiences, and because they fear repercussions for speaking out. Only when women unite in one voice and break the silence will cultural changes come about.

Thelma and Louise Helps Break the Silence About Violence Against Women

Violence against women in this culture creates an atmosphere of fear and distrust between males and females. Whether we look at the social myths or realities of culture, reasons abound for the maintenance and advocacy of violence against women. *Thelma and Louise* offers women an opportunity to become conscious of the extent to which violence is wielded against them in this culture, violence that both blinds and silences women while it provides power and control to men.

Thelma and Louise systematically raises women's consciousness about the daily violations they experience, whether from demoralizing husbands, emotionally distant boyfriends, aggressive rapists, disgusting truckers, or flirtatious strangers. It offers us an opportunity for awareness and, for a brief moment in time, a chance to feel some small sense of vindication for the daily aggressions against us. Women can enjoy the fantasy of taking revenge against men who violate them without enacting the behaviors themselves. As Morrison (1991) suggests to male critics who accuse the film of being nothing more than a male-bashing opportunity:

> You guys know fantasy, the movies have catered to yours for years. . . . Snap out of it, boys. Are we going to have to run smelling salts under your noses? Slap you until you stop screaming? It *is* only a movie. If we like it,

it's because it is a good one, a cathartic, blade edged *Field of Dreams* for women. A woman's idea of adult fantasy for a change. (p. A7)

At the very least, *Thelma and Louise* helps us to reflect on the omni-presence of violence in our culture. As Schickel (1991) explains:

Movies achieve this kind of historic stature not because they offer a par-ticularly acute portrayal of the way we live now or because they summa-rize with nuanced accuracy the opposing positions in an often flatulent quasi-political debate. They work because somehow they worm their way into our collective dreamscape, retrieve the anxious images they find there and then splash them across the big screen in dramatically heightened form. (p. 53)

It is clear that *Thelma and Louise* is part of our "collective dreamscape" based on the present-day existence of cultural artifacts in reference to it. There are bumper stickers, lapel pins, and T-shirts that state, "I'm Louise's Sister" or "Thelma and Louise Live." There are references to the movie in newer films, such as when Jane tells Holly in *Boys on the Side* that she isn't going over a cliff for her and her other female friend. And publications continue to come out on the topic (e.g., Griffin, 1995; Griggers, 1993; Russell, 1993; Willis, 1993).

Films like *Thelma and Louise* may help to empower women by increasing our consciousness of the staggering amount of violence wielded against us in our daily lives; it may even provide a moment's vindication for that violence. This, in turn, might give us the strength to begin to speak out about the violence we have suffered, thereby making the choice to not simply "get what we settle for."

Discussion Questions

1. When traveling, have you experienced incidents similar to those Thelma and Louise do in this film? If so, how did these incidents make you feel? Does the way such incidents make you feel affect your sense of personal power?

2. In what ways does psychological and physical violence silence women? Do you believe men are similarly silenced in this culture? Why or why not?

3. Do you think that Thelma was "asking for it" through her obvious flirtations with Harlan? Should women behave and dress in certain ways if they want to be safe?

4. Would two men going off on a fishing trip encounter similar interactions with people like Harlan, Earl, and J.D.? What kind of encounters might they have that would threaten their sense of safety?

5. Do you agree with Perry that films can provide people with experiences that help them resolve some issues in their own lives, or at least make them feel better about these issues for a brief time? Has a film done this for you? What film, and in what way?

References

Baber, A. (1991, August). Guerrilla feminism. *Playboy,* p. 45.

Baron, L., & Straus, M. A. (1987). Four theories of rape: A microsociological analysis. *Social Problems, 34,* 467–488.

Blair, K. A. (1986). The battered woman: Is she the silent victim? *Nurse Practitioner 11,* pp. 38, 40, 42–44, 47.

Brownmiller, S. (1975). *Against our will: Men, women and rape.* New York: Simon and Schuster.

Brownmiller, S. (1992). Victims: The setting. In M. Schaum & C. Flanagan (Eds.), *Gender images: Readings for composition* (pp. 277–278). Boston: Houghton Mifflin.

Carlson, M. (1991, June 24). Is this what feminism is all about? *Time,* p. 57.

Cohen, J. R. (1991). The "relevance" of cultural identity in audiences' interpretations of mass media. *Critical Studies in Mass Communication, 8,* 442–454.

Frye, M. (1992). Oppression. In M. Schaum & C. Flanagan (Eds.), *Gender images: Readings for composition* (pp. 51–61). Boston: Houghton Mifflin.

Goldner, V., Penn, P., Sheinberg, M., & Walker, G. (1990). Love and violence: Gender paradoxes in volatile attachments. *Family Process, 29,* 343–364.

Griffin, C. L. (1995). Teaching rhetorical criticism with *Thelma and Louise. Communication Education, 44,* 164–176.

Griggers, C. (1993). *Thelma and Louise* and the cultural generation of the new butch-femme. In J. Collins, H. Radner, & A. Collins (Eds.), *Film theory goes to the movies* (pp. 129–141). New York: Routledge.

Jerome, J. (1991, June 24). Riding shotgun. *People,* pp. 90–96.

Johnson, D. (1991). Rape. In E. Ashton-Jones & G. A. Olson (Eds.), *The gender reader* (pp. 518–527). Needham Heights, MA: Allyn and Bacon.

Kilpatrick, D. G., Best, C. L., Vernen, L. J., Amick, A. E., Villeponteaux, L. A., & Ruff, G. A. (1985). Mental health correlates of criminal victimization: A random community survey. *Journal of Consulting and Clinical Psychology, 53,* 866–873.

Koss, M. P. (1990). Violence against women. *The American Psychologist 45,* 374–380.

Malamuth, N. M., & Briere, J. (1986). Sexual violence in the media: Indirect effects on aggression against women. *Journal of Social Issues, 42,* 75–92.

McBride, A. B. (1990). Violence against women: Implications for research and practice. *Reflections, 16,* 10–12.

Morrison, P. (1991, June 24). Get a grip, gentlemen: *Thelma and Louise* is only a fantasy. *Portland Press Herald,* p. A7.

Mynatt, C. R., & Allgeier, E. R. (1990). Risk factors, self-attributions, and adjustment problems among victims of sexual coercion. *Journal of Applied Social Psychology, 20,* 130–153.

Page, C. (1991, June 24). *Thelma and Louise*: A reel-life tale of women and power. *Liberal Opinion Weekly,* p. 9.

Price, J. (1988). The importance of understanding the her-story of women. *Women & Therapy, 7,* 37–47.

Rich, A. (1979). *On lies, secrets, and silence: Selected prose 1966–1978.* New York: Norton.

Rivers, C. (1991, December 14). Are there no believable women? *Portland Herald Press,* p. A7.

Russell, D. E. H. (1993). From witches to bitches: Sexual terrorism begats *Thelma and Louise.* In D. E. H. Russell (Ed.), *Making violence sexy: Feminist views on pornography* (pp. 254–269). New York: Teachers College Press.

Russell, D. E. H. (1993). *Making violence sexy: Feminist views on pornography.* New York: New York Teaching Press.

Schickel, R. (1991, June 24). Gender bender: A white-hot debate rages over whether *Thelma and Louise* celebrates liberated females, male bashers—or outlaws. *Time,* pp. 52–56.

Scully, D. (1990). *Understanding sexual violence: A study of convicted rapists*. Boston: Unwin Hyman.

Shepherd, D. (1991, May 30). Movie reviews. *The Reader*, pp. 36–37.

Taubman, S. (1986). Beyond the bravado: Sex roles and the exploitative male. *Social Work, 31*, 12–18.

U.S. Bureau of the Census (1991). *Statistical abstract of the United States: 1991* (111th ed.). Washington, DC: *U.S. Government Printing Office*.

Willis, S. (1993). Hardware and hardbodies, what do women want?: A reading of *Thelma and Louise*. In J. Collins, H. Radner, & A. Collins (Eds.), *Film theory goes to the movies* (pp. 120–128). New York: Routledge.

Wilson, W. (1988). Rape as entertainment. *Psychological Reports, 63*, 607–610.

Note

1. Many men also have been wonderful to and supportive of me. However, in so far as this chapter is about the impact of crude, insensitive and/or violent men, I have purposely isolated here those negative experiences I have had in my lifetime, which epitomize those that keep me and most women from moving freely in this culture.

19

The Rhetoric of the "New Feminism"

Searching for a Cultural Backlash

Delia B. Conti, Ph.D.

Department of Speech Communication
Penn State–McKeesport

New opportunities

*A*s a working mother of three, I know only too well the divisions *between mothers who have a career outside the home and those who are at home raising their families. The issues facing women trying to balance work and family in contemporary society are unique. Decisions regarding marriage, children, and work face every American woman. These decisions are fundamentally moral, and therefore carry great potential to divide as well as unite. In my own community, there is an unspoken divide between mothers who have made these two different choices. It is not that friendships do not exist, for some certainly do. Lasting friendships, however, share at their core common interests and beliefs. Thus, the decision regarding working outside the home or raising a family often creates a gap between those who make different choices, and this decision carries with it profound implications in every aspect of a woman's life. The issue divides women as it does not men. In everyday conversation and in popular books and periodicals, these issues are pervasive. Women ask: Should I go out to work or stay at home? What is best for my children? Is there a return to the hearth? How can I decorate like Martha Stewart? Am I a feminist? Is there a return to "family values"? Thinking about these questions after having read magazines, newspapers, and books, I realized that for many these issues are still unresolved. I began to wonder, does a backlash against the women's movement truly exist, or is the idea of a backlash another way to keep women divided?*

With the publication of *Backlash* (Faludi, 1991), *The Beauty Myth* (Wolf, 1991), and *Revolution from Within* (Steinem, 1992); the media coverage of the Clarence Thomas hearings; the significant number of women in congressional races in the 1992 campaign; Vice President Quayle's focus on single motherhood; and the role of Hillary Rodham Clinton, there has been increased interest in "women's issues." Attesting to this expanded attention, women's studies is a rapidly growing major at many colleges and universities. Yet many magazines contain articles proclaiming women's return to the hearth. Books and magazines applaud or decry either women's entry into the workplace or return to the home. Is there a resurgence of a "new feminism"? To answer this question, this essay examines women's rhetoric, focusing on two areas: first, the making of a new feminist movement; and second, the ramifications of that new feminist movement. I both examine the rhetoric of best-selling books and major magazines and analyze this rhetoric, in the context of movement studies, to determine if the women's movement is indeed growing, remaining in abeyance, or actually declining under this presumed backlash.

In 1992, *Backlash, The Beauty Myth,* and *Revolution from Within* all appeared, and remained, on the *New York Times* best-seller list. All had a common thread: denouncing the backlash against women's rights that had been gained in the 1970s. All viewed the Reagan years as a period of conservatism, during which women fought to balance private and public responsibilities. Magazines proclaimed women's "return to the home" in a spate of articles, columns, and editorials. Yet by the 1990s women's issues had begun to resurface in the public sphere. Discussing the successes of Susan Faludi's (1991) and Gloria Steinem's (1992) books, *Time* ran a cover story on the backlash: "In popular culture, in politics—and among ordinary women—a backlash has hit the women's movement. Two unexpected best sellers explain why and raise the alarm" (Gibbs, 1992, p. 50).

As the 1990s progressed, evidence both for and against the existence of a backlash continued. The Clinton administration remained family friendly, yet the Republicans were resurgent with the 1994 "Contract with America." Hillary Rodham Clinton led the unsuccessful fight for healthcare reform, then retreated to the traditional role of "first lady." Increased funding for breast cancer research was one sign of government support for women, yet there were no significant increases in government support for child care. Scandals—for example, Tailhook and the Packwood hearings—continued to keep women's issues on the public agenda, yet women remained in the minority in the legislative arena and in executive positions despite their continued presence in the work force and their majority status in the population.

In the late 1980s and early 1990s, was there a resurgence of a "new feminism"? If so, was it in response to a backlash against women's rights? To answer these questions, I examine two issues in the 1991–1992 popular media: first, the making of a new feminist movement and the backlash to it and second, the ramifications of this new feminist movement.

The Making of the New Feminist Movement

Backlash (Faludi, 1991), *The Beauty Myth* (Wolf, 1991), *Revolution from Within* (Steinem, 1992), and news magazines all proclaimed the existence of a backlash against women's rights. The most prominent early recognition of the 1980s backlash was in Betty Friedan's *The Second Stage,* published in 1981. In this book, Friedan argued that women's initial breakthrough to the public sphere (the focus of her earlier book *The Feminine Mystique*, 1963) was not enough. It was time to reinvent the societal structure:

> There is no going back. The women's movement was necessary. But the liberation that began with the women's movement isn't finished. The equality we fought for isn't livable, isn't workable, isn't comfortable in the terms that structured the battle. The first stage, the women's movement, was fought within, and against, and defined by that old structure of unequal, polarized male and female sex roles. But to continue reacting against that structure is still to be defined and limited by its terms. What's needed now is to transcend those terms, transform the structure itself. (1981, p. 17)

According to Campbell (1973), women's demands were inherently in conflict with the existing societal structure. They were radical in themselves: "They threaten the institutions of marriage and the family and norms governing child-rearing and male-female roles. To meet them would require major, even revolutionary, social change" (p. 77).

In contrast to Friedan, Steinem, another founding member of the feminist movement, argued in her 1992 best-seller, *Revolution from Within,* that it was time to turn from the political to the personal. These views were not necessarily incompatible; witness the slogan of the women's movement: "The personal is political." Yet Steinem argued: "It's time to turn the feminist adage around. **The political is personal** [emphasis in original]" (p. 17). Steinem presented the women's movement as a series of steps, or stages. The personal was the essential first step in gaining political power:

> No matter who we are, the journey toward recovering the self-esteem that should have been our birthright follows similar steps: a first experience of seeing through our own eyes instead of through the eyes of others; telling what seemed to be shameful secrets, and discovering them neither shameful nor secret; giving names to problems that have been treated as normal and thus have no names; bonding with others who share similar experiences; achieving empowerment and self-government; bonding with others in shared power; and finally, achieving a balance of independence and interdependence, and taking one's place in a circle of true selves. (p. 45)

Steinem and Friedan agreed that the development of a woman's potential was critical to the success, and was indeed the primary goal, of the women's movement. Consciousness-raising was thus the first step in moving from the personal to the political. And narrative, or storytelling, was essential to consciousness-raising. Steinem's book, as did many of the articles on the women's movement, relied on narrative: "I combined this research with women's personal stories, which are, like all personal accounts of any group that has been marginalized, our best textbooks: the only way to make our experience central" (p. 4). Rosenwasser (1972) labeled this the "rhetoric of revelation."

Griffin (1969) emphasized the presence of division, or an unacceptable condition, during the inception period of a movement as resulting in a revolt against the status quo: "Movements begin when some pivotal individual or group—suffering attitudes of alienation in a given social system, and drawn (consciously or unconsciously) by the impious dream of a mythic order—enacts, gives voice to, a NO" (p. 462). Friedan's *The Feminist Mystique* (1963) gave voice to this "no" in the 1960s. In her 1989 best-seller *Roseanne: My Life as a Woman*, Roseanne Barr (now, Roseanne) wrote about her recognition of the unacceptable, her voicing of the "no": "What excited me, finally, was the thought of a woman, any woman, standing up and saying NO . . . a huge cosmic 'NO' and the first time I went on stage, I felt myself say it, and I felt chilled and free and redeemed" (p. 168). And again, in the early 1990s, Faludi's *Backlash* and Steinem's *Revolution from Within* gave voice to the "no."

According to Griffin (1969), this "no" must "itself be precipitated by some event or attitude, or cluster of events and attitudes," that symbolize "the unacceptable" (p. 462). In the 1980s, this "no" was precipitated by the backlash against women's rights, meticulously documented by Faludi (1991): "The truth is that the last decade has seen a powerful counterassault on women's rights, a backlash, an attempt to retract the handful of small and hard-won victories that the feminist movement did manage to win for women" (p. xviii). Faludi reaffirmed academic researchers' findings that the backlash was episodic, resurfacing after feminism's successes:

> But if fear and loathing of feminism is a sort of perpetual viral condition in our culture, it is not always in an acute stage; its symptoms subside and resurface periodically. We find such flare-ups are hardly random; they have always been triggered by the perception—accurate or not—that women are making great strides. (p. xix)

It was precisely because of this challenging of the status quo that backlashes occurred, especially as movements appeared to achieve successes. In examining antifeminist activism, Marshall (1991) argued that resistance to feminism followed significant successes of the movement—the winning of suffrage in 1916 and the advancement of the Equal Rights Amendment in 1972.

These two waves of antifeminist activism share some characteristics. In both cases, mobilization did not occur until feminist successes threatened the status quo. This crisis response is a general trait of countermovements but is especially true of antifeminism, which confronts the tactical dilemma of asking recruits to enter the political sphere in order to defend the traditional sexual division of labor. In both periods, opposition rhetoric recast the conflict from the abstract principles of equal rights to the defense of the traditional family, the homemaker role, and the protection of women from exploitation in the public sphere. (p. 52)

Antifeminists define themselves in contrast to feminists. Countermovements require scapegoats. For antifeminists, working women are easy prey for scapegoating, symbolizing material greed at the expense of family. Antifeminists deliberately downplay their level of political organization, preferring to rely on the impression of widespread grass-roots support. They explicitly disavow any interest in the public sphere (despite their activism), claiming the private sphere is the appropriate domain for women's interests.

Faludi (1991) recognized antifeminists' tactics of downplaying organizational strength and relying on dividing women:

Although the backlash is not an organized movement, that doesn't make it any less destructive. In fact, the lack of orchestration, the absence of a single string-puller, only makes it harder to see—and perhaps more effective. A backlash against women's rights succeeds to the degree that it appears **not** to be political, that it appears not to be a struggle at all. It is most powerful when it goes private, when it lodges inside a woman's mind and turns her vision inward, until she imagines the pressure is all in her head, until she begins to enforce the backlash, too—on herself.

It pursues a divide-and-conquer strategy: single versus married women, working women versus homemakers, middle- versus working-class. (p. xxii)

The essence of movement rhetoric, indeed the core of persuasion, is identification and division. The very definition of a successful movement therefore includes a backlash. As Simons (1970) wrote, backlash is inevitable for any movement because of cross-pressures and conflicting demands. Due to their society-induced primary responsibility for home and child care, women are subject to immense cross-pressures. Campbell (1973) identified this dilemma:

Feminist advocacy unearths tensions woven deep into the fabric of our society and provokes an unusually intense and profound "rhetoric of moral conflict." The sex role requirements for women contradict the dominant values of American culture—self-reliance, achievement, and independence. Unlike most other groups, the social status of women is defined primarily by birth, and their social position is at odds with fundamental democratic values. In fact, insofar as the role of rhetor entails qualities of self-reliance, self-confidence, and independence, **its very assumption is a violation of the female role** [emphasis in original]. (p. 75)

Faludi (1991) argued that these divisions were perpetuated through the media: "Three contradictory trend pairs, concerning work, marriage, and motherhood, formed the backlash media's triptych: Superwoman 'burnout' versus New Traditionalist 'cocooning,' the 'spinster boom' versus the 'return of marriages' and the 'infertility epidemic' versus the 'baby boomlet'" (p. 80). And Faludi believed that these media trends were derived from the "New Right":

The New Right leaders were among the first to articulate the central argument of the backlash—that women's equality is responsible for women's unhappiness. They were also the first to lambaste the women's movement for what would become its two most popularly cited, and contradictory, sins: promoting materialism over moral values (i.e., turning women into greedy yuppies) and dismantling the traditional familial support system (i.e., turning women into welfare mothers). The mainstream would reject their fevered rhetoric and hellfire imagery, but the heart of their political message survived—to be transubstantiated into the media's "trends." (p. 230)

The New Right increased in strength in the 1990s, as evidenced by the Republicans' 1994 "Contract with America" and their success in the 1994 midterm elections, gaining control of the House and the Senate. The contrast between the 1996 presidential contenders, President Bill Clinton and former Senate Majority Leader Bob Dole, despite the careers of both Hillary Rodham Clinton and Elizabeth Dole, magnified the generational divide in the assumptions concerning traditional women's roles. In *The Beauty Myth* (1991) Naomi Wolf detailed the reactionary nature of the backlash:

We are in the midst of a violent backlash against feminism that uses images of female beauty as a political weapon against women's advancement: the beauty myth.

The contemporary backlash is so violent because the ideology of beauty is the last one remaining of the old feminine ideologies that still has the power to control those women whom second wave feminism would have otherwise made relatively uncontrollable: It has grown stronger to take over the work of social coercion that myths about motherhood, domesticity, chastity, and passivity no longer can manage. It is seeking right now to undo psychologically and covertly all the good things that feminism did for women materially and overtly. (p. 11)

Wolf (1991), like Faludi (1991), recognized that backlashes against feminism have occurred throughout history: "Every generation since about 1830 has had to fight its version of the beauty myth" (Wolf, p. 11). The reason: "The beauty myth is not about women at all. It is about men's institutions and institutional power" (Wolf, p. 13). Narrative was also at the heart of Wolf's beauty myth:

The beauty myth tells a story: The quality called "beauty" objectively and universally exists. Women must want to embody it and men want to possess women who embody it. This embodiment is an imperative for women and not for men, which situation is necessary and natural because it is biological, sexual, and evolutionary: Strong men battle for beautiful women, and beautiful women are more reproductively successful. Women's beauty must correlate to their fertility, and since this system is based on sexual selection, it is inevitable and changeless. (p. 12)

The beauty myth was devastating to women's political power precisely because it divided: "**The beauty myth is always actually prescribing behavior and not appearance** [emphasis in original]. Competition between women has been made part of the myth so that women will be divided from one another" (Wolf, 1991, p. 14). Further, Wolf argued that the beauty myth was popularized through women's magazines:

Women's magazines for over a century have been one of the most powerful agents for changing women's roles, and throughout that time—today more than ever—they have consistently glamorized whatever the economy, their advertisers, and, during wartime, the government, needed at that moment from women. (p. 64)

Wolf suggested that magazines had deliberately replaced the feminine mystique with the beauty myth: "**The beauty myth, in its modern form, arose to take the place of the Feminine Mystique, to save magazines and advertisers from the economic fallout of the women's revolution** [emphasis in original]" (p. 66). Barr (1989) also recognized the negative impact of women's magazines:

Part of the reason that women are so confused these days is due to the horrid grotesque "women's magazines" and the type of mindnumbing bullshit they pour out on us month after hideous month. I just know they're a political conspiracy to keep women off base so we won't demand the arms race be stopped and the money it uses be spent more productively. (p. 149)

Thus the three best-sellers *Backlash, The Beauty Myth,* and *Revolution from Within* all recognized a backlash against women's rights fueled by women's successes in the 1970s and maintained by the conservatives of the 1980s. In analyzing this backlash, all writers acknowledged its episodic nature, the role of the media in perpetuating it, the reaction by antifeminists (often allied with the New Right and men), the division within the women's movement itself, and the importance of narrative in raising a woman's personal and political consciousness. In essence, the backlash against the women's movement was so powerful because the stakes were so high. The changes women were asking for—most notably, family-friendly work policies to allow women to continue in the public sphere—were changes in the fundamental nature of the division of labor in society. The evolving nature of women's private and public roles—and the resultant redefinition of gender requirements—has had many ramifications.

Ramifications of the New Feminist Movement

Women have been unable to translate popular support into political successes. Family issues, often referred to solely as women's issues, have been consistently defeated in the legislative arena. Admittedly, there are more women politicians, yet the numbers are not even close to representing 51% of the population. Even after the 1996 elections, women represent only 9% of the Senate and just under 11% of the House; they hold only two governorships.

Significantly, in 1980 there was for the first time a notable gender gap in voting for the presidential candidates. Approximately 8% more women than men supported the Democratic candidate. This gap continued in 1984, 1988, 1992, and 1996. Indeed, in 1996 the gender gap widened to 16%. In addition, in 1980 for the first time a greater number of women voted than men (Mueller, 1991, p. 24). Feminist groups encouraged media coverage of this gender gap, believing that this coverage would translate favorably in terms of women's influence (Mueller, 1991, p. 25). Yet women still ran primarily on "women's issues." Most important, in the 1980s there was little discussion about the women's movement; rather, talk remained on the level of specific issues. Although there is ideological support for mothers, the United States is one of the few nations without appropriate legislative support for working mothers. The distinction here is critical. Perhaps it is a measure of the success of the antifeminist movement that motherhood is revered, yet the legislative steps needed to enable working women to at the same time be mothers (for example, affordable child care and widespread flextime) are virtually nonexistent. And it is largely because of the lack of support from the public realm that women have found it difficult to balance public and private responsibilities.

Women in the work force is not a new phenomenon; historically, women have always worked. Day care is not a new phenomenon. What is new is the divorce of the workplace from the home:

> The majority of women have worked throughout U.S. history, first in the home, then in the shop and factory. The deeper change, according to Penelope Leach (1987), author of the popular parenting manual *Your Baby and Child,* stems from the Industrial Revolution, which forced a split between the home and the workplace. (Elmer-DeWitt, 1990, p. 74)

It is in the contemporary United States that combining working and mothering has become problematic for women. What is most remarkable, although not surprising, is that men have been excluded from the debate. It is women who are portrayed as abandoning children, as carrying immense burdens of guilt, and therefore as suffering from burnout in trying to combine family and career.

What is required is a revolution in thinking, making women's issues a concern for all of society. Thus, Faludi supported redefining the issues: "All family issues should not be women's issues. They should be human issues" (Gibbs & McDowell, 1992, p. 56). Steinem agreed: "This is a revolution, not a public relations movement. You have to speak to the constituency. If you say 'family issues' to most women, it's like going back to the past—and feeling guilty again. To make changes, you need new language" (Gibbs & McDowell, 1992, p. 56). *Time* acknowledged the importance of naming: "Issues like equal pay, child care, abortion, rape and domestic violence will no longer be cast as 'women's issues.' They will be viewed as economic issues, family issues, of equal resonance to men and women" (Blackman, Taylor, & Willwerth, 1990, p. 12).

Thus, a revolution in thinking requires new terminology, which is foreboding for the women's movement. Despite widespread support for the goals of the women's movement, there remains a widespread reluctance to identify with the women's movement itself. In a February 1992 *Time/CNN* poll, 63% of women did not consider themselves feminists (Gibbs, 1992, pp. 50–51). McGee (1983) wrote that for a movement to succeed, there must be a symbolic transformation, entailing renaming and redefining the environment (p. 76). Accepting "ideographs" ("slogan-like terms signifying commitment") is a prerequisite for belonging to a movement (Cathcart, 1983, p. 70). Thus coming to accept the term *feminism,* to call oneself a feminist, is a significant victory in itself.

In 1986, *Newsweek* found that 56% of women under age 45 called themselves feminists; in 1989, *Time* discovered that 82% of women said that feminism had improved their lives (Morgan, 1990, p. 1). Yet at the same time, *Time* reported that women rejected the feminist movement:

> Hairy legs haunt the feminist movement, as do images of being strident and lesbian. Feminine clothing is back; breasts are back; motherhood is in again. To the young, the movement that loudly rejected female stereotypes seems hopelessly dated. (Wallis, 1989, p. 81)

And in 1990, *Time* reported that women rejected the feminist label: "But while the goals are applauded by three-quarters of young people, the feminist label is viewed with disdain and alarm; the name Gloria Steinem is uttered as an epithet" (Blackman, Taylor, & Willwerth, 1990, p. 14). Thus, feminists were unable to translate popular support into an effective political movement in the 1980s, as evidenced by the failure of ERA passage in 1982, the 1989 Supreme Court *Webster* decision allowing state restrictions on abortion, and President Bush's two-time veto of the Family Leave Act.

Marshall (1991) observed that divisiveness among feminists weakened their chances for political victories, as suffragists in the 1930s and feminists in the 1980s fell victim to "internecine warfare," raising "similar questions about the viability of feminism" (p. 52). Campbell (1973) argued that this division was caused by the societal status of women: "Women are divided from one another by almost all the usual sources of identification—age, education, income, ethnic origin, even geography" (p. 78). Feminism's weaknesses due to division, however, were not significantly exploited by antifeminism. Most important, Marshall (1991) in her research review found "a relatively unstable antifeminist constituency" (p. 55). Indeed, she found considerable public support for feminist goals, despite low political successes:

> It is noteworthy that while Americans became slightly more conservative on some social issues in the 1980's, the backlash generally excluded women's issues. In 1985, for example, over two-thirds of both sexes said that women's roles should continue to change in the years to come, while

only 10 percent believed that changes had already gone too far. On the other hand, the pro-feminist majority has failed to transform these sentiments into political power. (p. 55)

Although women are slowly increasing their representation in local, state, and national government, percentages are minimal. Women are achieving some legislative successes, such as the 1993 passage of the Family Leave Act. However, family issues remain relegated to the fringes of the legislative agenda. Hillary Rodham Clinton, after heading the effort for health-care reform, returned to the traditional nonpolitical first lady role during President Clinton's first term. The prominence of "soccer moms" in the 1996 presidential election was more divisive for women than symbolic of political power, even when the soccer players were their daughters and with the gender gap in presidential voting in their favor. "Soccer mom" visibility promoted the image of affluent women toting their children to game after game—an image of passivity in which women were serving others rather than developing their selves. Still, there may be hope. President Clinton was reelected to a second term and remains supportive of women, nominating the first female secretary of state, hinting at a more significant role for Hillary Rodham Clinton, and suggesting expansion of flextime in the workplace.

A dispute over the nature of women and men is critical to recent legal controversy concerning the role of women in the work force. Felice Schwartz ignited this controversy in her 1989 *Harvard Business Review* article arguing for a "mommy track." In that article, Schwartz advocated a two-tiered system for working women, one which would allow women who choose to combine motherhood and career an easier path to follow. Critics believed this would result in a downgrading of women's status in the work force, relegating them to second-class status. Schwartz denied these consequences, arguing instead that employers should willingly adapt to working mothers' demands rather than lose them in the work force. Similarly, the debate over maternity leave and fetal protection hinges on how women are defined—as equal to men (for example, pregnancy treated as a disability) or as separate, which would allow special treatment (pregnancy treated as maternity leave).

Feminism has always been controversial precisely because it calls into question the appropriate roles for men and women in society. Currently, there is debate over the idea of women as nurturing versus men as competitive. Feminists themselves disagree on the issue. In her 1990 best-seller, *You Just Don't Understand: Women and Men in Conversation,* Tannen argued that women and men use language differently. Women aim for cooperation; men view language as a competitive display of dominance. Gilligan (1982) argued that women and men think differently and therefore experience life differently. Critics charged that Gilligan merely perpetuated old stereotypes. Even Paglia (1990), with her dismissal of contemporary feminists, was attacked for perpetuating stereotypes (Duffy, p. 62).

Although historically, women are probably closer to the ideal of equality than ever before, they are far from their goals. And whether equality can, or even should, be achieved given women's biological distinctiveness remains at question. What is not debatable, however, is that women are at a disadvantage in a patriarchal system. Men must give up inherently discriminatory privileges for women to gain equality. Women must relinquish patriarchal assumptions about their role to accept and demand this equality. Thus the backlash.

Ehrenreich (1990), in *Time,* warned that feminists had been co-opted by their successes:

> Women may be losing the idealistic vision that helped inspire feminism in the first place. Granted, every Out group—whether defined by race, ethnicity or sexual preference—seeks assimilation as a first priority. But every Out group carries with it a critical perspective, forged in the painful experiences of rejection and marginalization. When that perspective is lost or forgotten, a movement stands in danger of degenerating into a scramble for personal advancement. We applaud the winners and pray that their numbers increase, but the majority will still be found far outside the gates of privilege, waiting for the movement to start up again. (p. 15)

The women's movement is divided in the 1990s: between stay-at-home mothers and working mothers; between women confronting the system and women working within the system; between poor women, working-class women, and wealthy women. The divisions of class and gender were the hallmarks of the Clarence Thomas hearings. Surprisingly, the initial gender gap—with women supporting Hill—disappeared over the course of the Senate confirmation hearings. Instead, the dividing line became class. Working-class women supported Thomas; women in management positions supported Hill. Yet although the hearings were divisive for women, they also spurred women to run for office. Domestic violence, abortion rights, sexual harassment, fetal protection, child care, and elder care are all potentially galvanizing issues for the women's movement. In Griffin's (1969) terms, these issues provide the rationale for the movement, "symbolizing the unacceptable."

Conclusion

Is there a resurgence of a "new feminism" in spite of a backlash? There is a growing interest in issues that affect women (and therefore men and families) in the work force. There is not, however, a growing number of women who consider themselves feminists even though the majority of women identify with feminism's goals.

It is important to remember that a backlash, or countermovement, is integral to the definition of a successful movement. The hallmark of feminism's successes has been the recurrence of a backlash. What remains to be seen is how the women's movement will be able to take advantage of the resurgence of issues of concern to women, such as child care, domestic violence, abortion rights, and family leave. If the women's movement fails to broaden its political base and remains divided internally, its rhetorical task seems daunting. For the changes needed do indeed mean a radical restructuring of society. At the same time, the growing number of women in the work force mandates change—in 1996, this number was 60%. The success of women's books in 1991 and 1992 attests to an increased interest in women's issues. And, if women turned to private solutions for balancing work and family in the 1980s, the inadequacy of these solutions will return women to the public sphere in the 1990s.

Discussion Questions

1. Friedan argues that the appropriate level for change is political transformation of society; Steinem argues that the first step toward change is personal. With which view do you agree and why?

2. Narrative is the dominant mode of persuasion in the women's movement. Is this a strength or a liability? How can the women's movement bridge the divisions between women?

3. To what extent do you think there is and has been a backlash against the women's movement? What successes triggered it? Is the backlash capable of eliminating those successes? If you believe the backlash is relatively nonexistent, explain why.

4. To what extent have you been affected by the beauty myth? Has its influence been greater at certain stages of your life? To what extent does the beauty myth perpetuate divisions between women? Are men subject to the beauty myth?

5. Compare your life with your mother's (and even grandmother's). To what extent have the women in your life accepted or rejected the women's movement?

6. Would you call yourself a feminist? Must one be a feminist to be part of the women's movement? Must one be part of the women's movement to be a feminist?

References

Barr, R. (1989). *Roseanne: My life as a woman.* New York: Harper & Row.

Blackman, A., Taylor, E., & Willwerth, J. (1990, Fall). *Time, 136,* pp. 12–14.

Campbell, K. K. (1973). The rhetoric of women's liberation: An oxymoron. *Quarterly Journal of Speech, 59,* 74–86.

Cathcart, R. (1983). A confrontation perspective on the study of social movements. *Central States Speech Journal, 34,* 69–74.

Contract with America. (1994, November 12). *Congressional Quarterly, 52,* 3216–3219.

Duffy, M. (1992, January 13). The bête noire of feminism. *Time,* pp. 62–63.

Ehrenreich, B. (1990, Fall). Sorry, sisters, this is not the revolution. *Time, 136,* p. 15.

Elmer-DeWitt, P. (1990, Fall). The great experiment. *Time, 136,* pp. 72–74.

Faludi, S. (1991). *Backlash: The undeclared war against American women.* New York: Crown.

Friedan, B. (1963). *The feminine mystique.* New York: Norton.

Friedan, B. (1981). *The second stage.* New York: Summit Books.

Gibbs, N. (1992, March 9). The war against feminism. *Time,* pp. 50–55.

Gibbs, N., & McDowell, J. (1992, March 9). How to revive a revolution. *Time,* pp. 55–57.

Gilligan, C. (1982). *In a different voice: Psychological theory and women's development.* Cambridge: Harvard University Press.

Griffin, L. (1969). A dramatistic theory of the rhetoric of movements. In W. H. Rueckert (Ed.), *Critical responses to Kenneth Burke* (pp. 456–479). Minneapolis: University of Minnesota Press.

Leach, P. (1987). *Your baby and child.* New York: Knopf.

Marshall, S. E. (1991, May). Who speaks for American women? The future of antifeminism. *Annals of the American Academy, 515,* 50–62.

McGee, M. C. (1983). Social movements as meaning. *Central States Speech Journal, 34,* 74–77.

Morgan, R. (1990, July/August). Ms. lives! *Ms.,* pp. 1–2.

Mueller, C. (1991, May). The gender gap and women's political influence. *Annals of the American Academy, 515,* 23–37.

Paglia, C. (1990). *Sexual personae: Art and decadence from Nefertiti to Emily Dickinson.* New Haven: Yale University Press.

Rosenwasser, M. J. (1972). Rhetoric and the progress of the women's liberation movement. *Today's Speech, 29 (3),* 45–56.

Schwartz, F. N. (1989, January). Management women and the new facts of life. *Harvard Business Review, 67,* 65–76.

Simons, H. W. (1970). Requirements, problems, and strategies: A theory of persuasion for social movements. *Quarterly Journal of Speech, 56,* 1–11.

Steinem, G. (1992). *Revolution from within: A book of self-esteem.* Boston: Little, Brown.

Tannen, D. (1990). *You just don't understand: Women and men in conversation.* New York: Morrow.

Wallis, C. (1989, December 4). Onward, women. *Time,* pp. 80–89.

Wolf, N. (1991). *The beauty myth: How images of beauty are used against women.* New York: Morrow.

20

La Malinche Revisited[1]

María Cristina González, Ph.D.

Campus Community Program
Arizona State University

$\mathcal{I}$ can already hear the feminists getting on my case, even before I state it. They will say that what I'm writing "could be true about *all* women. . . ." Maybe so. But I am writing about myself right now. And I am thinking about Mexicanas and Chicanas. I am thinking about cruel coincidence and the power of layered patterns and defenses. I am talking about the fact that as I have dealt with my learned helplessness, dissociative responses, re-victimizations, other-based identity and worth, and the many, many symptoms of having been the victim of sexual abuse, the persona of the victim is so much like . . . like the persona of the traditional Mexican woman's role.

Yes, I have thought and talked and written about how my worth has often been wrapped up in a man's approval of me . . . and this approval has been wrapped up in my secrets so I wouldn't suffer if the truth about the perpetrator were known. As a Chicana, or Mexican American woman, I learned early that it was best to maintain an illusion of the man as king. If that illusion were disturbed, I would suffer . . . (and I *have*).

There's a saying in Mexico that there are women that men have sex with, and there are women that men marry. The ideal woman is the Madonna, the virgin mother. Participating in sex and revealing her sensuality and sexual vigor is a sign of a woman's less-than-pure nature. Yet, the wife is expected to "provide" whenever the fragile-egoed, male husband requires proof of his virility. If the woman attempts to refrain from show-ing enjoyment in order to maintain an image of propriety . . . well then, of course this stud of a man must go elsewhere to find satisfaction for his insatiable male drive.

As a sexual abuse victim, I became a dirty little girl because men used me to demonstrate *their* power and virility with my body. Later, my learned script of fear of sexual contact justified that a man I truly loved would believe I did not care about him. My dissociative trances . . . proof to him that I was unfaithful. My perpetrators' actions, my consequences.

This is just me thinking on paper . . . but this whole thing about guilt and dysfunction and tangled webs of responsibility . . . always ready to take the blame (*por mi culpa, por mi culpa, por mi gran culpa*) because somehow the abuse set me up to become my own victimizer. *La sufrida* . . . long-suffering woman.

Wasn't the Mexican culture of *mestizaje,* mixed-blood people, founded on generations of sexually violated and abused women? Isn't it common Mexican folklore that priests always have a few illegitimate "children of God" in every parish? Could it be that the defenses Mexican women have developed, combined with a misogynistic religious system, led to the devel-opment of a cultural role ideal that is devoid of voice and esteem . . . and whose worth is based almost totally on a woman's response to the power-ful male other?

I think I can better understand now, perhaps, why a friend once asked me how someone as smart as I am could be so trapped by my religious beliefs and an abusive relationship in a marriage. Or why it was so hard for me to talk openly about my sexuality. Because not only was I raised within a misogynistic religious setting in Roman Catholicism, not only was I victimized sexually repeatedly as a child and an adolescent, but I was socialized within a culture that had incorporated the role of a silenced raped woman forced into "conversion" to Roman Catholicism as the appropriate role for a proper woman.

I am convinced that this has to be related to the reason that lesbian Chicanas have written so much of the empowering literature regarding women in our culture. Being lesbians, they have had to reject the symbolic perpetrator who has lived in our collective unconscious for many genera-tions. *Gracias, mis hemanas . . . ahora a mi me toca.* Thank you, my sis-ters . . . it's my turn now. You have motivated me to seek for the voice in writing that will empower those of us attracted to men . . . those of us who choose to believe in God and belong to the Church . . . those of us who wish to remain modest in our sexuality . . . but who do not wish to live out our lives living out the role of *la chingada.*[2]

You see, our language even has a word for it.

Reference

Paz, O. (1985). *The labyrinth of solitude.* New York: Grove Weidenfeld.

Endnotes

1. *La Malinche,* or Marina, the name given to her by the Spaniards, is the Aztec woman who bore the children of the conquistador Hernán Cortez. She was traditionally known as "she who favored foreigners, the betrayer, the whore," and only in recent history has her persona as the mother of a new race of mixed-blood Mexicans been seen as arche-typal for Mexican and Chicana women seeking to deconstruct the patriarchal, xenophobic, and misogynistic cultural myths that have camouflaged their multicultural strength and indigenous dignity.

2. *Chingada,* a Mexican colloquialism meaning, literally, "the raped one," or in the words of Octavio Paz (1985), "the violated Mother" (p. 85).

Bird of Paradise

A stem in my left hand,
a jar to my right, I cut
first flower, then leaf,
flower, then leaf,
arranging the heavy stalks
in the rising water,
turning the jar
to the afternoon sun
until each flower
reflects the steady light.

—*Phyllis Kahaney*

TEXT CREDITS

Reading 1 The author acknowledges the Board of Trustees of the Connecticut State University for granting permission to print this essay based on the article "Connecticut's Canterbury Tale: Prudence Crandall and Her School," published in the *Connecticut Review*, vol. X, no. 1, Summer 1987.

Reading 9 "That's The Way I've Always Heard It Should Be," written by Carly Simon and Jacob Brackman. Copyright ©1970 Quackenbush Music Ltd./Maya Productions Ltd. Administered by BMG Music.

"The Girl You Think You See," written by Carly Simon and Jacob Brackman. Copyright ©1971 Quackenbush Music Ltd./Maya Productions Ltd. Administered by BMG Music.

"It Was So Easy," written by Carly Simon and Jacob Brackman. Copyright ©1972 Quackenbush Music Ltd./Maya Productions Ltd. Administered by BMG Music.

"Embrace MeYou Child," written by Carly Simon. Copyright ©1972 Quackenbush Music Ltd. Administered by BMG Music.

"Older Sister," written by Carly Simon. Copyright ©1974 Ces't Music. Administered by BMG Music.

"Think I'm Going To Have A Baby," written by Carly Simon. Copyright ©1974 Ces't Music. Administered by BMG Music.

"Slave," written by Carly Simon and Jacob Brackman. Copyright © 1975 Ces'tMusic/Maya Productions Ltd. Administered by BMG Music.

"Cow Town," written by Carly Simon. Copyright ©1976 Ces't Music. Administered by BMG Music.

"Fairweather Father," written by Carly Simon. Copyright ©1976 Ces't Music. Administered by BMG Music.

"Tranquillo," written by Carly Simon and Arif Mardin/James Taylor. Copyright ©1978 Ces't Music/Country Road Music. Administered by BMG Music.

"Jesse," written by Carly Simon and Mike Mainieri. Copyright ©1980 Quackenbush Music Ltd./Red Eye Music. Administered by BMG Music.

"Vengeance," written by Carly Simon. Copyright ©1979 Ces't Music. Administered by BMG Music.

"Take Me As I Am," written by Carly Simon, Mike Mainieri and Sid McGinnis. Copyright ©1980 Quackenbush Music Ltd./Red Eye Music/Mohisse Music. Administered by BMG Music.

"Coming To Get You," written by Carly Simon. Copyright ©1979 Ces't Music. Administered by BMG Music.

"Them," written by Carly Simon and Mike Mainieri. Copyright ©1980 Quackenbush Music Ltd./Red Eye Music. Administered by BMG Music.

"It Happens Every Day," written by Carly Simon. Copyright ©1983 Ces't Music. Administered by BMG Music.

"Hello Big Man," written by Carly Simon and Peter Wood. Copyright ©1983 Ces't Music/Hythefield Music. Administered by BMG Music.

"Give Me All Night," written by Carly Simon and Gerard McMahon. Copyright ©1987 Ces't Music/BackMack Publishing. Administered by BMG Music.

"Don't Wrap It Up," written by Carly Simon. Copyright ©1970 Ces't Music. Administered by BMG Music.

"Back That Way," written by Carly Simon. Copyright ©1992 Ces't Music and TCF Music. Administered by BMG Music.

"Tired of Being Blonde," Words and Music by Larry Raspberry. Copyright ©1984 Screen Gems-EMI Music Inc. All Rights Reserved. International Copyright Secured. Used by Permission.

Reading 10 "Three Babies," words and Music by Sinead O'Connor. Copyright ©1990 EMI Music Publishing (Holland) B.V. All Rights Controlled and Administered by EMI Blackwood Music Inc. All Rights Reserved. International Copyright Secured. Used by Permission.

PHOTO CREDITS

pg. 19, © The Granger Collection, New York; pg. 23, © TheGranger Collection, New York; pg. 35, © Moorland-Spingarn Reserch Center, Howard University; pg. 55, Courtesy of the Illinois Labor History Society; pg. 69, Courtesy of Gwendolyn Clancy; pg. 87, © Chase Statler. Permission granted by the Margaret Chase Smith Library; pg. 101,© Omaha World-Herald; pg 129, Courtesy Thuy-Phuong Do; pg. 142, Courtesy Thuy Phuong-Do; pg. 145, © Peter Simon/Retna, Ltd.; pg. 182, Courtesy of Patricia Geist; pg. 185, Courtesy of Michelle Freund; pg. 235, © McLaughlin/The Image Works; pg 253, Courtesy of Rachel Lundberg; pg. 301, Courtesy of Holly J. Nichols;pg. 321, courtesy of the authors.